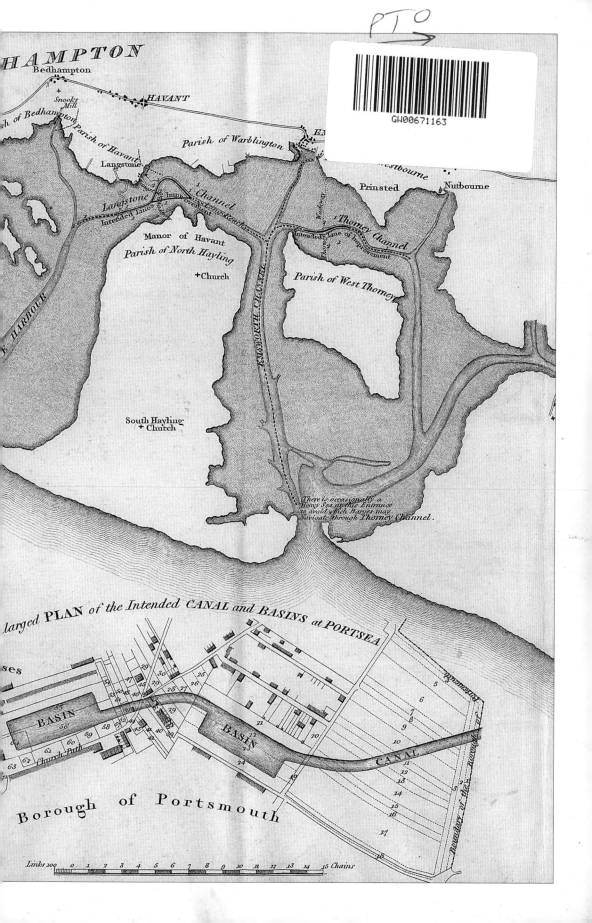

LONDON'S LOST ROUTE TO PORTSMOUTH

SURREY
COUNTY COUNCIL
Community Services

Charges will be payable at
the Adult rate if this item
is not returned by the
latest date stamped above.

L21B

Artist's impression of a bullion barge guarded by Red Coats on the Portsmouth & Arundel Canal, c.1825.

London's Lost Route to Portsmouth

*An historical account of the
Portsmouth and Arundel Canal Navigation
including the story of the
ill-fated Portsea Ship Canal and
the Chichester Ship Canal*

P.A.L. Vine

Phillimore

2005

Published by
PHILLIMORE & CO. LTD
Shopwyke Manor Barn, Chichester, West Sussex, England

© P.A.L. Vine, 2005

ISBN 1 86077 283 8

Printed and bound in Great Britain by
THE CROMWELL PRESS LTD
Trowbridge, Wiltshire

*This book is dedicated to
the voluntary workforces
who have so far laboured
for more than thirty-five years
to restore the derelict
Wey & Arun Junction Canal
and the Chichester Ship Canal*

The Seal of the Portsmouth & Arundel Navigation Company

CONTENTS

Appendices

LIST OF ILLUSTRATIONS

LIST OF MAPS

Front endpaper: Plan of the Intended Arundel and Portsmouth Canal (Portsmouth-Itchenor), 1815.

Rear endpaper: Plan of the Intended Arundel and Portsmouth Canal (Birdham-Ford), 1815.

Chronological Table

PREFACE

The Portsmouth & Arundel Canal formed the final link in the chain of inland waterways joining the Thames to the English Channel. The story of this line of navigation was outlined in *London's Lost Route to the Sea*, first published in 1965, which dealt primarily with the rise and fall of the Wey & Arun Junction Canal. This account tells in greater detail how the waterway joining Arundel to Chichester and Portsmouth was built and why it failed. The venture was a brave but foolhardy speculation. Projected while Britain was still at war with France, its *raison d'être* appeared to many to be unanswerable; however, its success depended on the belief that merchants would favour a storm-free route rather than brave the hazards of the North Foreland Passage and the Goodwin Sands. By the time the waterway was officially opened, peace was assured, steam power was superseding sail and even the roads were being improved. The fall in coastal freight rates put in jeopardy the company's financial viability and the utter failure of the Portsea ship canal heralded disaster. Strenuous efforts were made to raise more capital to complete the navigation through the Portsbridge Channel into Portsmouth Harbour. However, by the time the new cut was successfully completed in 1830, the waterway's commercial value had all but vanished. The arrival of the railway ended local trade, after which the company's existence simply faded away. Only the Chichester Ship Canal has survived as a drainage channel but which it is hoped will soon be reopened for pleasure craft.

This, then, is a tale of mismanagement and misfortune but it nonetheless reflects the optimism of the speculators who risked their capital to build what they believed would form part of a national highway linking London and Portsmouth. In this they were to be sadly disappointed, but if war had broken out again (as it had in 1793, 1803 and 1814), the waterway might have played a useful strategic role.

PALV

Quito
March 2005

PORTSMOUTH AND ARUNDEL
Navigation.

TOLLS AND WHARFAGE DUES
ON
THE LOCAL TRADE,

Between Ford, on Arundel River, and the Company's Basin, at the Half-way Houses, Portsea.

	per Ton.		per Ton.
On ALL GOODS, except what are especially rated or agreed for passing the whole of the above distance	6 8	SALT	2 0
		STRAW	1 6
CORN and GRAIN, say five Quarters	3 0	TIMBER, say one Load	2 0
CHALK, for Lime	1 6	TAR	2 0
FLOUR, say eight Sacks	3 0	WOOL, say seven Sacks	3 0
MALT	3 0		
MANURE of all kinds	1 6	PITCHERS, CHALK, DUNG, GRAVEL, AND MANURE,	

	per Ton.		per Ton.
On ALL GOODS, except what are especially rated or agreed for passing the Sussex Line from Ford to Chichester or Birdham, or vice versa	3 8	From Ford to Yapton	0 4
		Barnham	0 6
ASHES	2 0	Lidsey	0 8
BEER	2 6	any greater distance	0 8
BARK	3 0	From Chichester to any place between Birdham and Merston	0 4
BEANS, say five Quarters	2 0		
BRICKS, say 500 No.	1 6	Colworth	0 6
CORN and GRAIN, say five Quarters	2 0	Lidsey	0 8
	per Chaldron.	any greater distance	0 8
COALS	2 6		
	per Ton.	All BARGES or VESSELS, of every description, if empty, to pay for each Lock that they pass in the Sussex Line	1 0
DEALS, say 30 No. 14 feet 3 inches	2 0		
FELLIES	2 6		
FLOUR, say eight sacks	2 0	VESSELS having delivered Cargoes on any part of the Navigation, and returning light, to pass	Free
HOOPS	2 6		
PEASE, say five Quarters	2 0		
SPOKES	2 6		

TOLLS AND WHARFAGE DUES

On the Portsea Canal, from Langstone Harbour to Half-way Houses.

	per Ton.		per Ton.
GOODS generally	1 6	MANURE	0 6
CORN and GRAIN, say five Quarters	1 0	GRAVEL	0 6
FLOUR, say eight Sacks	1 0	All BARGES or VESSELS of every description, if empty, to pay for each Lock that they pass in the Portsea Line	1 6
	per Chaldron.		
COALS	1 0		
	per Ton.	But Vessels having delivered Cargoes therein, and returning light, to pass	Free
CHALK for Lime	0 10		
STONE	0 6		
SAND	0 6		

In reference to the List of Tolls for the Chichester Branch, published on 21st May, 1822;

The Following Articles passing to and from the City of Chichester to the Harbour at Birdham, are from this date reduced to the Tonnage set against them,

viz.
CORN
GRAIN
MALT
FLOUR
TIMBER
DEALS
} . . . 1s. per Ton.

BY ORDER OF THE COMMITTEE OF MANAGEMENT,

JACKSON M. WILLIAMS,
CLERK TO THE COMPANY.

CANAL OFFICE, PORTSMOUTH,
13th June, 1823.

HOLLINGSWORTH, PRINTER.

Notice of tolls and wharfage dues on trade between Ford and Portsea 1823. Fellies are the outer circles of a wheel, pitchers are paving stones.

ACKNOWLEDGEMENTS

My interest in the history of British Waterways was fostered initially by both Tom Rolt and Charles Hadfield, to whom I am much indebted. Membership of the Railway & Canal Historical Society, the Sussex Industrial Archaeology Society and the Inland Waterways Association widened my knowledge and gave me the opportunity to meet fellow adventurers. Over the years there have been many who have kindly answered my enquiries and assisted my research. I would particularly mention: John Ascoli, Alan Bell, A.M.J. Chapman, Hugh Compton, Edwin Course, P.S.M. Cross-Rudkin, Ron Davis, Roger Dunbar, Dendy Easton, Roger French, Rosemary Gilmoor (Chichester District Museum), Gerald Griffith, Martin Hayes, Douglas Hayler, John Herniman, Ron Iden, Alan King (Portsmouth Historical Collections), Kim Leslie, Ann Lowther, Klaus Marx, Alison McCann (WSRO), Hugh McKnight, Cecil Parkinson, Ian Plenderleith, Nigel and Caroline Proddow, Roger Reed, H.E. Roberts, Fred Saigeman, Roger Sellman, Judy Talbot, Michael Tibbs, C.E.C. Townsend, Edwina Vine, Judy Wallace, Frank Westwood, Guy Whitaker, Linda Wilkinson, Frank Worley. It was Frank who in October 1963 generously provided photographs of the Chichester Canal taken by his father in 1898.

I would also wish to place on record the extensive help accorded to me at various times, and often over many weeks, by the librarians and staff of Arundel Castle muniment room, the Bodleian Library, British Library, Institution of Civil Engineers, Chichester Library, Guildhall (London), House of Lords, Portsmouth Central, the National Maritime Museum, and the National Library of Scotland and by the archivists and staff of the county record offices of Hampshire, Lincolnshire, Surrey and West Sussex.

A special mention to Jeremy Stuart Smith who kindly flew me along the lost route from Ford to Milton. The problem of navigating barges from Chichester Harbour round Thorney and Hayling Islands into Langstone Harbour when the tide was on the ebb can well be imagined; also to The Author's Foundation (trustees Antonia Fraser and Michael Holroyd) which supplied a generous grant to assist with the costs of travel and research. I have also had the benefit of reading Marcus Gillespie's unpublished thesis written in 1995 on the 'Evolution of the Buildings and the Landscape

Development on the site of the Portsea Canal'. The Governors of Christ's Hospital have kindly consented to the inclusion of extracts from the London Guildhall file MS 13325.

My thanks are also due to John Olston and Huw Williams, librarians at the Oxford and Cambridge Club, and to Susan White and the staff at Pulborough Library who have taken great pains to obtain books long out of print. Tribute too to my wife, Kay, who has spent many hours accompanying me on arduous journeys, deciphering my notes and transferring the copy to her laptop, and to Edwina Vine who found time to improve my presentation.

Illustration Acknowledgements

I wish to express my thanks to those who have kindly lent or sent me illustrations. Arundel Museum, 51; Mr Roy Barton, 10; Mr A.A.F. Bell, 75, 76; Chichester District Museum, xiv, 60, 66-7; Mike Codd and West Sussex County Council, frontispiece and jacket; Edwin Course, 84; Hampshire County Record Office, 32, 42, 65; *Illustrated London News*, 54; Lincolnshire County Record Office, 16, 41; Littlehampton Museum, 58; Mrs Nellie Lofting, 64, 83; Mr Klaus Marx, 71; National Maritime Museum, 39; Portsmouth City Library, 1; Railway & Canal Historical Society, 62, 73; Dr Roger Sellman, 55-6; Sotheby's, 52; Sussex Canal Trust, 70; Mrs Doreen Turner, 59, 69; West Sussex County Record Office, 45; West Sussex Institute of Higher Education (Bognor Regis), 12; Worthing Public Library, 53. The remainder are from my own collection.

I

PLANS TO LINK LONDON
AND PORTSMOUTH
1785-1815

First attempts to link the Thames with the English Channel (1641) – Portsmouth's
strategic value – transport of military stores to Godalming by water, and thence by
road to Portsmouth during the American conflict – plan for canal from Reading
to Portsmouth (1785) – canal or iron railway? – William Jessop's proposal (1799)
– John Rennie's project (1803) – Robert Marshall's view (1803) – The Grand
Southern Canal Bill (1810) – publication of prospectus for linking the Wey and
Arun rivers (1811) – The Wey & Arun Junction Canal Act (1813).

Plans to provide a navigable link between London and the English Channel
date from the 17th century. In 1641 attempts were made to obtain an Act
of Parliament to make 'a river' navigable for boats and barges from Arundel
Haven through Surrey to the Thames. It was argued that water carriage
would be much cheaper than land carriage, that for every 20 tons moved
by barge, the cost of keeping 120 horses would be saved. And that, since
only two miles separated the streams at Cranleigh and Dunsfold which
flowed into the Wey and Arun rivers, a canal could be formed with little
difficulty.[1] However, the bill failed to obtain a third reading in the House
of Lords, as did most of the navigation bills introduced into Parliament
during the 17th century.

The strategic value of Portsmouth Harbour over the centuries changed
according to the prevailing continental enemy. In Queen Elizabeth I's reign
when Spain succeeded France as England's major adversary, Portsmouth
played little part in the actions against the Spanish fleet guarding the
Netherlands. The lack of a dry dock required ship repairs to be carried
out at nearby creeks, which had to be temporarily walled off at low tide.
It was not, therefore, until the second half of the 18th century, after
major improvements had been made to the dockyard at Portsmouth, that
it was regarded as the principal naval port in Great Britain.[2] Indeed the
Rev. William Gilpin, passing by in 1774, counted between fifty and sixty
sail of the line. However, the naval use of the harbour greatly limited its
development as a commercial port.

The extension of the Wey Navigation from Guildford to Godalming
was completed in 1763. The American War of Independence (1776-83)
gave a considerable impetus to trade to Godalming, due in large measure

to the transport of Government stores and ammunition from London to the naval arsenal at Portsmouth. In February 1780, carriers Messrs Collins & Davis advised the Board of Ordnance that they had barges ready at Bull Wharf, Upper Thames Street in the City of London (see map on page 113) to carry stores to Portsmouth in eight days at £3 a ton (or £5 a ton by land the whole way). In March it was reported that a quantity of Government stores had already arrived and that since many more were expected a warehouse was to be built at Godalming. Indeed, between 1779 and 1782 receipts on the Guildford section of the Wey Navigation increased by 25 per cent and the amount of goods carried in the year rose from 22,000 to 36,000 tons. However, the Treaty of Versailles of 1783, coupled with the disadvantages of transferring goods from water to land half-way to Portsmouth, caused traffic to diminish and in 1789 the Wey Navigation sold their three-quarter interest in the warehouse to the Wey Godalming Commissioners at less than cost.

However, the end of the French War prompted the Basingstoke Canal Navigation Company to publish 'An address to the Public' which foresaw an extension of the canal from Basingstoke to the English Channel via the Itchen Navigation. Rumours abounded. In March 1785 the *Derby Mercury* announced that they were well informed 'that the Minister is in possession of a Plan for making a navigable canal from Reading to Portsmouth, by which in time of war, provisions and stores may be conveyed to the Fleet at no hazard, and at less expense. The cargoes also of the Norway and West India Ships may be transported to London by the same Communication'.[3]

Phillips, in his 1792 edition of the *General History of Inland Navigation*, had envisaged the Basingstoke Canal forming part of a system to connect London with Southampton and Portsmouth. 'And if the proposed canals through the county of Hampshire should take place (which I hope I shall live so see), goods and stores of all kinds, from the magazines of London, Woolwich, etc may then be certainly conveyed to Portsmouth, thereby avoiding a long, circuitous and hazardous navigation'.

The completion of the Andover Canal in 1796 linked the market town with Southampton Water at Redbridge, a distance of 22 miles. All that remained to ensure a through-passage from London to Southampton was to link Basingstoke with Andover, only 17 miles away. Such a canal, said Phillips, might be finished in 12 months and 'in time of war would save the public several millions, by accelerating expedition and saving convoys employed between the two ports. Sometimes an expedition is deferred for want of gunpowder, another time for want of guns, a third time for army necessaries. It also requires a variety of winds to proceed from the Thames to Portsmouth whereas the whole of any convoy through this canal will arrive there in three days time'.[4]

A variety of abortive schemes to link London and Portsmouth was considered during the first decade of the 19th century.* Initially there

* See P.A.L. Vine, *London's Lost Route to Basingstoke* (1994), chapter V.

was doubt as to whether the link should be by rail or canal. As early as 1799 William Jessop had proposed a horse railway from Wandsworth to Portsmouth by way of Croydon, Reigate and Arundel. In May 1801 the Act was obtained for making the Surrey Iron Railway, which was opened in July 1803 and ran from Wandsworth Creek as far as Croydon. But at a meeting on 3 June 1802 it was announced that 'it had been thought advisable to enquire whether the Iron Railway now establishing from Wandsworth to Croydon might not be extended through Surrey, Sussex and Hants, so as to open a communication with seaports in the Channel and particularly with Portsmouth.'[5]

The simultaneous promotion of the Croydon Canal and the Surrey Iron Railway encouraged rival schemes for a communication between London and Portsmouth. In 1803 John Rennie proposed extending the Croydon Canal through Horsham, Pulborough and Chichester to the port 'just above His Majesty's Dockyard'. Its length was to be 100 miles with 41 locks and a 2½-mile tunnel through the North Downs at Merstham. The cost was estimated at over £500,000 for a narrow and £720,000 for a broad canal. The *Lewes Journal* doubted whether there would be sufficient tolls to pay the interest on the capital[6] and, when in March 1804 the bill was presented to Parliament, it failed. There had been strong protests from the millers on the river Wandle and various landowners. Doubts were also expressed about the wisdom of so lengthy a tunnel, not only on the grounds of cost and the possibility that the borings might meet quicksand where there ought to be rock, but of the difficulty of working through a tunnel of this length by manpower. In the event the urge to reach Portsmouth faded with Nelson's victory at Trafalgar.

Five weeks after the Surrey Iron Railway had been authorised the Croydon Canal Act was passed, but it was not until October 1809 that the waterway was opened. *The Times* correspondent attended the celebratory dinner and reported the occasion when it was announced that circumstances were now favourable for the extension of the Croydon Canal to Portsmouth; and the prodigious advantages of such a measure, both as affecting public commerce and the commercial and agricultural improvements of counties through which it would pass, being universally acknowledged, the following toast was accompanied by the most lively acclamation: 'The union of the River Thames and the English Channel through the Croydon Canal'.[7]

The problem was to decide whether a horse-drawn railway would be a better investment than a canal. There was a lack of reliable information. Pamphlets setting out the merits of both forms of transport considered that the railway would be cheaper and quicker to build and probably more reliable, while a canal, although more expensive and requiring more land, would be better capable of carrying heavier goods such as timber, coal and manure at less expense. Although speed was not of prime importance, railway waggons were more likely to reach Portsmouth in 24 hours than barges in 65 hours, due to the regular occurrence of floods, ice or drought.

COMPARATIVE VIEW

OF THE RESPECTIVE

QUALITIES AND ADVANTAGES

OF

An Iron Railway and a Canal;

WITH REFERENCE IN PARTICULAR, TO THOSE PROPOSED BETWEEN

LONDON and PORTSMOUTH.

Statement in favour of the proposed Canal.

Statement in favour of the proposed Railway.

1ft. If the fupplying a cheap mode of communication to many confiderable Towns, and through a country abounding in articles of general confumption—if the improvement of the prefent ftate of Agriculture of the country, and alfo bringing into cultivation large tracts of land now lying wafte for want of manure—if the affording an important affiftance to national commerce—if any of thefe circumftances can juftify the expenditure of a large fum of money, furely the country through which a Canal from London to Portfmouth is intended to be made has fuperlative claims to fuch an expenditure. But though this is the cafe with refpect to a Canal, it will not be found fo with refpect to a Railway; as it is hoped it will be found in the fequel that a Railway is not capable of anfwering the purpofes of conveyance on terms fo cheap as on a Canal; befides the expenfe will be found,

1ft. It is queftionable whether the commerce of this part of the kingdom will be fufficient to juftify the expenditure of fo large a capital as muft be funk in making a Canal; if it is but barely doubtful, it may amply warrant half the expenditure in making a Railway. An eftimate has been made of the probable coft of completing a Railway from London Portfmouth; and to fhew that the Committtee for carrying the fame into effect, are warranted in ftating to the public that the fame will not exceed 400,000l. the following eftimate is fubmitted:

The eftimate for making an Iron Railway from near Reigate to Portfmouth, is calculated not to exceed 299,000l. The eftimate for making a Railway from Wandfworth to London, is calculated not to exceed 26,000l. which calculation exceeds that for any other part of the Road, as land near the Metropolis is known

1   *The first page of a pamphlet setting out the pros and cons of the proposed canal and railway between London and Portsmouth, c.1803.*

Robert Marshall, a major user of the Godalming Navigation, stated that he preferred canals to other modes of conveyance over level country where the land was of little value and the 'bowels of the earth contain valuable mines and quarries and with the advantages of plenty of water on a retentive soil, and', wrote Marshall, 'as did the Croydon Canal and its proposed extension to Portsmouth possess these advantages, some hopes might be entertained of its success'. But the likely route was far from level. He estimated the total expense of a canal from Croydon at £800,000, compared with £450,000 for a railway. His arguments in favour of the railway were threefold; that the journey would be completed in one day instead of five, that it would take one-tenth of the time to build and that it would require 40 as against 75 horses to operate. The writer's experience of the Godalming navigation was that barges could be detained for up to two months in winter and that few barges could perform more than 13 voyages a year to London.[8]

From about 1810 to 1835 the Croydon Canal and Surrey Iron Railway operated in direct competition with each other, and the results over this period gave no positive proof that mule-pulled trucks were any more efficient than horse-drawn barges. However, both projects were dropped and the link between the two great cities was postponed.

In 1810 Rennie revived his 1803 project in the form of the Grand Southern Canal. This waterway would have stretched 95 miles from the river Medway at Tonbridge to Portsmouth through Edenbridge, Horsham, Pulborough, Arundel and Chichester. 'I propose', wrote Rennie, 'for the canal to be of a size capable of admitting the Thames barges to navigate.'[9] The canal would have avoided using the Arun Navigation by being built along the eastern bank of the river to within 1¼ miles of Arundel. Rennie remarked that 'barges navigating it, experience great detention, from the floods in winter and droughts in summer and, as the length is greater by about eight miles, I can scarcely suppose any saving in cost by the use of this navigation when put in competition with the detention and inconvenience the trade of so great an inland navigation would be likely to sustain by barges navigating the Arun between Newbridge and Arundel, on their voyage to and from Portsmouth. 'It is true', wrote Rennie, 'that the Arun might be improved, but no improvement which could be made would ever render it so certain as the proposed canal for the through trade; but a branch may be made to join it below Pulborough which will cost but little while it will open an extensive district of country to its benefits.'

Although subscriptions were received for some £650,000, the bill was defeated on second reading by 100 to 17 votes.[10] Rennie attributed the failure of this scheme to the 'powerful opposition of certain proprietors'[11] but there was considerable doubt whether the canal was an economic proposition. The intended route was extremely circuitous and passed through agricultural areas with few industries.

In 1791 the 3rd Earl of Egremont had obtained his own Act of Parliament to build the Rother Navigation and planned to extend a branch from Petworth to the Godalming Navigation. However, after William Jessop had surveyed the proposed line, his lordship decided in 1796 to buy a controlling interest in the Arun Navigation, which had been opened to Newbridge in 1787. Only 17 miles now separated the navigable portions of the Wey and Arun rivers. The failure of the Grand Southern Canal project left the way open for Egremont to take the lead in promoting the Wey and Arun Junction Canal bill for which he drafted the prospectus. In this he stressed 'the advantage likely to accrue to the public from a communication by inland navigation between the River Thames and Portsmouth'.[12] On 1 April 1813 the Bill received the Royal Assent.

II

THE PORTSMOUTH & ARUNDEL CANAL PROJECT
1815-1817

Provisional Committee formed – John Williams, the projector of the scheme
– John Rennie consulted – survey carried out by Netlam and Francis Giles (1815)
– Huskisson's plea to the prime minister – formation of group to oppose the
intended canal – Rennie's report to the initial subscribers (1816) – the proposed
route – estimate of cost – his very favourable conclusion – lively correspondence
for and against the project – opening of the Wey & Arun Junction Canal (1816)
– toast drunk to the intended Portsmouth Canal – Lord Egremont corresponds
with the Clerk of Christ's Hospital.

The construction of the Wey & Arun Junction Canal gave fresh impetus to
plans to link the Thames with the great naval dockyard at Portsmouth. In
January 1815 it was announced that a canal to London by way of Chichester
and Arundel was being contemplated as promising very great advantages to
the port. The report went on to say that people in Portsmouth had alone
subscribed for shares totalling £20,000.[1] Gates, the local historian, relates
that the proposition was received with great favour and some sanguine
spirits prophesied that half the sea trade of London would pass along it.[2]
Others were less enthusiastic. Lake Allen, a contemporary Portsmouth
historian, had only this to say: 'If the design is entered upon, it will have
at least one beneficial effect, viz: that of employing a number of the poor
and labouring classes of society'.[*3]

A provisional committee was formed, from those subscribing for five
or more shares, to press ahead with the plan. William Turner acted as
its chairman and included John Williams, the Comptroller of Customs at
Portsmouth, who is credited as being the projector of the scheme.[4] In March
this committee drew up a memorial which they submitted to the Admiralty
for their observations. The main concern of the naval commissioner, Sir
George Grey, was that Portsmouth Harbour might suffer if the tide was
allowed to ebb through Portsbridge Creek eastwards, contrary to the present
southward flow. John Rennie, asked for his opinion, felt that this possible

---

[*] It was Lord Palmerston who in 1857 when prime minister condemned the Suez Canal scheme as
an undertaking which 'may be deemed to rank among the many bubble schemes that from time to
time have been palmed upon gullible capitalists'. (*Hansard's Parliamentary Debates*, 7 July 1857.)

2 *John Rennie (1761-1821), civil engineer, whose initial projects to link the river Thames with Portsmouth failed. However, his report in January 1816 to the subscribers of the Portsmouth & Arundel Canal would, he believed, give them 'an ample return' on their speculation.*

injury could be prevented by erecting either a sluice or pairs of gates at the junction of the cut with Fareham Lake. And so he replied to the Naval Secretary that he could see no disadvantages, only the advantages, as by making Langstone Harbour the principal commercial port it would abate many of 'the nuisances and obstructions occasioned by merchant shipping in Portsmouth Dockyard'.[5] Meantime Rennie instructed Francis and Netlam Giles to take the levels* and in October Lord Keith chaired a meeting to receive their report. The next step was for Rennie to meet the Inspector-

---

* The Giles's had previously carried out various surveys for John Rennie including that for the proposed Weald of Kent Canal from the Medway to Rye Harbour in 1802. When in 1824 Francis surveyed the route for the intended Hants & Berks Junction Canal counsel for the Bill's opponents asserted before the parliamentary committee that 'he had never been employed by the judicious engineer in the execution or super-intendance [*sic*] of any of his works; nor had he since the death of Mr Rennie in 1821, as yet executed any canal of his own'. In 1830, Francis Giles became engineer of the Newcastle & Carlisle Railway and in 1834 of the London & Southampton Railway whose directors forced his resignation in 1837 for mismanagement.

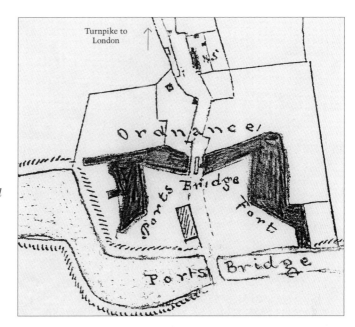

MAP 1 *Portsbridge Fort. Plan of the fortification (1815) protecting Portsbridge which had precluded using the shortest route through Portscreek to Portsmouth Harbour. Instead Rennie proposed building the Cosham Canal to provide access to the harbour.*

General of Fortifications, General Gother Mann, to discuss what would be the best line to adopt between the two harbours to alleviate any concern over the possible breaching of the island's defences.[6] There was a danger that mounds of excavated soil and the erection of warehouses and keepers' cottages could interfere with the line of fire from Fort Cumberland.[*]

Towards the end of August a list of 169 subscribers was published but no indication was given of the amount tendered by each applicant.[7] Notice of the intended application to Parliament for a bill was published in September[8] but unfavourable attitudes to the scheme had caused new subscriptions to dwindle and the application was postponed until the following year. Lord Egremont voiced his concern to William Huskisson (1770-1830), MP for Chichester since 1812, who had been appointed Minister of Woods and Forests in Lord Liverpool's administration in 1814.[†]

In the aftermath of Waterloo (18 June 1815) Huskisson was concerned with the plight of soldiers returning from the war. Writing to the prime minister, he drew his attention to the national importance of the waterway and pointed out that its construction would provide employment to many artisans, bricklayers, carpenters, etc. As it appeared probable that the subscription list could not be filled by individuals due to the present state of the economy, Huskisson proposed that the Boards of Admiralty and Ordnance should each subscribe £15,000 for shares in the canal. If the Government would support this measure 'it would be the means of securing

---

[*] Fort Cumberland had been built to guard the entrance to Langstone Harbour, c.1747 and was further enlarged between 1794 and 1820.

[†] Huskisson, who lived at Eartham, was well known to Egremont with whom he both corresponded and whom he visited on several occasions at Petworth House.

the execution of such a work in the interval of peace, when labour and materials are cheap'; and help those

> who by the cessation of the war are thrown out of work at Portsmouth and its
> neighbourhood, as well as to country labourers, of whom there is now a great
> excess. The case is simply this – that the advance of a comparatively small sum
> by Govt. for a work in which it is admitted the State has a material interest, is
> necessary at this moment to enable individuals to lay out a much larger sum of
> their own in the same work, and without any other inducement than the probable
> benefit they expect to derive from the speculation; a benefit which, whatever it
> may be, will be equally shared by the Govt. in proportion to its subscription …
> . If between this time and the meeting of Parliament the subscription should
> be filled by individuals, no advance will be asked, but it is essential to obtain
> the assurance that this aid will not be refused, in case it shall be wanted to
> complete the amount of private subscription.[9]

The Government was not prepared to act, so the navigation's provisional committee decided to make up the deficiency themselves. In October there was a report that many subscribers had been added to the list but no details were given.

Whereas there had been little opposition to the Wey & Arun Junction Canal Bill during its progress through both Houses in 1813 this was not the case with the proposal to extend the navigation to Portsmouth. Indeed, before John Rennie could report to the promoters , an influential opposition group of landowners and farmers had been formed which held its first meeting at the *Fleece Inn*, Chichester on 22 November 1815. Thirty-six people attended the meeting, chaired by Mr George Thomas M.P. for Chichester (1784-1812) of Yapton Place (who also owned Ford Wharf), at which it was agreed that the intended canal would 'be attended with great detriment to the country through which it passes without any adequate benefit derived from it'. It was argued that much valuable farmland would be left either dried up or, if the canal was carried into effect, the district would be drained of water in dry seasons. Twenty-nine gentlemen subscribed the substantial sum of £1,224 to meet the expense of opposing the scheme. Both Thomas and John Gustavus Crosbie* subscribed £200 each and John Peachey £100, while the farmers John Staker of Yapton and John Boniface of Climping† put their names down for £50 apiece. The land, at the point where it was proposed to begin the canal, belonged to Christ's Hospital and before the meeting took place Thomas was writing to Richard Corp, the Clerk to the Governors, stating that he understood from their tenant that the Hospital was against the intended canal.[10]

---

* General Sir John Gustavus Crosbie (1765-1843) was seized of property in Donnington through whose land the Chichester Canal was built 1818-23. He married Frances, daughter of George White Thomas of Yapton Place in 1802. The *Gentleman's Magazine* described him as a 'gallant officer' who joined the army in 1780 and was nominated a Grand Cross of the Hanoverian Guelphic Order in 1837.
† The Boniface family were farmer, millers and meal men in Ford and Yapton.

Early in the New Year, John Rennie reported favourably to the initial subscribers to the project. He referred to the Wey & Arun Junction Canal which was 'now under execution' and which would 'avoid those parts of the country where the greatest difficulties arose to the former schemes'. The benefits of the proposed navigation would be to avoid:

• The uncertainty of the coasting voyage from Arundel to Portsmouth.
• The loss, detention and inconvenience of having to transfer goods from barge or coaster at Arundel.

Rennie believed that the trade through this intended navigation 'will give an ample return to those who may be inclined to adventure their money on the project: while to the merchants of London and Portsmouth, as well as to the trade in all the towns near which this canal will pass, and to the country in general, the advantages will greatly exceed any reasonable calculation that may be made'.[11]

Rennie pronounced the line of country through which the canal would pass as 'very favourable' but mentioned the fact that he preferred the line he had first surveyed in 1803 and improved on in 1810.[12] However, the Government having 'recently purchased all the land which is contiguous to Portsbridge, thereby occasioned a difficulty not easily to be surmounted', but which Rennie proposed to overcome by building the 1¼-mile Cosham Canal with two locks to give direct access from Langstone Harbour into Portsmouth Harbour.

The new line from Ford was to pass some 13 miles through Yapton and Barnham to Chichester Harbour. Rennie drew attention to the lengthy cuttings required near Yapton, at Lidsey and at Donnington; 'also to several valleys of some magnitude to embank at Denges Burn near Yapton, another west of Barnham, one near Lidsey and one at the sewer dividing the parishes of Bersted and Oving'. A barge canal would form a branch line from Hunston to Chichester.

The navigation from Chichester Harbour was to be made through dredged channels in the tideway to the north of Thorney and Hayling Islands to near

A REPORT

TO

THE SUBSCRIBERS TO A CANAL

FROM

ARUNDEL TO PORTSMOUTH,

&c. &c. &c.

By JOHN RENNIE, Esq.

PORTSMOUTH:

PRINTED BY MOTTLEY, HARRISON, AND MILLER.

1816.

3 *It was Rennie's report which set out the case for building the navigation.*

the Convict Watering Place on Eastney Lake in Langstone Harbour. From here a canal was to be dug across Portsea Island to the Halfway Houses on Portsea Common, 'a central point between the towns of Portsmouth and Portsea'. Rennie estimated the cost at £118,990 (see Appendix B) to which £6,500 was later added for the branch to Chichester, bringing the total to £125,490.

In March, William Turner chaired a meeting of subscribers to explain Rennie's proposals for the Portsea and Cosham canals and how Fareham's inhabitants and 'its populous vicinity' would be supplied with goods without having to go up the length of Portsmouth Harbour through the anchorage of H.M. ships.[13] However, in spite of Rennie's encouraging report, critical comment was not silenced and in March John Staker, who farmed 347 acres at Ford, reported to his landlords (the Governors of Christ's Hospital) that George Thomas had informed him a few days ago that the Portsmouth Canal was not likely to take place, 'which I was happy to hear of'.[14] Six months later he was apologising for not answering the Hospital's enquiry and thought that the proposed canal had been given up until he read the notice in the *Lewes News* that week. Even so, he felt there would be strong opposition by the landowners in these parts as it will be very 'pridiges' to their estates.[15]

Notice of the intended application to Parliament for the Bill in September 1816 resulted in the columns of the *Hampshire Telegraph* being filled with a lengthy and mostly repetitive correspondence between 'Zeno', 'Atticus' and 'Vetus' on the merits and stupidity of the proposal.[*]

'Zeno' (who chose to remain anonymous) began by stating that, however much it was desirable to employ the labouring poor, the primary object must be to ensure that either the money laid out was recoverable or alternatively the public utility was equal to the money expended. He considered that the proposed navigation was not viable on the following grounds:

- The coastal trade was already sufficient to meet the current needs. The canal could cause eight costing smacks to be laid up and sixty or seventy horses prevented from being yoked to the waggon trade.
- Valuable agricultural land would be destroyed by the canal's construction.
- The canal's advantage over the coastal route would be dissipated if the open water route through Chichester and Langstone Harbours was retained.
- The money would be better spent in relieving poverty by providing the poor with cheap provisions and by assisting the fishing industry.[16]

'Atticus' repudiated 'Zeno's' statements the following week and recommended 'Zeno' to follow the precepts of his master.[17] 'Zeno' replied a week later disagreeing with 'Atticus' and repeating the well known doggerel written about the Redbridge branch of the Southampton and Salisbury Canal:

[*] Only John Williams, who used the pseudonym 'Vetus', revealed his identity.

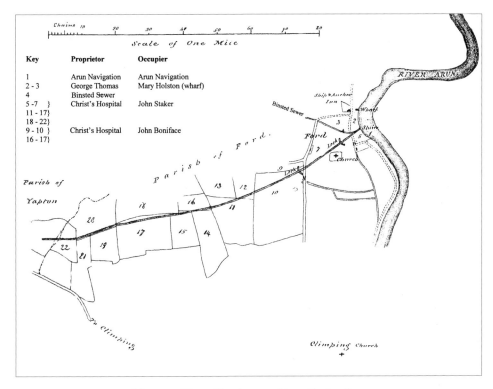

MAP 2 *Plan of land ownership at Ford, 1817.*

Southampton's wise sons found their river so large,
Tho' 'twould carry a Ship, 'twould not carry a barge.
But soon this defect their sage noddles supply'd,
For they cut a snug ditch to run close by its side.
Like the man who, contriving a hole through his wall,
To admit his two cats, the one great, t'other small,
Where a great hole was made for great puss to pass through,
Had a little hole cut for his little cat too.[18]

The correspondence was concluded by 'Vetus' in a lengthy article entitled 'The Intended Canal' which, while admitting that many projects had failed, others could be shown to have succeeded in the highest degree.[19] Williams (quoting himself) wrote that documents, proving that upward of £30,000 had been paid for transporting goods between London and Portsmouth in 1815, were open for inspection and that between 17 and 18,000 tons had passed by coasting vessels. The cost of carriage by land averaged £4 10s. 0d. a ton. 'Vetus' rashly claimed that water would be supplied 'with the trifling expense of two steam engines'.

'Zeno' was accused of self-interest in his mis-statements to the public relative to the canal and challenged to reveal his identity, so that the public could judge whether the completion of the canal could conflict with his own self interests, but to no avail.

Three weeks before the official opening of the Wey & Arun Junction Canal, the *Hampshire Telegraph* reported that 'several gentlemen' had set out from Littlehampton to Weybridge on a trial voyage through the new canal and returned to the port within three days. The party reported that they passed each lock in the average space of five minutes and saw loaded barges with 'upwards of 45 tons of goods' pass through in the same space of time. 'Frivolous objections indeed have been urged against, and erroneous opinion entertained, upon this part of the communication by those who were prejudiced or who had taken but a superficial view of the subject', concluded the report.[20]

While this correspondence was keeping the readers of the Hampshire press bemused, the management committee were concerned about the attitude of the Governors of Christ's Hospital, the owners of the land at Ford which would be required for the entrance to the canal from the river Arun. As Lord Egremont had been a Donation Governor of the Hospital since 1805, he was clearly the person to try to obtain their agreement, and so in September he wrote to Richard Corp. His lordship proposed that the treasurer, James Palmer, and Corp might like to attend the dinner being given at the *White Hart Inn* in Guildford to celebrate the completion of the Wey & Arun Junction Canal. He went on to suggest that they might care to return to Petworth House before visiting the Hospital's property.[21] Corp attended the dinner on Saturday 28 September but was unable to accept his lordship's invitation to Petworth. Egremont wrote to him after the dinner saying he was very sorry that he had not seen more of him 'in the bustle of yesterday and that as Petworth was only one stage beyond Guildford he would be very happy to see him there whenever it might be convenient'.[22]

It was not surprising that Egremont had been unable to talk to him. There had been 127 guests. His lordship was in the chair with the Earl of Onslow and Lord Grantley, the High Steward of Guildford, seated on either side. Among the many distinguished people present had been William Huskisson, Vice Admiral Sir George Murray who had served with Nelson, Lord Melville, the First Lord of the Admiralty (1812-26) and Lord Musgrave, a previous First Lord (1807-10) and now Master of the Ordnance (1810-18).

The *Hampshire Telegraph* reported 'with great pleasure' that when Lord Egremont gave the toast of Lord Melville and the Admiralty, he averred that

> the noble Lord and the Board were fully aware of the benefit which the public service will derive from this canal if it should be extended but a very few miles further to Portsmouth, both in peace and war. All present then drank to the 'Success to the Intended Portsmouth & Arundel Canal and Health to its Promoters'. The *Hampshire Telegraph's* correspondent observed that 'this sentiment of approbation of the plan was warmly expressed by all present'.[23]

It is evident that during the year Lord Egremont had been using his best endeavours to obtain the approval of both the Admiralty and the Board of Ordnance to the plan to extend the canal into Portsmouth Harbour.

There was opposition to the idea on the grounds that the safety of the country's great port and arsenal should not in any way be lessened by barges breaching its defences. The Government had only recently (1814) purchased the land contiguous to Portsbridge. To overcome this difficulty it had been agreed that Portsmouth Harbour should be reached by a canal built behind the defences at Wymering.

Egremont wrote again to Corp in the New Year explaining in detail the position regarding the land required by the canal company. Egremont began his letter by stating that the Bill was going before Parliament in the ensuing session 'under the most promising auspices with the entire approbation and good wishes of the Board of Admiralty' and emphasising that the new navigation was 'an object of great public importance and benefit'.

His lordship then went on to explain how, being a 'very old resident in the neighbourhood of those canals', he had devoted considerable attention to subjects of this nature and pointed out that the Hospital would receive a much larger rent for the few acres required than it did at present. As for their land being cut asunder, the only difference for the tenants would be that they would have to pass over flat bridges instead of through the present gates. Egremont concluded by stating that he would be 'ready and happy' to attend on the Governors at their convenience.[24]

Egremont was unwell the following day and wrote to say that he was unable to travel 'or I would certainly have gone to London to attend the committee tomorrow'. The following week he was still unwell and 'cannot depend upon my health from one day to another'. He thereupon wrote again to Corp a lengthy letter of seven pages which set out the pros and cons of the canal project as he saw it.

Egremont listed the advantages of the canal to the Hospital as being the provision of cheap water carriage for their farm produce and the increase in value of their farmland as a result of their being able to considerably augment the rent to their tenant farmers. The earl then went on to list the benefits.

Firstly, the removal of mercantile shipping from Portsmouth to Langstone Harbour, 'a measure highly advantageous to the public service as well as to the trade of Portsmouth and long wished for by the Board of Admiralty'.

Secondly, the provision of a cheap and easy conveyance for many heavy articles which now pass in waggons at great expense between Portsmouth and London on Admiralty and Ordnance business.

Thirdly, the prevention of smuggling.

> The coast from Littlehampton to the neighbourhood of Portsmouth is well known to be the shallowest upon the coast in the whole Channel, so that no ships but those of little draught can approach within many miles of the shore and the smugglers take advantage of this to land their goods upon the peninsular [sic] which is now their principal resort, but the canal by cutting the whole peninsular [sic] across and leaving only the passes over the bridges where the Customs Officers will be sure of meeting them, will certainly have the effect of

preventing a great fraud upon the revenue as well as great injury to the morals
of the people by whom this fraud is carried on.*

Egremont went on to state what he considered to be the objections of
those against the canal. Firstly, he felt that tenants were not much interested
in land improvements as improvements were generally attended with an
increase in rent; secondly, that they felt they were liable to suffer from the
depredations of the navigators (the labourers building the canal). Thirdly,
they disliked the valuation which took place between the canal company
and the landlords since they were placed in an awkward dilemma, on the
one hand wanting to exaggerate the value of the land taken from their
farm but 'having a contrary feeling with respect to the rent of the whole
farm upon which that land is taken'; other objections were interference
with their sports and another was the 'feeling which probably many of the
committee have observed in persons of a higher station than farmers, that
although they would not upon any account engage in smuggling, they are
not unwilling to avail themselves of the convenience of sometimes having
opportunities of purchasing from the smugglers'.[25]

Egremont's experience of inland navigation went back over thirty years from
the time he had invited William Jessop to Petworth House to discuss the viability
of waterways and the benefits they could bring to agriculture. In 1791 he had
obtained an Act of Parliament to make the River Rother navigable at his own
expense from the River Arun at Stopham to Midhurst and, although thwarted
in his attempt to link Petworth directly to the Wey Navigation and the Thames,
his substantial shareholdings in both the Arun Navigation (36 per cent) and
the Wey & Arun Junction Canal (25 per cent) gave him a sound understanding
of waterways and the benefits they brought to the community.

One of the farmers' worries, that the canal might spoil their sport, gave
Egremont the opportunity to express his wry humour. He now foresaw
that hares when hunted would 'take a different course upon that they
have been used to'; in spite of that he felt that they would be quite as
numerous and quite as 'good for the table, and will, I believe, afford as
good diversion though perhaps in a different direction'. And then in more
serious vein he went on to say, 'I am warranted as saying they will be as
numerous, because I and many other gentlemen in Sussex† have lands
close to navigable canals on which there are as many pheasants and hares
as before the canals were made'.[26]

---

* At the time that Egremont was writing (1817), smuggling threatened to escalate out of control
along the south coast. Roy Philip describes in detail in *The Coast Blockade* (see Bibliography) how the
government countered the threat by empowering the Royal Navy to guard the shores from Sheerness
to Chichester. Many attacks on customs officials were reported in the local papers but one particular
success was achieved in April 1823 when John Bide, a Temporary Riding Officer stationed at the
port of Chichester, came upon a group of smugglers unloading tubs of brandy in Mundham parish.
He bravely waded into the sea, climbed into their boat and, after being thrown overboard and then
knocked down, eventually succeeded in securing it. The customs commissioners offered a reward of
£100 for the apprehension of any of the offenders (*Hampshire Telegraph*, 2 June 1823).

† Both Egremont's son-in-law Sir Charles Merrick Burrell and Lord Selsey were leading proprietors in
the nearby Baybridge Canal whose Act was granted in 1825.

III

PARLIAMENTARY PROGRESS
1817

Petition for bill (1817) – petitions against – second reading – referred to committee – sent to the House of Lords and returned without amendment – Act obtained in July 1817 – summary of main sections – the list of subscribers.

The petition for the bill was brought to the House of Commons on 14 February 1817. Referred to committee, it was reported on 19 February that it complied with standing orders. On 24 February the subscribers met at the Old Town Hall in Portsmouth to give their formal approval and confirm their support. However, Nathaniel Atcheson, the parliamentary agent, warned the canal's management committee that the Bill was going to be opposed, and, in view of the efforts being made to procure signatures against the Bill, it was urged that the inhabitants of Gosport, Portsea and Portsmouth should sign the counter-petition which had been left in the *Blacksmith's Arms* at the Halfway Houses.[1] On 4 March the Bill had its first reading. During the next few weeks two petitions, one from the inhabitants of Chichester and the other from those of Portsmouth, were lodged in favour of the navigation but there were also no fewer than five against; of these, 'three came from owners and occupiers of property along the proposed line of the canal and two were from the ship owners, ship builders and persons connected with the coastal shipping trade in New Shoreham and Littlehampton.

Another body alarmed by the prospective bill was the Commissioners of Littlehampton Harbour. They called a special general meeting, held at the *Norfolk Arms Inn* in Arundel on Monday 24 February 1817, which was attended by 33 commissioners. After a long discussion it was resolved that the proposed bill should be 'vigilantly watched' and that eight named individuals should be empowered to direct the clerk (Richard Holmes) to act on any point which might need to be dealt with without him having to call a general meeting.

The Commissioners felt that the proposed navigation would 'most materially reduce' the port dues at Littlehampton by reducing the amount of traffic entering the port. The likelihood of increased barge and other traffic up the river would also accelerate the need to repair the timber

ANNO QUINQUAGESIMO SEPTIMO

GEORGII III. REGIS.

****

Cap. lxiii.

An Act for making and maintaining a Navigable
Canal from the River *Arun* to *Chichester* Harbour,
and from thence to *Langstone* and *Portsmouth*
Harbours, with a Cut or Branch from *Hunston*
Common, to or near the City of *Chichester;* and
for improving the Navigation of the Harbour
of *Langstone*, and Channels of *Langstone* and
Thorney.   [7th *July* 1817.]

WHEREAS the making and maintaining a Canal navigable for
Boats, Barges, and other Vessels from the River *Arun*, at or
near to a certain Public House called *The Ship and Anchor*, in
the Parish of *Ford*, in the County of *Sussex*, to the Harbour of *Chichester*,
at or near to a certain Place called *The Salterns*, in the Parishes of *Birdham* and *Itchenor*, in the said County of *Sussex*, in, to, or through the
several Parishes of *Ford*, *Yapton*, *Barnham*, *Aldingbourn*, *Birstead*, *Oving*,
Merston, *North Mundham*, *Hunston*, *Donnington*, *Appledram*, *Birdham*, and
Itchenor, or some or one of them, in the said County of *Sussex;* and also
the making and maintaining another or Branch Canal, navigable for Boats,
Barges, and other Vessels, from and out of the main Line of the above-
mentioned Canal, at or near to a certain Place called *Hunston Common*,
in the said Parish of *Hunston*, to or near to a certain Place called *Southgate*, in the Parish of *Saint Bartholomew*, at or near the City of *Chichester*,
in the said County of *Sussex*, in, to, or through the several Parishes of
Hunston, *Donnington*, *Rumboldswyke*, *Saint Pancras*, *Saint Peter the Great*
[*Local.*]   17 P   or

4   *Preamble to the Portsmouth & Arundel Canal Navigation Act 1817.*

piers (which having been erected in 1734 were now old and dilapidated)
and create more wear to the towing path up to Ford. The Commissioners
resolved to seek powers to impose a toll of 3d. a ton on those articles now
liable to pay pier dues.

The House of Commons Committee met to consider the clauses of
the Bill and the points made by the petitioners in late April and agreed

> Fresh Water tobe supplied the Canals between the River Arun and Chichester Harbour.
>
> LVI. Provided also, and be it enacted, That in order to preserve the Water of the said intended Canals and Cuts between the River *Arun* and *Chichester* Harbour from any Mixture of Salt Water, the same shall not be supplied with any Water out of the said Harbour of *Chichester*; and in case the same is supplied from the River *Arun*, then it shall be supplied at such Times of the Ebb Tide as shall be not less than Two Hours after High Water, and from thence until not exceeding One Hour after Flood; and that in order to prevent the Water of the said intended Canals and Cuts from becoming putrid and stagnant, and thereby noxious to the Health and offensive to the Persons inhabiting the Vicinity thereof, the said Company of Proprietors, or their Committee of Management, shall from Time to Time cause the said Canals or Cuts to be furnished with a Supply of such Water as aforesaid, fully sufficient to keep the Water of the said Canals and Cuts pure and free from noxious and offensive Qualities; the Extent and Sufficiency of such Supply, in the Event of any Dispute, to be determined by the said Commissioners appointed under or by virtue of this present Act.

5   *The extract from the 1817 Act relating to the fact that only fresh water was to be pumped into the barge canal whereas there was no prohibition on pumping salt water into the Portsea Canal which was later the cause of its failure.*

that clauses should be inserted into it to protect the interests of riparian landowners and occupiers.

The Bill was passed to the House of Lords on 24 June 1817, and examined by a committee of 16 which included Lord Egremont. Six days later the Earl of Shaftesbury reported the Bill without amendment. 'An Act for making and maintaining a Navigable Canal from near the City of Chichester Harbour, with a Cut or Branch from Hunston Common, to or near the City of Chichester, and for improving the Navigation of the Harbour of Langston, and Channels of Langstone and Thorney' received the Royal Assent on 7 July 1817. By now £101,250 had been subscribed toward the estimated cost of £125,450.

The Act contained 150 sections, designating both the means to be employed in building the canal and the manner in which it was to be maintained. The subscribers to the undertaking were constituted 'The Company of Proprietors of the Portsmouth & Arundel Navigation' and were now empowered to purchase all lands and acquire rights of way wherever necessary for the construction and maintenance of the waterway (Section I).*
The company was authorised to raise £126,000 by the issue of 2,520 shares of £50 each. If this sum proved insufficient, the company could either raise up to £10,000 by issuing further shares or by mortgage of the navigation; alternatively the company, 'for the more speedy completion of the canal', could borrow up to £40,000 by mortgaging the tolls (LVII).

The names of the 269 subscribers, who were required to pay a deposit of £1 a share, were listed by rank and in alphabetical order. The list was headed by the Duke of Norfolk and the Earl of Egremont. There was

* Figures in parentheses denote the section of the Act.

strong naval support. Besides Admiral Keith there was Admiral Exmouth, Commander-in-Chief Plymouth (1817-21) and Vice-Admiral Sir Alexander Cochrane, who was promoted admiral in 1819 and became the Commander-in-chief Portsmouth in 1821. Rear Admirals Peter Halkett and Home Popham, seven naval captains and four officers from the Royal Marines were included in the list. Other distinguished speculators included Dame Catherine Prevost, Sir Edward Tucker, several doctors of divinity and one Member of Parliament, Henry Howard Mollineux (*sic*) who had represented the City of Gloucester in seven parliaments until 1818 when he became one of the Members for Arundel.*

Subscribers who were shareholders in the adjoining waterways included Richard Wardroper, the clerk and William Cutfield, the treasurer of the Arun Navigation; James Mangles, MP for Guildford, and William Newland, management committee members of the Wey & Arun Junction Canal. James Hollinsworth, shortly to be appointed resident engineer, was also named. However, the names of two leading local landowners do not appear – the Duke of Richmond of Goodwood House and Lord Selsey of West Dean House – for reasons that are not apparent.

Most of the sections in the Act were intended to provide a sound basis for the running of the company, protection for landowners and occupiers of property and penalties for malfeasance. General meetings were to held annually in May in Portsmouth (LXVI); shareholders to have one vote for every share and a chairman to be appointed at every meeting (LXIII). A Committee of Management, elected from those possessing five or more shares, was to control the workings of the company and to meet in August, November and February. Ten individuals were named in the Act (LXVI) and were to hold office for three years together with five others to be elected within six weeks of the passing of the Act. Five members present were needed to form a quorum. Notice of meetings had to be published in the Sussex and Hampshire newspapers ten days in advance (LXVI). Commissioners were to be appointed to settle differences between the company and landowners (XVII). Where landowners disagreed with the commissioners' determination, appeal could be made to a jury of 12, whose assessment would be final (XXII).

The Admiralty had insisted that no weirs or dams should be erected between Portsmouth and Langstone Harbours which might obstruct the natural flow of water and which might reduce the depth of water in Portsmouth Harbour (II). The company also had to expend two-thirds of the capital raised to ensure the completion of the section of the canal between the river Arun and Chichester Harbour 'with as much expedition as possible' (LXXIX).

---

* He was the younger brother of the 12th Duke of Norfolk and died in 1824. In October 1817 the Prince Regent ordained that he could take the title of Lord Henry Thomas Howard Molineaux Howard and act as deputy Earl Marshal of England. (C. Wright, *The History and Description of Arundel Castle*, second edition, 1818, pp.139-40, J. Dallaway and E. Cartwright, *Rape of Arundel*, 1832, Vol.II part the first p.184.)

Sections were devoted to making watering places for cattle (XLVIII), ways of obtaining capital (LVII), issuing shares (LVIII), mortgaging (LXI) or letting the tolls (XCIX); to authorising the Company to dig or erect, if required, all manner of objects like soughs, water stanks, watch-houses, weighing beams, dry docks, cranes, and fire engines (I); to permit the employment of rollers or inclined planes instead of locks (III). Maximum toll and wharfage rates were fixed; manure could be charged at 2d. per ton-mile; merchandise and commodities at 4d. per ton-mile; parcels not exceeding two cwt at one penny a mile (XCIV). Empty boats were to pay one shilling a lock while passenger boats had to be licensed (CV).

Egremont's recent difficulties with barge-master William Stoveld of Petworth over the method of calculating tolls and gauging tonnage and the identification of barges on the Rother Navigation account for the exactness of Section XCVI. This required posts to be fixed at quarter-mile intervals and tolls to be paid for a full quarter mile even if not actually passed; likewise cargoes were to be weighted to the nearest full quarter of a ton.* Furthermore, every barge had to have its name and number painted in white on its stern and two indexes of graduated figures to denote the tonnage of the cargo carried (CX). Any person guilty of defacing the marks (which is what had also occurred on the Rother Navigation) could be fined up to £5.

The importance of the new steam vessels was recognised but clause CIX ensured that the use of high pressure engines in boats impelled by steam would not be lawful if 'the steam is blown into the atmosphere instead of being condensed by cold water, or in which the steam used to work the engine is of a strength equal to double the pressure of the atmosphere'. Lock-keepers giving undue preference to any barge could be fined up to twenty shillings (CXIV). Fines of up to £5 could be levied on persons leaving open swivel-bridges of which sum one moiety was to be given to the informer and the other to the poor of the parish where the offence was committed (CXVIII). The stiff penalty of transportation for a term not exceeding fourteen years was reserved for anyone convicted of destroying canal property (CXX).

Lords of the Manor were entitled to retain their right of fishery (CXXV), but anyone having on board his boat any fishing tackle could be fined five pounds (CXXII). Several measures had been included to appease or meet the objections of landowners and tenant farmers. For instance, in places where the company would have to spread excavated clay over adjoining or nearby land, the land had to be restored by covering the spoil with at least nine inches of soil (L). Where the canal divided an owner's land, a bridge was to be made (XLV) unless the land measured less than an acre of 50 yards in breadth, in which case it was to be bought by the company and, if necessary, resold (VIII). Private wharves could be erected by landowners

---

* See *London's Lost Route to Midhurst* (1995), chapter VIII, pp.97-100.

(CI), who were granted the fishing rights (CXIX) and allowed to keep pleasure boats on the canal *gratis*, unless passing through the locks. Boats of husbandry could also be used for conveying cattle or manure to any other farm or land in their possession toll free provided that the boats did not exceed five feet in breadth and twelve feet in length and were not employed in carrying goods to market (CXXVI).

The marriage or death of proprietors could cause the clerk difficulty in ascertaining to whom dividends ought to be paid. It was, therefore, required that an affidavit containing the copy of the marriage register or a copy of the will and letter of administration had to be produced and shown to the company's clerk (XC). The company was entitled to make bylaws to regulate its affairs with power to impose fines of up to £5 in the event of contravention (LXXXIV).

Finally, the Act specified that, if the canal should not be completed within ten years, then the powers of the Act would become void, except for that part of the canal which had been completed (CXXXI).

IV

FORMING THE COMPANY
1817-1818

The Committee of Management – Rear-Admiral Peter Halkett – his distinguished
naval career – Admiral Keith – the 3rd Earl of Egremont – his advice sought
– subscription list filled – Rennie reports on the Portsbridge Creek proposal
– James Hollinsworth appointed resident engineer – his background – Dyson
& Thornton engaged as contractors.

At the company's first general meeting held at Portsmouth on 5 August 1817,
the proprietors invited Rear-Admiral Peter Halkett (1765-1839) to take the
chair.* In addition to the other nine members listed in the Act (namely Sir
Lucius Curtis Bt, William Turner, Trevor Lethem, Moses Greetham, John
Williams, William Cutfield, John Snook, Thomas Edgecombe, Robert Park)
who were to hold office for three years, the Earl of Egremont, Viscount
Keith, James Brown, William T. Williams and Benjamin Goodeve were
elected to the management committee.

At this first meeting the opportunity was taken to congratulate those
who had enabled the company to obtain its Act. William Thomas Williams
of Blendworth House thanked both Lord Egremont and Lord Keith for
their valuable support, Sir John Jackson for his zealous attention to the
Bill as it passed through the House of Commons, and Sir Lucius Curtis
and the members of his sub-committee for their unremitting exertions. A
shareholder, Mr Hopkins of Gosport, thanked John Williams for having
proposed the construction of the canal and he in turn expressed 'his
high sense of the honour done him'. Lastly, Sir Lucius Curtis recalled
William Turner's 'indefatigable' exertions in explaining the great public
utility of the measure to the different government departments whose
support he had obtained.[1]

The committee was thus composed of a group of noblemen, landowners,
attorneys and farmers rather than men of business. It had little or no
experience of building a navigation of such magnitude nor of the canal

---

* The Committee elected one of its number to act as chairman at each meeting. Lieut. Peter Halkett,
RN made the first recorded trip in a rubber boat cloak from Kew to Westminster Bridge in June
1844 (P.A.L. Vine, *Pleasure Boating in the Victorian Era* (1983), pp.1-4).

trade. The only salaried executive was – the clerk, G.L. Greetham, who acted as secretary to what by present-day standards would be regarded as a body of unpaid non-executive directors.

Peter Halkett (1765-1839) was a distinguished naval officer. The admiral had commenced his naval career during the war with the American colonies. On the outbreak of hostilities with France in 1793 he was lieutenant of the frigate *Syren* in which HRH the Duke of York sailed to Holland to take command of the British troops sent there to help the Dutch. After successfully commanding 28 small gun boats in the defence of Williamstadt, HRH recommended him for promotion and the Prince of Orange awarded him a handsome gold medal and chain worth 500 guilders. He next took command of the *Echo* sloop of war and then the 28-gun frigate *Circe*, in which in 1797 he took part in the decisive victory of Admiral Duncan over the Dutch fleet at Camperdown. In January 1799 he survived shipwreck when the *Circe* ran aground off the Texel without loss of life.

Appointed to a new frigate, Halkett sailed to the West Indies. There, and in the Gulf of Mexico, he succeeded in capturing numerous Spanish warships and privateers before the Treaty of Amiens brought a temporary respite from war and he returned to England in 1802. He resumed active service in 1806, took part in the second battle of Copenhagen (1807) where he commanded the 64-gun *Ganges*, joined the fleet off the Tagus blockading Lisbon and in 1809 accompanied the grand, but unfortunate, expedition to the island of Walcheren. Promoted to rear-admiral in 1812, he became second-in-command at Portsmouth in 1814. In July 1821 he attained the rank of Vice-Admiral of the Blue* and lived at Catherington House near Horndean which had been built by Admiral Lord Hood.

Another distinguished naval officer was Admiral Lord George Keith (1746 -1823). Joining the navy in 1761, he had been largely responsible for suppressing the Sheerness Mutiny of 1792. Promoted admiral in 1801, he became Commander-in-Chief of the North Sea Fleet responsible for coastal defence 1803-7, was a colleague of Horatio Nelson when in the Mediterranean and from 1812 to 1815 was Commander-in-Chief of the Channel Fleet. Created a viscount in 1814, he was, after Napoleon's defeat at Waterloo, one of those who met the former emperor at Plymouth in August 1815 and ensured his departure to St Helena. Keith was held in high regard as a meticulous administrator. However when elected to the management committee he was over seventy and had terminated his naval career to spend time in improving Purbrook Park, his estate at Farlington which stood within sight of Portsmouth Harbour. He had amassed a small fortune (£177,000 in prize money alone between 1803-6) which he later also lavished on his castle on the banks of the Firth of Forth. Among

---

* Admirals seldom retired in the early 19th century and in 1837 at the age of 72 Halkett became Admiral of the Blue and served as Commander-in-Chief North America (W.L. Clowes, *History of the Royal Navy* (1901), vol.VI, p.204).

Portsmouth and Arundel Navigation.

The Committee think it proper to communicate to Mr. Brooks *that of* Two Thousand Five Hundred and Nine Shares, *which are required to complete the amount of the Estimate for this undertaking, only* Four Hundred and Fifty-five *remain unengaged at this date. They therefore send herewith the Statement of the Trade, accompanied with observations resulting from their enquiries, and are induced to hope that he will have no objection to recommend the same to the consideration of his Friends, with a view to the more expeditious completion of the Subscription List.*

PORTSMOUTH, August 8th, 1817.

6 *Work on building the canal could not begin until £125,450 had been subscribed.*

the other committee members, the most influential was George O'Brien Wyndham, 3rd Earl of Egremont (1751-1837), who was the company's largest shareholder. The story of the vital part Egremont played in the development of inland navigation in Surrey and Sussex will be found in *London's Lost Route to the Sea* and *London's Lost Route to Midhurst* (see Bibliography).

Of the others John Williams was a senior customs official at Portsmouth at a time when smuggling was rife; William Cutfield was a major landowner and farmer at Climping, who had been the Arun Navigation's treasurer since 1813 as well as its largest shareholder. Benjamin Goodeve was a Gosport brewer. Moses Greetham and Thomas Edgecombe were Portsea solicitors.

The committee's first tasks were to raise the capital, to appoint a resident engineer, to start negotiations for the purchase of land and to engage one or more contractors. The passing of the Act of 7 July 1817 and the attendant publicity had given rise to a flurry of interest in the project. However, work could not begin until the full amount of the estimated cost had been subscribed. £101,250 was promised at the time the Act was passed, left £24,200 still required.[2] Early in August the management committee dispatched a circular, prepared by John Williams, to all interested parties setting out the company's trading expectations in some detail.[3] This document described the trade which had been carried on by land and sea in 1816 (both in the locality and between London, Chichester and Portsmouth) from which the canal's revenue would be derived. The committee confidently expected that half of the 80,000 tons carried would pass to the navigation. If this was so the annual income would exceed £10,000 (£5,000 less than the expectation published in the *Hampshire Telegraph* two months before) and provide a return of 'nearly' ten per cent per annum to the shareholders on an outlay of £125,000. The

7 *Ticket issued on receipt of subscriber's deposit of £1 a share, 1817.*

canal would, it was thought, supersede the local coasting trade by obviating the expense of transhipment at Arundel and the delays of 'several weeks if the wind set on the shore'. However, it was admitted that some of the estimates were uncertain, such as the amount of the corn traffic to be expected between Arundel and Chichester Harbour. A printed covering note dated 8 August, and personally addressed to each subscriber, hoped that he would recommend the purchase of shares to his friends 'with a view to the more expeditious completion of the subscription list'.

Local commercial interests had also been hesitant in their support but in November John Williams informed Lord Egremont that Godwin's Bank in Portsmouth who had always treated 'our measures very slightingly' had changed their mind and requested 20 shares 'which were a great acquisition to our strength'. Meantime Williams was concerned that, if the public thought that all the shares had been taken up and if the present holders later surrendered them to the company, it would be 'most prejudicial to the concern'. Williams suggested that Egremont should write to him to this effect so that he could show them his letter and bring them into line and then 'the world is assured that every share is bona fide sold'.[4] Slowly the subscription list was filled and its completion announced on 6 January 1818; Egremont retained 315 shares but it was not until 3 March 1818 that the first call of £3 a share (which included the £1 deposit made before the passing of the Act) had to be paid.[5] The other principal shareholders included the Cutfield family of Climping who held 125 shares. Twelve speculators held over 20 shares apiece and other investors included the Duke of Norfolk, Viscount Keith, Viscount Exmouth and 'very many Gentlemen and Ladies of great respectability', among them Captain John Bligh and other senior naval officers.

In late November 1817 John Williams told the *Hampshire Chronicle* that work was planned to begin 'very early in the ensuing spring'. However, this was optimistic thinking, since no contractors had yet been engaged. It did, however, give the newspaper the opportunity to sing the canal's praises and how it would allow merchandise to be sent more safely than by sea. 'No person that is conversant with Inland Navigation, will hesitate to affirm that a barge housed, and with hatches battered down, is one of the safest modes for the conveyance of goods that can be resorted to; but the real benefit to the Owners of Goods of that might pass on this canal cannot be fully appreciated, but by a clear view of the casualties to which the sea voyage is subject. It would be superfluous to dwell on the great risque [*sic*] that will ever attend the navigation of the narrow part of the Channel from the privateers of the enemy in war time. We shall therefore only lay before our readers the actual risque to which goods by the coasting voyage are now subject from the elements. It appears by the General Shipping Lists, from the commencement of the present year to the 31 October last, that the following casualties have occurred between Portsmouth and London River, to such vessels only as were bound to or from some port in the British channel, viz. twenty-one driven into port with loss of anchors and cables, or otherwise disabled; six aground; eleven sprung leaks or much damaged in hull and cargo; four only were to the Westward of Dover – a sufficient indication as to where the greatest danger exists. We submit, therefore, that it is a very strong feature in favour of the Canal that it will present the means of forwarding goods from the metropolis to Chichester and Portsmouth, so as to avoid the sea voyage altogether, and the Western ports in the British Channel so as to avoid the most dangerous parts of it.'[6] Although work on raising the capital was still in hand and digging the canal had not begun, advertisements started to appear in the New Year offering for sale barges and lighters which would be suitable for use on the proposed canal.[7]

James Hollinsworth was appointed resident engineer in July 1818 at the substantial salary of £500 p.a. with an additional £50 p.a. for house rent and taxes. Born in the 1760s, he had married Ann Stanfield in 1797 and worked as a mason in Banbury before being employed in 1785 as a supervisor, under William Jessop's direction, on the Grand Junction Canal.[8] The company's minute book refers to his usefulness and conscientiousness, but also refers to him being reprimanded for negligence for failing to supervise remedial work to straighten Braunston Tunnel. Two years later

8   *The 3rd Earl of Egremont in 1825 when he was 64 years of age.*

he was recommended by John Rennie to be an inspector of masonry, earthwork and carpentry on the Kennet & Avon Canal. However, in April 1798 the committee proposed to arrest him for false accounting. In 1799 he carried out at John Rennie's instigation an admeasurement survey of the Southampton branch of the Salisbury & Southampton Canal.[9] Later in 1805 he was also, on John Rennie's recommendation, appointed resident engineer of the Crinan Canal. This canal had been opened in an unfinished state in 1801 and was not pronounced finally complete until 1809. However, the waterway had been built so badly that heavy expenditure was often

9   A 1,350-ton East-Indiaman bound for China, when driven ashore by a heavy gale near Eastbourne in February 1822. After the navigation was opened the following year it was hoped that such vessels would sail from Portsmouth after receiving their cargo by barge from Deptford or Queenhithe. In 1817 40 vessels were disabled or run aground between Dover and Portsmouth of which four were a total loss.

required for repairs. After a violent gale in January 1811, a collapsed embankment had caused the canal to be closed to navigation, at which point of time[10] James Hollinsworth junior succeeded his father who had become the resident engineer supervising the construction of Waterloo Bridge (1811-17).

It was the resident engineer's task to direct and supervise the work of the contractors, to attend all meetings of the management committee, to advise the committee on how the works were proceeding, of the difficulties being met and on how well the contractors were faring. Such skills were rarely found and the history of canal building is filled with more examples of incompetence than of success. However, this was not always the engineer's fault, because management committees had a habit of changing their minds and of not always promptly passing on details to the persons most concerned.

Digging the canal had not begun, and it was not until May that advertisements appeared for contractors to execute the works.[11] The contract, which

was awarded to Dyson & Thornton and signed on 4 August 1818, related
to only part of the navigation.* The cost of land, the branch at Wymering,
the basin in Chichester and the erection of the steam pumping engines
at Ford and Milton were excluded. The sums agreed for the remainder
were:

From the river Arun at Ford to the tideway in Chichester Harbour	£40,520
The branch barge canal from Hunston to Chichester	£4,170
The Portsea Canal	£11,960
The dredging of the wadeways of Thorney and Langstone	£7,400[†]
Total	£64,050

Payment was to be made monthly (less 10 per cent until half the work
was finished) and the contractors had to deposit £10,000 as a guarantee
for carrying out the work 'sedulously and diligently and in a good and
workmanlike manner.' The building was to be completed in 2½ years from
the date to be fixed by the resident engineer. In other words, digging could
not begin until the land was purchased and possessed and Hollinsworth had
been given the go-ahead. Whether Hollinsworth informed the contractors of
the actual date in writing or orally remains open to doubt – the contractors
later claimed that no date was ever mentioned.[12]

---

* Hollingsworth (sic), Bough and Dyson had on Rennie's recommendation been contracted to build
the Royal Military Canal in 1803 but when the famous engineer had inspected the works, three
months later, he was aghast. 'They have greatly disappointed my expectations', he wrote, 'and many
charges in the accounts at Shorncliffe unreasonable and ought not to be paid.' Consequently, the
contractors were dismissed and the work was completed by the Royal Staff Corps and the Royal
Sappers and Miners (P.A.L. Vine, Royal Military Canal (1972), pp.61-3).
† Rennie had allowed nearly £13,000 for this work (see Appendix B).

V

Building the Waterway
1818-1823

First sod cut at Ford – second Act of Parliament (1819) – valuation of land by sheriff's jury – steam pumping engine at work (1819) – boats used at Yapton to carry away spoil (1820) – agreement with the Arun Navigation embodied in third Act (1821) – its purpose – Thomas Telford's recommendation – Lord Egremont to the rescue.

The construction of the canal was a mighty task. Although the lie of the land was relatively flat and the engineering works unexceptional, there was nonetheless considerable cutting, excavation and puddling to be done. Six brickworks were established to provide for two substantial basins, six locks, 17 bridges and the abutments for 21 iron swivel bridges as well as 22 culverts. Three-storey buildings were required to house the pumping engines at Ford and Milton together with ancillary cottages, drains and wells. The excavation of the basins at Southgate and Halfway Houses required the removal of over 15,000 cubic yards of soil and two aqueducts were needed to cross the rifes at Aldingbourne and Lidsey. However, the most difficult work was to dredge the winding channel from Birdham through Chichester Harbour and around Thorney and Hayling Islands to provide a draught of 3 feet 6 inches at low water.

The first sod of turf was ceremoniously removed by John Williams at Ford on 18 August 1818. A fortnight later digging had begun at Merston; the bells of Chichester Cathedral rang a merry peel to celebrate the news and in the evening a quantity of beer was given away at the Market Cross.[1]

Meantime Rennie had drawn up the specification for the entrance lock at Birdham. Its length was to be 76 feet, its breadth 18 feet 6 inches. The requirement for building the bottom, cills, side walls, gates and trunking were minutely described on five pages of foolscap totalling 138 lines. The mortar was to be made with Lyme Regis lime, well burnt and unslacked but ground into powder and mixed with clean sharp river sand.

The front mortar to be one part of lime and three of sand and the backing four parts of sand – the lime and sand to be mixed together in their dry state and no water to be put to it until it is to be worked into mortar – it is then to be well beat and mixed until no white specks are to

MAPS 3(i) TO 3(v) *provide a comparison of the line of canal as surveyed by Netlam and Francis Giles in 1815 with the first edition of the one-inch Ordnance Survey (1813) on which are superimposed both the Portsmouth & Arundel Canal opened in 1823 and the Shoreham to Chichester Railway opened in 1846.*

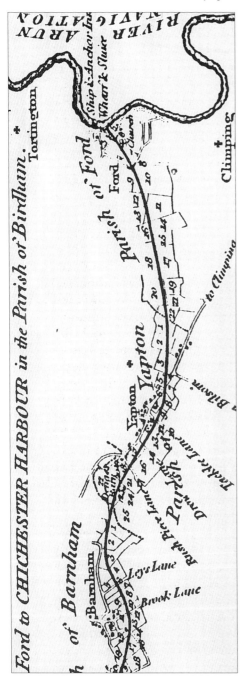

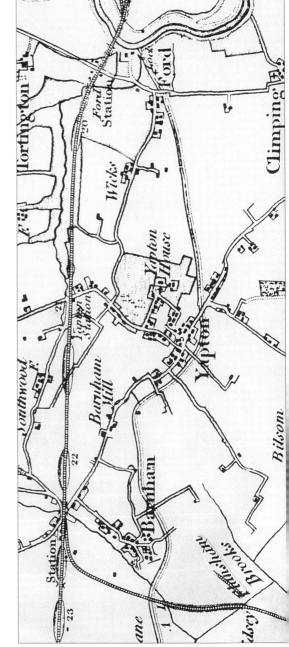

(i)   *Ford to Barnham.*

be seen in it – but no more is to be worked up than what can be used in one day; the heap is to be covered with sand to keep it from the air.

The stone was to be Bramley Fall, Cornish or Devonshire granite. Rennie concluded by stipulating that if the contractor failed to comply with his directions or ask an unreasonable price for any of them or not proceed with the works to the full satisfaction of the resident engineer, he is to have the power of taking the work out of the contractors hands and settle the amount in such manner as he shall think proper and all the measurements are to be made by him of the net solid contents without any allowance for curved work or extra labour.[2]

Work was going on apace elsewhere. On 17 November the *County Chronicle* reported that the works were proceeding 'with celerity' at seven different places and that the first bridge had been completed. By the following summer bricks were being made in large quantities at six different sites; two bridges were finished, two others were built up to the 'springing of the arch' and two were in progress.[3]

What the original Act of 1817 failed to include was any reference to the Arun Navigation and the Wey & Arun Junction Canal, although it did mention that barge owners had the right to use the Wey Navigation, without procuring a licence, upon payment of the tolls (CXXXVII). It was not, therefore, surprising that in June 1819 a second Act had to be obtained. The preamble stated that the proprietors of the Portsmouth & Arundel and Wey & Arun Junction Companies having entered into an agreement dated 1 September 1818 to reduce certain tolls on their respective navigations, 'it would be very beneficial to the public that such agreement should be confirmed and made binding'. The purpose of this arrangement was to enable the Wey & Arun to borrow £10,000 to pay off its outstanding debts and to complete new works which the clerk John Smallpeice told the House of Lords Committee examining the bill (11 June 1819) totalled £8,716. At the same time the Portsmouth & Arundel Navigation Company were empowered to levy higher tolls; on merchandise the rate was to go up by 50 per cent to 6d. a ton-mile, empty boats to 1s. 6d. a lock; manure was, however, reduced by 25 per cent to 1½d. a ton mile. The Act did not extend the reduced toll rates to goods conveyed out of the Arun Navigation which became the subject of two further agreements enacted in 1821 (see Bibliography).

The termination of the war with France had brought one benefit to the proprietors. Both the Admiralty and the Board of Ordnance had previously opposed granting direct access to Portsmouth Harbour through Portsbridge Creek because of the risk of weakening the defences and of lessening the draught of the inner harbour where the fleet was moored. For this reason Rennie had proposed the building of the Cosham Canal to overcome this objection and this had been sanctioned.

With hostilities over, Admiral Keith, together with signatories Lucius Curtis, William Turner, John Williams, Robert Park and Greetham, the

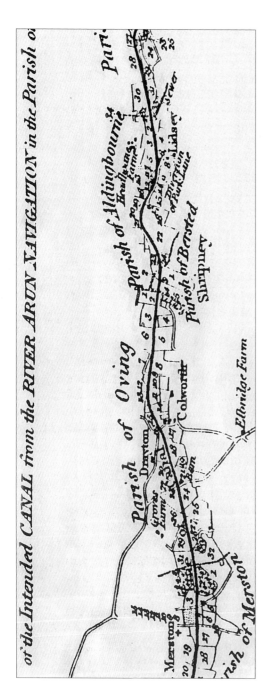

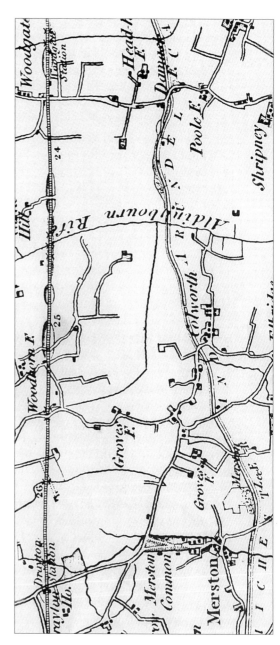

(ii)   *Aldingbourne to Merston.*

company's clerk, wrote in February 1818 to Lord Melville, the First Lord of the Admiralty, to enquire whether the Board would allow a realigned Portsbridge Channel to be deepened to allow the passage of barges and so save the cost of building the Cosham Canal and a bridge across the turnpike road to Petersfield.[4] The Board referred the matter to Rennie. He replied that, although he had 'never examined the Ditch correctly' himself, he saw no objection to the proposal provided that stop gates were erected by the canal company to control the flow of water out of, or into, Portsmouth Harbour. Rennie also drew attention to the need either for the provision of a tow-path or that the cut should be dug wide enough to preclude 'the paddle wheels of the steamboat' lacerating the banks.[5]

The next step was to obtain the agreement of the Board of Ordnance. Both the Commanding Royal Engineer (Colonel Sir Alan Bryce) and his superior, the Inspector General of Fortifications* (Lieut-General Gother Mann) opined that from a military point of view the proposal offered 'a very considerable advantage'.[6] The navigation company intended to erect a wooden hut for the toll-collector by the 'tête du port' and to rebuild Portsbridge while agreeing to defray half the cost of its future maintenance. It also undertook to allow the Board of Ordnance and its tenant farmers at Hilsea toll-free passage for its stores and agricultural implements.

Rennie was again asked to examine the clauses of the second canal Bill which related to the security of Portsmouth Harbour. He replied that he had 'distinctly stated' in his previous report that a lock might need to be erected at the Langstone entrance to Portsbridge Creek and that the clause in the draft Bill was not sufficient. However, he considered that there was little danger from steam vessels coming near the floating magazine as there was ample breadth to work in, which would not be the case if boats attempted the channel between Hornsea Island and the magazine at Tipner, as they would be liable to ground on the ebbing tide (but see pages 103-4).[7]

And so it was agreed, when the second Act came to be granted in June 1819, that Section XI repealed the authority to build the Cosham Canal and Section XII empowered the company to make Portsbridge Creek navigable. The Admiralty, while approving the work in principle, was wary as to the effect it might have on Portsmouth Harbour. It was therefore stipulated that the canal company should ensure that the bottom of the channel at its junction with Portsmouth Harbour should be on the same level at low water and two feet above this level at its junction with Langstone Harbour.

If necessary, a lock was to be built at the entrance to Langstone Harbour with the gates pointed towards the naval base (Section XV). It was a further condition that none of the excavated spoil should be deposited within 1,200 yards of the Board of Ordnance's fortifications without their consent.

---

* 1811-30; he was promoted General in 1821.

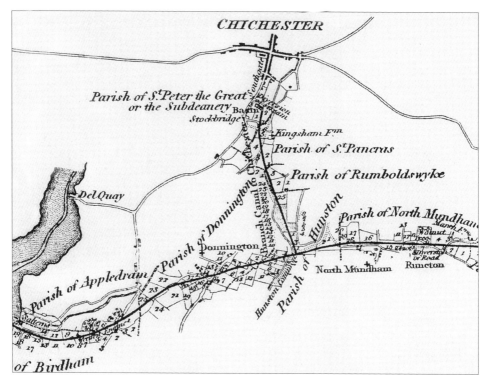

(iii)   *North Mundham to Birdham.*

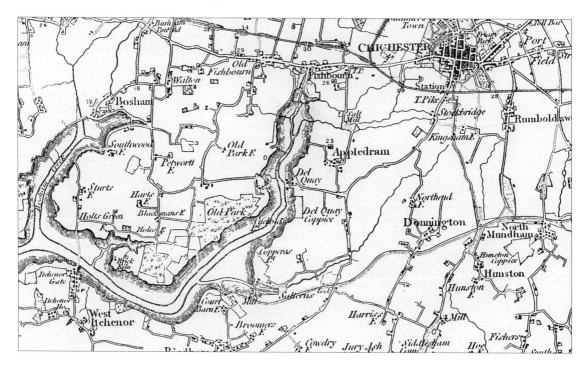

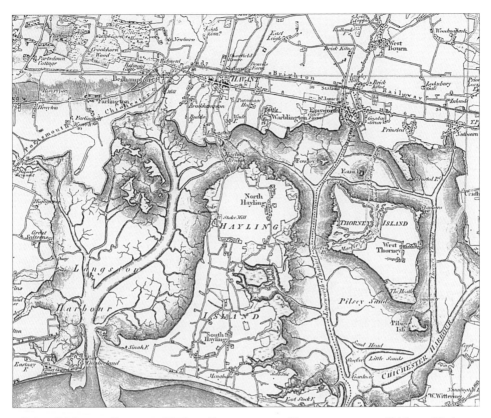

(iv)   *Chichester to Langstone Harbour. Barges were towed by steam tug across Chichester Harbour to the Emsworth Channel and north of Hayling Island where the dredged channel under the bridge is still known as the 'new cut'. The Wadeway to Thorney Island is marked 'road for carriages at low tide'.*

The creek was also forbidden for vessels with standing masts as the cut was intended only for 'boats, barges and lighters' (Section XVII). Lastly, it was agreed that Portsbridge should be jointly maintained by the Government and the company (Section XVIII).

The original proposal had been for the Ford-Birdham section to be built as a barge canal for boats carrying up to 40 tons. However, in September 1818 the Mayor of Chichester and his colleagues requested that the canal to the city should be widened and deepened to eight feet to admit sea-going vessels of 100 tons burthen and suggested as recompense the levying of an additional toll of one shilling a ton.* John Rennie advised Hollinsworth to widen the locks to 18 feet and provide five passing places. The company approved the proposal and also agreed to build a new road from Southgate

---

* A ship canal to Chichester to avoid coasting vessels transhipping cargoes into lighters at Itchenor and for goods to be then carted by the turnpike road from Dell Quay into the city had been considered at various times (see Heneghan, *The Chichester Canal*, pp.1-5). In July 1805 Rennie had instructed James Florance of Chichester to carry out two surveys which indicated that even a draught of 16 feet would be insufficient to allow shipping to enter the city at all states of the tide.

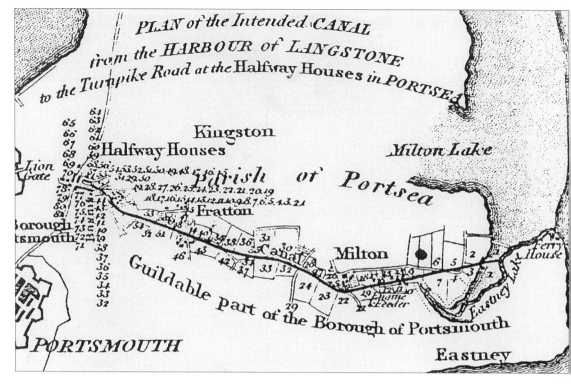

(v)   *Milton to Halfway Houses.*

basin to the city. It was considered that the extra cost would not exceed
£7,000.[8]

It was also agreed in May 1819 to increase the size of the Portsea Canal
so that sea-going vessels of 150 tons burthen could reach the centre of
the city at Halfway Houses. The draught was to be increased from five to
10 feet, the width from 40 to 60 feet, and swivel bridges provided; the
additional cost was estimated at £8,804. However 'in consequence of the
strong representation of several commercial gentlemen' of Portsmouth, it
was decided in January 1820 to further increase the draught to 12 feet to
allow vessels drawing 11½ feet to reach the basin. The contractors undertook
to execute this additional work for the surprisingly low consideration of
£200.[9]

Rennie was not consulted about this change and was later to question
the motive for expending so great a sum in the belief that it would increase
the water supply and so save the expense of working the steam pump. This
benefit was, he thought, rather questionable; 'the engine must after all be
looked to as the only legitimate means of supply'.[10]

For the past year or so the canal company's surveyors had been trying to
agree a fair valuation with the owners of the 15 shops and houses needed
to give access to the basin as well as for the land taken for excavating the
Portsea Canal. This was never an easy task and, in cases where agreement
could not be reached, a sheriff's jury had to be empanelled to arbitrate.
In September 1819 such a jury heard a dozen or so cases at the new Session Room in Portsmouth. One of the larger landowners was Miss White
of Southwick. Her property contained a brick yard and five acres of arable
land for which she claimed £1,500 to £1,700 with damages included. The
company surveyors offered £775. Mr Serjeant Pell appeared for the canal
proprietors and questioned many witnesses 'with his usual ingenuity and
ability'. To some avail, for after six hours, the jury awarded only £1,100.
This decision was regarded as a 'manifestation of the jury's sentiments'
since they ruled in the remaining 12 cases that awards should be 'rather
less than one third of the difference between the sum offered and the
amount demanded'.[11] Nevertheless, the company had to pay £6,110 for
the land compared with Rennie's estimate in January 1816 of £1,800.[12]

The brick yard, established by Ford Church in March 1819, remained in
use for three years. In August the steam engine at Ford began pumping up
water from the Arun 'while the excavation and brickwork were carrying on
in the drain' which was to feed the well. This drain was to open into the
river through one of the wings at the tail end of the lower sea lock. However,
'the land soaks' at this time produced so much water that the engine was
continuously employed.[13] The company arranged a demonstration of the
steam pump in the presence of several shareholders 'and many other
persons assembled', to prove its powers. The *Hampshire Chronicle* reported
that the result of the trial was highly satisfactory 'as the volume of water
raised and discharged by the pumps was more than equal to twenty tons a

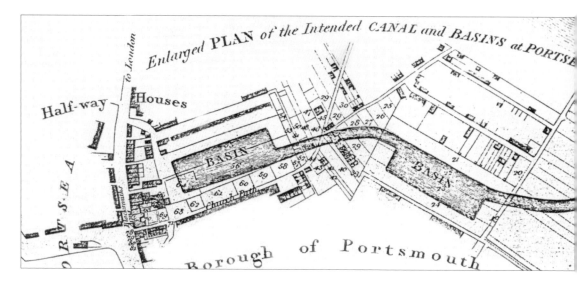

(vi)   *The upper map shows the proposed basin at Halfway Houses 1815 of which only one was built. The lower map formed part of a one-inch sketch of Portsmouth Dockyard in 1823. The basin was filled in in 1830 and the land sold to become part of Arundel Street.*

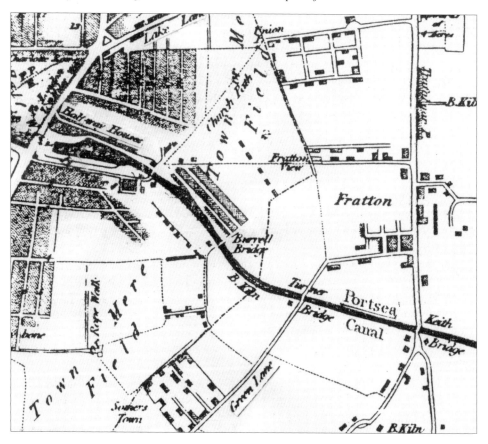

minute, filling the whole width of the canal and rushing along its bottom
with an impetuosity equal to that of a rapid river'. The paper optimistically
concluded that 'the working of the engine but half a day a week will
replace the consumption of water which the transit of numerous vessels and
barges would occasion; we therefore feel real pleasure in congratulating
the canal company on this satisfactory completion of one important part
of this undertaking.'[14]

Sufficient water from the pumping engine at Ford had reached Yapton
by 18 March 1820 to enable boats to carry away the excavations from
the west of the village to the embankment being built over the valley at
Denges Barn. An aqueduct with a span to ten feet had been made over
the rife dividing the parishes of Barnham and Aldingbourne. At Hunston
Common the bridge was causing trouble: 'The bridge standing on very
low ground has taken a great quantity of earth to make the approaches,
which necessarily being boated from the deep cutting toward Donnington,
has occasioned a long and tedious process.' The sea lock at Salterns was
half-built and bricks were being made from earth excavated from the canal
for building the upper lock. A brick arch had been turned over the river
Lavant where it passed under the new road from Southgate Basin towards
the city. The basin at Halfway Houses, which was to be 517 feet long and
77 feet wide, was nearly excavated and much of the basin walls built but
progress at the engine house at Milton had been held back for want of
bricks. In July it was agreed that the land purchased for the proposed
second basin should be appropriated for building a bonding warehouse
and timber wharf, 120 feet in length, provided with wooden fenders and
indented walls. In October the steam engine at Milton which was to supply
the canal with sea water underwent its first trial. After six hours pumping
it was possible for the contractor's barges to be floated in three feet of
water over three-quarters of a mile.[15]

In December an unattributed article in the *Hampshire Telegraph* attempted
to bolster enthusiasm for investing in canal shares.[16] The writer referred
to the prices listed in the *London Courier* and noted that, of the £100
shares of 18 companies, 13 were priced above par and five below. He
concluded that this fact could not fail to be good news to the P & A
shareholders 'as it offers the completed contradiction in the opinion
... that canal property is very generally unprofitable'. However, the list
favoured shares from the industrial regions; the only Hampshire navigation
mentioned was the Andover Canal whose £100 shares were quoted at £5;
nor was there reference to the Basingstoke whose shares barely fetched
£10 or to the Wey & Arun Junction whose stock had already lost a third
of its value.

The iron swivel bridges were built by C.H. Tickell of Southampton and
dated 1820. All 21 were named after local landowners or leading supporters
of the project. The seven over the Portsea Canal included Burrell, Keith
and Williams;[17] over the Chichester Canal, Casher, Crosbie, Cutfield, Dudley,

Egremont and Poyntz, and over the barge canal, Hollinsworth. The names of those not on the management committee were landowners like General Sir John Gustavus Crosbie (Donnington), William Poyntz (Cowdray House) and Sir Charles Merrick Burrell (West Grinstead), who had married Lord Egremont's eldest daughter.

Progress was now frustrated by various incidents and the work fell behind schedule. Many of the contractor's difficulties were caused by numerous unforeseen obstacles which were not unusual in this type of work. In May the *Hampshire Telegraph* reported that an incredibly heavy hailstorm had stopped work at Donnington and Mundham. It only lasted four minutes but every window in the neighbourhood was shattered and fruit destroyed. Hailstones three inches in circumference covered the ground to a depth of six inches. Dyson & Thornton claimed, after excavating the basin at Halfway Houses to a depth of eight feet, that flooding had halted the work until a drain could be dug. The accounts reveal that the contractors had to pay Mr Hack £40 'as a recompense for flooding his meadow adjoining the basin which, if it had not been done, the basin would not have been made'. More serious was the damage to the canal banks near Bersted which were 'riotously destroyed after the line was wholly completed and work on the basin was in progress. The contractors claimed £181 for repairs and £364 for law expenses, incurred at the recommendation of the management committee, against the offenders.[18]

There was also it appears indecision by Hollinsworth in deciding the mode of deepening the channels through Chichester and Langstone harbours. There were delays too in obtaining possession of land and impediments from landowners. In addition porous soil, springs, floods and lax communications between the committee, the resident engineer and the contractors added to the company's problems.

There is no record of Hollinsworth's contract being extended after December 1820.[*] However, in May 1821 the management committee reported that Dyson & Thornton had 'adopted a more energetic mode' of carrying on the company's works by offering certain sums in the way of bonus to the different sub-contractors under them, provided that the parts they had engaged to perform were finished by specific periods. This stimulus had the effect of having double sets of men, working day and night. Consequently, it was hoped that the Portsea line would be finished by about the following Michaelmas and the whole line in about 40 weeks. At the same time the committee were well aware of the need to ensure that the bed was watertight and observed that the bank would be lined both bottom and sides to a thickness of three feet to prevent leakage when the canal was filled.[19]

[*] Neither newspaper reports nor the company's circulars to the proprietors (except that of 4 August 1818) mention Hollinsworth by name. However in the summer of 1820 he surveyed the Arun Navigation from Burpham to Newbridge and also provided a design for the timber Hayling Island viaduct.

Meantime the steam tug which was to tow craft round Thorney and Hayling Islands was under construction. Shortly before Christmas 1820 the *Egremont* was launched at Milton and fitted up in Portsmouth Harbour.[*][20] She had one deck, one mast, measured 78 feet in breadth and weighed 16½ tons. Her registration certificate was granted on 24 March 1821 and James Bowyer named as her first master.[21]

In the taverns of Chichester and Portsea much speculation was voiced as to whether the tug would be able to tow with safety a string of barges through Chichester and Langstone harbours. In April the management committee arranged for trials to take place and was very pleased to announce at the annual meeting in May that the *Egremont* in a single operation had towed two large sailing lighters, each of 120 tons, a cutter of 40 tons and six boats from their anchorage in Portsmouth Harbour to Spithead against the flood tide.[22]

In February 1818 John Williams had proposed that the company should consider applying for parliamentary authority to operate its own barges and collect freight charges in addition to tolls at Portsbridge. This he felt would ensure 'certainty with which goods can be conveyed as to time and cheapness as to freight'. He advocated a fleet of 15 barges costing about £4,500 to secure 'the whole trade to the company and to avoid the tolls of the proprietors not being endangered by the avaricious charges of the barge masters'.[23]

Not perhaps unexpectedly those proprietors, who were also merchants, rejected this plan and, when Williams raised the matter again in 1821, the idea was to have only eight or so barges. This time he pointed out that 'it is to be distinctly understood that such an arrangement is not meant to engross the conveyance of goods to the company exclusively or to prevent a general competition among proprietors of barges'.[24]

It was also reported that the sea lock at Ford had been a work of 'great labour and expense owing to the quantity of water produced by cutting into the bed of chalk or marl, which nearly baffled every exertion that could be applied by means of manual labour'. There was other disappointing news. The excavation of earth to form the banks from Hunston Common toward Donnington had been a 'very slow operation' and the decision to deepen the Portsea Canal had occasioned much delay.

The work continued to be beset by problems. A year later in May 1822 the Committee regretted that the navigation remained unfinished but concentrated in its report on what remained to be done rather than what had been achieved. Considerable time would be needed to complete the works at Barnham and Bersted Valleys due to the ground 'having proved to

---

[*] A letter in the archives of the National Science Museum Library dated 25 December 1820 (ref GOODA928) mentions that one of Mr Field's men is going down to fix the engine in a boat at Emsworth for the Arundel Canal Company. 'It is the most unpleasant season of the year to execute any work of this kind and steam boats tho' so pleasant in the summer make one shudder to think of them just now.'

be of an open and porous description' and where 800 yards of excavation
and 400 yards of embanking were still required. However, the bricks and
iron swivel bridges were in place and the pump engine houses built at
Ford and Milton.

As William Huskisson had noted earlier in his letter to the prime
minister (see pages 9-10), the financial slump which followed the end of
the Napoleonic Wars had made it extremely difficult to raise capital for
new ventures. Consequently many projects came to a standstill for lack of
finance and, with the troops returning from the war seeking work, there
was a growing risk of serious unemployment. It was to counter this threat
that the chancellor of the exchequer, Nicholas Vansittart, had instigated in
1817 the setting up of the Exchequer Loans commission and empowered
it to make loans to undertakings which would relieve unemployment.[25]
The first loan of £2,000 was made in August to Sir Robert Heron MP to
erect a House of Industry for the parishes between Grantham and Newark.
Thomas Telford was appointed technical adviser 'on all works requiring
the information of a civil engineer'. Between 1817 and 1828 some 20
projects were examined by Telford of which 17 were granted loans varying
from £6,000 (Folly Bridge, Oxford) to £250,000 (Regent's Canal). Not all
applications were successful. In 1818 the Thames & Medway Canal Company
was refused a loan of £40,000.

The Portsmouth & Arundel Navigation Company received £40,000. The
first loan was applied for in November 1820 and £24,000 was advanced in
May 1821. A further sum of £16,000 was applied for in October 1822 and
granted a month later. These loans had to be repaid by annual instalments
of 5 per cent with interest at 4 per cent. This gave rise to ten proprietors
requisitioning a special meeting in Portsmouth on 9 October to 'arrange
and make effectual the securities' to be given for this loan, which a special
meeting on 19 June had approved.[26] It would appear that it was at this point
that Lord Egremont had to step in personally to guarantee the loan.*

In December 1821 the management committee resolved to dispense with
the deepening of the channel though the wadeway at Thorney,† unilaterally
annulled that part of the contract with Dyson & Thornton, and determined
to excavate a channel through the Hayling wadeway and erect a bridge for
£6,400, a saving of £1,000 on the original estimate. The contractors began
building the bridge in January but, after most of the piling had been driven,
abandoned the contract to allow another company (the Hayling Bridge
company) to erect their own bridge and causeway between Langstone and
Hayling to which the canal company contributed £3,080 as well as £500

---

* The company accounts for 1824 show that Lord Egremont had repaid £3,600, in three instalments, of the £24,000 loan and £800 in respect of the £16,000 loan. He had also made an interest
  payment to Government of £64, but it is not clear how this figure was calculated.
† The Committee chose to ignore the Gileses warning on the 1815 plan that the occasional heavy sea
  at the entrance to Chichester Harbour could be avoided by navigating the Thorney Channel.

toward the cost of future repair. This was a more satisfactory arrangement for both parties as the canal company's bridge would merely have had to cross the dredged channel, leaving the existing wadeway on either side (see page 65).

An unforeseen expense was the decision to oppose the Bill introduced into the House of Commons in 1822 to construct a bridge across the river Arun at Littlehampton. Trade between the towns and villages along the seaboard between Worthing and Bognor was hampered by the need for wheeled traffic either to ford the river at low tide when weather conditions permitted or to have to cross the river at Arundel which increased the distance between the two towns by 3½ miles. Whereas from Littlehampton to Bognor was only 6½ miles as the crow flies, via Arundel it was twice that. However, the inhabitants of Arundel, Petworth and Midhurst all opposed the Bill as they feared a loss of trade.

The management committees of the Arun, Wey & Arun and Portsmouth & Arundel companies together with the Earl of Egremont, who owned the Rother Navigation, were more ambivalent but feared that a bridge might hinder navigation. The day before the committee hearing in the House of Commons (24 April) every member of the Parliamentary Committee was sent a circular letter urging the Bill's rejection 'as the establishment of the bridge could not fail to check the rising tide and decrease the depth of water, thus preventing at the upper parts thereof the passage of barges to and from London'. The Bill was lost but in 1824 Littlehampton obtained an Act to establish a ferry which remained in use until 1908.

The building of the giant basin at Halfway Houses had taken three years and had transformed the area. By the time this tremendous work was completed those living in the locality pursued a diversity of occupations. Pigot listed over thirty which included blacksmiths, brewers, brush and clay pipe makers, carpenters, coal and corn merchants, hatters, linen drapers, iron-founders, masons, millwrights, painters, pawn brokers, rope makers, saddlers and tin-smiths. There were also 11 grocers and general stores, and no fewer than 12 taverns which included the *Battle of the Nile*, the curiously named *Heart in Hand*, the *Valiant Soldier* (later changed to the *Valiant Trooper*) and the *Canal House* managed by William Phillips.[27]

At the 1823 Annual Meeting the committee had 'great cause to regret' that the canal was still unfinished.* Nevertheless, it was announced that 26 May had been 'named by the contractors' when the whole line from London to Portsmouth would be ready for the passage of 'suitable' barges of about 40 tons burthen. The word 'suitable' was not defined until much later as some barge masters trying to navigate through Hardham tunnel were soon to discover.

---

* Gates relates how on 28 December 1821, 'the sea burst its bounds between Southsea Castle and Lumps Fort and inundated all the low-lying land ... Farlington marshes were completely covered and much damage done to the works of the Portsmouth Canal by the falling in of the banks'. (*History of Portsmouth*, p.640.)

VI

OPENING CEREMONIES
1822-1823

Filling of Southgate Basin (1821) – opening of Chichester Canal (1822) – a disastrous incident – the steam tug *Egremont* runs aground in Emsworth Channel – Mr Williams tries to explain – Portsea Canal opened (1822) – closed by storm – completion of Ford to Hunston barge canal (1823) – inauguration ceremonies and dinners.

Slowly but surely the waterway had neared completion. More than three years after work had commenced on digging the navigation, the day at last arrived; late in the afternoon of 27 December 1821 nearly 1,000 spectators watched the filling of Southgate Basin.[1] However, it was not until Tuesday 9 April 1822 that the Chichester Ship Canal was officially opened. The local newspaper carried advertisements inviting subscribers to the enterprise and the general public to take part.

In the event it was not an auspicious occasion. The local press wrote that they had been requested to invite 'such gentlemen as are engaged in trade in Portsmouth, Portsea and Gosport', who receive merchandise from London, to take passage on this occasion 'that they might judge of the safety with which goods can be conveyed thereon'. The invitation was extended to any interested lady or gentleman and included a return passage to Portsmouth set to leave at noon on the following day.[2] The plan was for the gathering of supporters to embark at Eastney Creek by the entrance to the Portsea Canal. From here a flotilla of boats was to be towed by the steam tug across Langstone Harbour and around Hayling and Thorney Islands to enter the Chichester Canal at Birdham.

The day's outing was organised by the navigation's promoter, John Williams. His party of 132 guests were accommodated in three gaily decorated barges, suitably furnished with chairs, parasols and cushions. A band enlivened the party as they waited to set off at ten o'clock. It was a long wait.

The arrangements were perhaps left rather too much to chance. Apparently, although Williams had planned an early start in order to take advantage of the tide, shortly before sailing a Mr Burnett appeared on the deck of the tug *Egremont* and offered his services to Williams, claiming

46

10 *A busy dockside scene at Arundel c.1820 shortly before the opening of the Portsmouth & Arundel Canal.*

knowledge of the tricky route through Langstone and Chichester harbours. Williams, anxious to spend time with his guests, was glad to hand over the task of steering the 150-yard-long procession to a man he thought to be an experienced pilot. Burnett's first action was to delay the start because of his concern about the depth of water by Hayling Island, so not until after 11 a.m. did the vessel enter Langstone Harbour. Here more doubts were expressed about the depth and a further stoppage occurred.

However, both Williams and a passenger, Mr Hicks, were dubious about this further delay since they considered there was six feet of water and the *Egremont* only drew 4ft. 4ins. With all these delays it was not until 5 p.m. that the tug left the Emsworth Channel to enter Chichester Harbour. Then disaster struck as it turned the last angle of the lake. The canal entrance was in sight 'at little more than a quarter of a mile distant', when the pilot steering the vessel himself ran the boat aground on a mud bank even though he was negotiating a deep channel 150 yards wide. The procession held fast waiting until the tide turned or some larger vessel came to the rescue, and so those aboard were precluded from participating in the principal object of their excursion.

While John Williams and his party lay stranded, the yacht *Sylph* owned by William Johnson led a procession of trading and pleasure craft up the canal to Southgate Basin to be greeted by cannon fire, bands of music and the acclamations of an impatient crowd. The 12 barges included the *Mayflower* laden with deals, the *Prosperous* with grocery and the *Chichester* with

36 chaldrons of coal. Dinner tickets costing one guinea each had been sold by Mr Hudson, landlord at the *Dolphin Inn*, but since the advertised time was five o'clock it seems improbable that any member of the management committee participated.

The company had to take great pains to try to refute the 'many erroneous reports' that began to circulate. Williams tried to explain away the fiasco by stating that he had been duped by Burnett, that the procession had to struggle against a north-easterly gale and the ebb of a spring tide. 'We were towing three barges of forty tons each, which although not laden, were the less manageable on account of the wind. Added to all this there were various boats hanging on the different vessels throughout the voyage amounting at one time to two sailing boats and eleven rowing boats.'[3]

All in all it was a most unfortunate beginning that only confirmed what many thought, that the navigation of the twisting tidal channels would always be a hazard on ebb tides and when the weather was foggy or stormy. Another problem arose. No sooner was the Chichester Canal completed than the banks were 'riotously destroyed' by hooligans. The cost of repairs was £181 but law expenses incurred against the ruffians who had ravished the berms totalled £364.[4]

The Chichester Canal, however, soon proved its utility. Twenty vessels discharged their cargoes of coal, deals and grocery at the company's wharves in April. However, its opening brought a demand from the bargemen, who had hitherto transported coal from colliers at Itchenor to Fishbourne, for an extra one shilling a chaldron for carrying it through the canal to Southgate Basin. The navigation company refused their request since the men could now 'avoid the risks, labour and delays … from the winds and tides' by using the canal. In any case, most small vessels such as schooners, sloops, ketches, brigs, cutters and smacks could use the canal and only the larger colliers required to have their cargoes transferred into barges.[5] On Friday 19 April the 86-ton schooner *Richmond* was launched at Southgate Basin by the Duke of Richmond and Mr Hudson again provided a dinner to be held at three o'clock, tickets half a guinea each, to celebrate the occasion.

Meanwhile, work was proceeding with the Portsea Canal. In May it was hoped that it would be completed in July but this was not to be, and it was not until Thurday 19 September at two o'clock that the opening took place. The week before, it was announced that, following the opening, a dinner would be held at the *George Inn*, Portsmouth at six o'clock at which the committee and some of the subscribers intended to be present. The invitation was extended to 'any gentlemen who may feel disposed to be of the party'. Tickets were available from the bar at 17 shillings each to include wine. It was also reported that the depth of the canal was about nine feet 'which will be gradually increased on each succeeding day till it reaches the permanent depth of twelve feet'.[6]

On the great day the steam tug *Egremont*, followed by several gaily decorated barges filled with passengers and with a band playing on board,

11 *The entrance to the Portsmouth & Arundel Canal at Ford, c.1830. In the background can be seen Ford road bridge and the substantial three-storey engine house and chimney.*

passed in procession up the canal watched by 'many thousand spectators' lining the banks throughout its entire length. The opening being successfuly accomplished, the correspondent of the *Hampshire Chronicle* was able to write wryly, 'with pleasure, we add, no accident occurred'. John Frattle's sloop *Beehive*, which entered to take up a cargo, and the schooner *Richmond*, which discharged a cargo of coals at the basin, were listed as the first trading vessels to use the canal. However, even though the two ship canals had been completed, the barge canal was still unfinished: 550 yards of excavation and embanking still remained to be done.[7]

The navigation was finally opened throughout its entire length on Monday, 26 May 1823. The week before a notice had appeared in the *Hampshire Telegraph* under the clerk's full name, Jackson Muspratt Williams, to advise both shareholders and the public that a celebratory dinner would be held at the *Swan Inn*, Chichester (Mr Hewlins) at four o'clock and on the following day at five o'clock at the *George Inn*, Portsmouth (Mr Billett) and that tickets to include 'wine and all charges' were available from inns in Arundel, Emsworth and Havant – price 12s. 6d.

Not until 4 June did a detailed account of the proceedings appear in the London press. 'OPENING OF THE PORTSMOUTH & ARUNDEL CANAL, being the last portion of the whole line of inland navigation from London to

12   *A closer view of the engine house at Ford, c.1860. The steam pumps were built over a well which was fed by a brick drain from the river to the tail of the lock. The engine house was reported to be partially dismantled and quite out of repair when it was surveyed in 1888.*

Portsmouth', ran the announcement in the *Morning Post*. The reader can well imagine the splendid sight as on that sunny May morning 18 boats and barges, decorated with gay streamers and colours, assembled at the entrance to the canal at Ford; some were filled with the county's aristocracy and civic dignitaries, others laden with chalk for farmers on the line and five contained goods for Chichester, one of which had reached Ford from London in three days. Leading the way was the Earl of Egremont in his brightly painted pleasure barge with a large party of his friends on board; close behind was that of the Duke of Norfolk* who was accompanied by the Mayor of Arundel (William Holmes). The Mayor of Guildford had many of his townsmen in his boat and there were numerous parties from the local gentry in others, all of whom were entertained by bands of musicians who filled two more craft.

> The procession was handsomely decorated with colours, and it glided along upon the smooth surface of the canal through a country possessing every beauty, which high cultivation, interspersed with occasional plantations, could give it; while from the decks of the barges, the charms of a beautiful day were heightened by a very extensive and delightful varied prospect.

At Hunston Common the flotilla was met by the schooner *Richmond* and five sloops which had come up from Chichester Harbour. The whole entourage then moved majestically along with bands playing and colours flying towards Southgate Basin, where they were greeted with a discharge of cannon and by a 'very numerous assemblage of spectators, entirely covering the wharves and adjoining land'. In the basin it was found that a sloop and two barges were in the midst of discharging their cargoes.

> The proceedings of the day passed without the slightest interruption and appeared to give entire satisfaction to everyone; it being a matter of no small congratulation to the tradesmen of Chichester that where five years before nothing but meadows and corn fields appeared, there is now a channel that will float their commerce to and from the Metropolis and the manufacturing districts of the country at comparatively little expense. At five o'clock, about seventy Gentlemen, amongst whom was the Noble Earl, sat down to an excellent dinner at the Swan Inn and the evening was spent in a way suited to the occasion.

An elderly inhabitant, reminiscing on the event in 1887, said:

> The first thing that took place was the digging of the canal, and when that was finished there was a grand 'to do'. It was a pretty sight, the vessels being towed down with scores of people on the decks, bands playing and flags flying. There was a fair held there that very day, which was kept up afterwards for years. There was jumping in sacks, diving for oranges, donkey racing and so on.[8]

The *Morning Post*'s report continued:

> On the following morning his Lordship and about fifty Gentlemen proceeded in one of the barges down the canal into Chichester Harbour, and having embarked in the Company's steam vessel, to which a barge of forty tons burthen, and fully

_____
* The 12th Duke who had succeeded to the title in 1815 when 57 years of age.

laden, was attached; the light barge was, for the accommodation of passengers, made fast to her, and at about eleven o'clock, the steam vessel got under weigh, and proceeded with this charge against a strong flood tide, making a good passage in five hours, through Chichester Harbour, Hayling Channel, and Langstone Harbour, to the Sea Lock of the Portsea Island Canal. The whole having passed the locks, proceeded through this branch, of two miles in length, between banks covered with spectators; to the amount of at least twenty thousand. On reaching the basin they were greeting with a discharge of cannon and the acclamations of the persons assembled, amongst which were at least three hundred who covered the masts, rigging and deck of a large collier brig that lay therein.

   The proceedings of this day also passed without any impediment, and the evening terminated with an excellent dinner at the George Inn, to which about sixty persons sat down to partake of some fine venison which his Lordship had handsomely presented to this assembly, as he had previously done to that of Chichester.

The newspaper concluded its lengthy account with the comment that, although the navigation was not yet entirely completed, it was in such a forward state as to be navigable and that,

the arrival at Ford of the before mentioned barge from London in three days, together with the result of several trials, by which it has appeared that a barge can conveniently go from Ford to Portsmouth in one day, has placed beyond all doubt the point that it is practicable to transport goods from London to Portsmouth in four days; and even in less time by means of the Fly Barges, which are intended to travel by night as well as by day.

Some additional gossipy details were provided by the *Hampshire Chronicle*'s reporter.[9] Lord Egremont had entertained the Management Committee and a large party of his personal friends with 'an elegant cold collation' on his pleasure barge while it was thought worthwhile to mention that the Duke of Norfolk included ladies in his party. The long train of boats filled with 'elegantly dressed females' occupied nearly a mile while the Sussex Militia Band was joined by private bands from Arundel. On the second day Lord Egremont himself sailed on the steam tug to the Portsea Canal up which the vessel proceeded 'slowly and majestically, with colours flying'. 'The approach to the basin was the finest part of the scene. Many thousands had assembled to greet the entrance of the vessels, which were received, amidst the repeated shouts of the multitude, by a salute of cannon from the shore, and thus terminated the joyful occurrence. A brig, lying in the basin, was literally studded with people from the deck to the mast heads; the appearance was peculiarly novel, and while it afforded accommodation for seeing, to those who could find no footing so good on shore, it very appropriately served to close a scene which must have gratified every one who witnessed it.' Lord Egremont attended the dinner at the *George Inn* with George Grant, a Treasurer of the P. & A., in the chair. The Marine Band and a party of glee singers enlivened this pleasing close of a most interesting day; and, aided by the able Chairman, and the judicious arrangements of the Stewards, the party was kept in good humour to a late hour.

It was also announced that goods, with the exception of a few articles of special value, could now be conveyed by the Arundel Lighter Company, from the wharves of Randells, Howell & Co, Queenhithe, Upper Thames Street, and W.J. Hall near the Custom House, Lower Thames Street, London, to those of the canal company at the Halfway Houses, Portsea, for 22s. 6d. a ton including the expenses of shipping and landing; and that arrangements were being made by which goods 'destined for Western Ports in the British Channel, and for Guernsey and Jersey' as well as Paris (via the Seine) would be received and forwarded by vessels belonging to these places.

VII

THE PROSPECTS FOR SUCCESS
1823-1825

The start of barge traffic between Portsmouth and London – fall of coastal
freight rates – formation of Portsmouth Fly Barge Company – the main carriers
– bullion traffic – Lord Selsey sounds a warning – the company's dire financial
plight – the dispute with the contractors – efforts to raise more capital initially
thwarted.

No sooner had the celebrations ceased and the cheering died away than
the Committee of Management met at the Old Town Hall in Portsmouth
to reassess the canal's prospects. Eight years had elapsed since the project
had been formulated during which period the country's economic and
political situation had materially changed. So now that the two ports had
at last been linked, what were the prospects of success? Unemployment was
now high and trade depressed. The advent of peace had removed what
was really the *raison d'être* of building the navigation but the committee
did not think so. John Williams and his fellow committee members
believed there was trade to be had if only they could convince the
London and Portsmouth merchants to use the bargeway instead of the
coastal route.

However, even before the canal was fully open Williams had admitted that
tentative enquiries had shown the unwillingness of both the Government
and traders to change their normal method of transporting goods by
coaster. Nevertheless, he remained convinced that the canal could beat
the coaster out of the field if only all the connecting navigations would
grant toll concessions. This, however, was to be a stumbling block. With
the war over, shipping charges had fallen as low as 10s. to 16s. per ton
and 'unless a strong case can be made', wrote Williams, 'it will be next to
an impossibility to induce a departure from the old and beaten track'.[1]
The post-war years had seen a boom in coastal traffic. What had not been
foreseen was the sudden availability of hundreds of sailors discharged from
the navy readily available to man merchant vessels.

Estimates of the canal's potential trade prepared by Williams, and based
on 1816 returns,[2] now bore little relation to the current situation. In May
1822 the Basingstoke Canal Committee had likewise reflected on the

depression of inland trade generally and 'the encouragement afforded in peace to the conveyance of goods coast wise'.

The same edition of the *Hampshire Advertiser* which had announced the opening of the canal contained an extensive article entitled 'Annals of Commerce – Canals', which sought to remind readers of the benefits of water carriage and attempted to refute some of the criticisms levelled at the project. The writer, after detailing the development of inland waterways in England and their benefits to commerce, took issue with the critics of this new means of conveyance. It had been argued that the canal would diminish the number of draught horses, reduce the coastal trade and consequently weaken the navy, cause loss of capital and loss of land which could be better used in raising corn. But, said our correspondent, these objections had been well and truly laid over the past thirty years when they were first mooted. Canals invigorate and create trade.

Another problem for the company was that their toll charges were higher than on the other connecting navigations. In a letter to the proprietors of the Wey Navigation in March 1823 Williams explained why. The canal had cost, he said, £45,000 more than the estimate. Furthermore the running costs were higher than expected because of the enormous expense involved in supplying water from the two pumping stations;* in addition the steam tug, which had cost over £5,000, had to be kept in a constant state of readiness. An added difficulty was that mud in the tideway channels between Milton and Birdham could only be dredged at low-water spring tides.[3]

The canal office was established at 22 Lombard Street, Portsmouth. Management committee meetings were also held there but not those of the proprietors which took place at the Old Town Hall.† However, an ominous indication of the casual manner in which the company was being run is shown by the fact that more than a fortnight elapsed from the date of the official opening before a list of tolls for local traffic was published (see page xiv); one reason, perhaps, why James Fowler was appointed clerk to succeed J.M. Williams (salary £200 p.a.) soon after the opening of the navigation. The goods expected to be carried between Ford and Portsea was mainly agricultural. Timber products included hoops, spokes and fellies.‡ Seemingly arbitrary rates were charged on some items. The method of calculating the amount of tolls on a mixed cargo must have been daunting. For example, peas were rated at so much per five-quarters while wool was charged per seven and flour per eight sacks.

One of the great inconveniences of sending goods between London and Portsmouth was the necessity to pay tolls, totalling 13s. 6¼d. a ton, to six different navigations made up as follows:

---

* Each station cost £20 per day to operate.
† The old Town Hall in the High Street replaced the 16th-century timber building in 1739. Its council chamber was regarded as both 'ill contrived and excessive small' but was rebuilt in 1796. A new town hall was opened in 1838.
‡ The parts of the wheels to which spokes are attached.

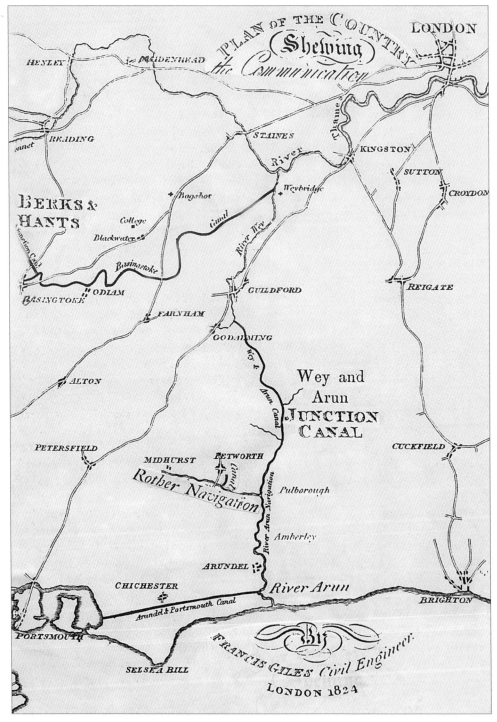

MAP 4   *Part of the 1824 plan by Francis Giles indicating the inland water route from London to Portsmouth.*

Portsmouth & Arundel	5s.	0d.
Arun	1s.	2d.
Wey & Arun	3s.	6d.
Godalming		6d.
Wey	2s.	8d.
Thames		8¼d.

Add the freight charge of 8s. 11¾d. a ton and the total of 22s. 6d. could be up to double the coastal freight charge. A reduced toll of 8s. 8¾d. was payable on goods of 'much weight and little value' and only 5s. 11¼d. on goods of 'much weight and extremely small value' (e.g. chalk) but of these items there was very little through-traffic. If, as often happened, the exact weight or nature of a cargo carried varied from one navigation to another, different calculations came into play which created additional uncertainty as to the exact amount required. Furthermore, potential customers were discouraged by the problem of finding carriers to quote inclusive and competitive rates.

The opening of the navigation had nevertheless produced several immediate benefits. Land carriage became less expensive. On 4 June the trustees of the turnpike roads from Chichester to Dell Quay, to Farnhurst (Fernhurst) and to Cosham each announced reduced toll rates.[4] The following year the trustees of the London Road to Portsmouth turnpike resolved to lower the road over Portsdown Hill by ten feet.[5]

At the annual meeting in May 1823 the committee commented on the low prices of forage, provisions and pay which was resulting in 'very low and unprecedented' freight rates for both land and sea carriage. Consequently they sought a proportional reduction of tolls by the inter-connecting navigations. To promote trade they had published and circulated to every port between Arundel and Land's End, as well as to the Channel Islands and Normandy ports, a pamphlet setting out the benefits of using the navigation.

The Arundel Lighter Company had begun advertising a twice-weekly goods service between London, Chichester and Portsmouth as soon as the navigation was open. Barges were to be loaded on Wednesdays and Thursdays for departure the following day. On the Chichester Canal the opening soon brought benefits to the town. On 15 September *The Sussex Weekly Advertiser* reported that 'The streets and various of the shops in the City of Chichester were on last Thursday evening, for the first time illuminated with gas, and presented a very brilliant appearance to a great number of perambulators'. On 17 November the same newspaper stated that the cutter *The Royal Gift* had arrived at the basin where its owner, a disabled naval warrior, gave a display of seamanship 'alike amusing to the visitors and profitable to himself'.

The canal company tried hard to convince potential users that it would be quicker and safer to send goods by inland water. Early in 1823 it had built its own fly barge which, while smaller than the Arun barges, was

PORTSMOUTH, PORTSEA, GOSPORT, AND WEST
OF ENGLAND
COMMERCIAL FLY BARGE COMPANY.

THE Subscribers to this Undertaking are
informed,—That their FIRST GENERAL
MEETING will take place on Tuesday the 15th inst.
at seven o'clock precisely, at the Old Town Hall, in
the High-street, Portsmouth, to choose a Committee
of Management, regulate the number and size of the
Barges, and many other important matters, relative to
its future direction. The Friends to this Concern will
be gratified to hear, that, after only a very partial can-
vass (owing to the shortness of the time), the majority
of the Shares (exclusive of those expected to be taken
by Mercantile Men at Plymouth, and the Ports adjacent), are already subscribed for.—Those Persons who
have not yet joined the Concern, are invited to attend
the Meeting; and (if satisfied) with the advantages
offered), to an early subscription.

The principal advantages which this Company will
afford to all the parties interested, and to the Public
in general, are—a regular Conveyance of light Goods
at least twice, and probably thrice, a week, with a
dispatch equal to the common waggon, at about ONE
THIRD of the expence; and a certain conveyance of
the heavier Articles at a price equal to the Coasting
Vessel, without its anxiety or delay.

PORTSMOUTH, 12th July, 1823.

13 *Announcement of the first meeting of the Portsmouth, Portsea, Gosport and West of England Fly Barge Company 1823. Edward Casher, wine merchant and member of the navigation's management committee, became its secretary.*

designed to carry general merchandise and which by using relays of horses could travel by day and night. In June the company carried out a trial run and publicised the fact that its barge had performed the distance up to Queenhithe* in 2 days 16 hours and back down to Portsmouth in 2 days 20 hours. However, it did not hesitate to point out that this was achieved notwithstanding 'the delay in getting horses and the necessity of using some that had already finished their day's work'.[6]

Following this successful trial Edward Casher,[†] wine merchant and member of the management committee, was one of those who instigated the establishment of the Portsmouth, Portsea, Gosport, Arundel & West of England Commercial Fly Barge Company. Shares were offered to the public at £10 each payable in five instalments. The company's aim was to provide a regular conveyance of light goods at least twice a week 'with a dispatch equal to the common waggon at about one third of the expense and a certain conveyance of heavier articles at a price equal to the coasting

* Locate upstream of Southwark Bridge.
† Casher was one of the original subscribers to the company; he lived at Froddington House in Fratton and became mayor of Portsmouth 1842-44.

vessel without the anxiety of delay'.[7] Casher was elected company secretary and Erasmus Jackson treasurer.

Some of the items carried on the Fly were of a cryptic nature. The Rector of Pulborough received a firkin sent down from London; two bottles (contents unknown) were destined for Coldwaltham together with a 'bundle of Stoveld's left overs'. (William Stoveld was a well known Petworth timber and coal merchant who operated his own barges.)

However, it was soon evident that the route was not really suitable for fly boats for only one was ever built, and in February 1824 the company was advertised without the 'fly barge' appellation while stating that barges were 'regularly' arriving within seven days 'so that in about ten days goods could be conveyed by packet to Plymouth, Falmouth, Exeter, Guernsey and Jersey at about a quarter of the expense of land carriage'.[8] The problems were, of course, the need for the tug to tow the fly barge around Hayling and Thorney Islands and for horses to be led over Hardham tunnel. Causes of delay were manifold, not least being the hazard of adverse weather (ice, floods, drought, fallen trees, the state of the tides and the failure of any lock gates).

Road transport, too, had improved. By 1823 the introduction of lighter, better-sprung fly waggons could carry packages and light goods daily (Sunday excepted) between London and Portsmouth in 36 hours.[9] The following year the *Hampshire Telegraph* reported that the trustees of the Portsmouth Road claimed that lumbering stage waggons drawn by eight horses could provide the kind of carriage offered by barges – only, however, at twice or thrice the cost. Even so, road carriers could offer a wider range of collection and delivery points while providing slightly less risk of pilferage than barge traffic and, because road transport was likely to be less affected by drought or ice, they offered a more frequent and reliable service than by water. The time taken of four days was roughly the same whichever means of transport was preferred.[10] However, goods delivered to the receiving wharf might have to wait two or three days before being loaded even when a twice-weekly service was offered.

The distance from Portsmouth to London Bridge by river and canal was 116 miles. The distance by road to Hyde Park Corner was listed by Paterson as 74 miles. Since the coastal voyage to the capital was a hundred miles further, there appeared to be good reason for avoiding wintry seas, contrary winds, and the dangers of the North Foreland by conveying goods along this shorter but ofter slower route – slower because barges rarely travelled by night, and because cargoes had to be transhipped at least once more than was usually necessary by coaster. Barges leaving Portsmouth at daybreak hoped to spend the first night at Ford or Arundel, the second above Loxwood, the third at Weybridge so that Queenhithe would be reached late the following afternoon if conditions were normal. But they seldom were. Delays were manifold; shoals or floods in the Arun valley, shortage of water on the summit level, fog in the Thames, slackness by the barge captains – these were the causes of many.

The Wey Navigation ledgers record the slow start to through-traffic. Initially only two barge companies began to carry goods between London, Chichester and Portsmouth. Dyson & Company's new barge *Chichester* was the first to arrive at Guildford from the Thames on 22 May bound for Chichester; she carried 13½ tons of groceries and drew three feet of water. She was followed by the *Union* and the *Commerce*. Between the navigation's opening and the end of the year Dyson's made 38 trips to Chichester carrying a total of 526 tons, an average load of less than 14 tons and a maximum of 25 tons. Meantime, Seward & Co of Arundel had been advertising a twice-weekly goods service and were operating their fleet of ten barges rather more successfully. Their first barge reached Portsmouth on 9 June and by the end of the year had carried 475 tons to Chichester and 1,000 tons to Halfway Houses. The average load of 24½ tons (with a maximum of 39 tons) meant, however, that barges were rarely more than two-thirds full.

In the first six months of operation some 1,500 tons of corn and groceries reached Chichester and Portsmouth from the capital. Smaller quantities of porter, wine, and pottery initially arrived with some degree of regularity from London; but consignments to the capital were harder to secure and consequently more variable, ranging from ships' timber and planks to more unusual items such as furniture, soldiers' baggage, marble and Indian cotton.

However, trade did not develop as had been expected. The hopes and aspirations of the promoters were rudely shaken when in 1824 – which incidentally was the most successful year – only 3,650 tons and not the hoped-for 55,000 tons were carried between the Portsmouth & Arundel Navigation and London. Nevertheless, what was insignificant in weight was to some extent made up in value. In June 1824 the first of 29 cargoes of bullion left the Halfway Houses bound for the Bank of England (Appendix E). The *Windsor & Eton Express* reported in October that 'silver bars to the value of £300,000 passed up the Portsmouth & Arundel Canal on Tuesday in a lighter from Portsmouth to London having recently arrived from Spanish America'.[11] This lighter would have been the Arundel Barge Company's *Arun*, shown in the lock-keeper's diary at Guildford as carrying 13 tons. Whereas 20 or 25 tons was the usual consignment, one day in February 1825 the *Union* and the *Portsea* went through together with 72 tons on board. Each bullion barge carried an armed guard of four 'redcoats' who slept on board at night. No attempted hold-ups were reported but a greater deterrent for any bank robber would have been the problem of carrying away the booty over land. The bullion traffic continued, albeit spasmodically, until 1838.

At the special general meeting held the week before Christmas 1824 Lord Selsey[*] informed the shareholders of the company's dire financial

---

[*] Henry Peachey had succeeded his father in 1816 as the 3rd Baron Selsey at the age of 29. Although he was not one of the original subscribers, his interest in the navigation would have arisen from the canal being built close to the family seat at West Dean House. He was a former captain in the Royal Navy, a substantial landowner and much interested in land improvement. He died in Italy in 1838.

Number of Shares.	Names of Canals.	Amount of Share.	Average Cost per Share.	Price per Share.	Div. per Annum.	Dividend Payable.
		£ s.	£ s. d.	£ s.	£ s. d.	
1,482	Ashby-de-la-Zouch	100 0	113 0 0	80 0 0	4 0 0	Ap. Oct.
1,766	Ashton and Oldham	- -	113 0 0	100 0 0	5 0 0	Ap. Oct.
720	Barnsley	160 0	-	220 0 0	10 0 0	Feb. Aug.
1,260	Basingstoke	100 0	-	5 0 0	-	
—	Ditto Bonds	100 0	-	-	-	April.
400	Chelmer and Blackwater	100 0	-	106 0 0	5 0 0	January.
1,500	Chesterfield	100 0	-	170 0 0	8 0 0	
500	Coventry	100 0	-	795 0 0	44 0 0	May, Nov.
1,851	Crinan	50 0	-	2 0 0	-	
440	Cromford	100 0	-	420 0 0	19 0 0	Jan. July.
4,546	Croydon	100 0	31 2 10	1 17 6	-	
11,810	Ditto Bonds	100 0	-	50 0 0	5 0 0	
600	Derby	100 0	110 0 0	130 0 0	6 0 0	Jan. July.
2,060	Dudley	100 0	-	52 0 0	2 15 0	Mar. Sept.
3,575	Ellesmere and Chester	133 0	133 0 0	72 0 0	3 15 0	September.
11,600	Grand Junction	100 0	-	243½ 241½	13 0 0	Jan. July.
1,521	Grand Surrey	100 0	-	40 0 0	-	Apr. Oct.
120,000	Ditto Loan	-	-	97 0 0	5 0 0	Jan. July.
2,849	Grand Union	100 0	-	21 0 0	1 0 0	1st Oct.
3,096	Grand Western	100 0	89 0 0 pd.	8 0 0	-	
749	Grantham	150 0	150 0 0	195 0 0	10 0 0	May.
	Hereford and Gloucester	100 0	-	-	-	
6,238	Huddersfield	100 0	57 6 6	15 10 0	0 10 0	September.
148	Ivel and Ouse Beds	100 0	100 0 0 pd.	115 10 0	5 0 0	Jan. July.
25,328	Kennet and Avon	100 0	39 18 10	25 10 0	1 5 0	September.
70	Loughborough	-	142 17 0	2100 0 0	180 0 0	Jan. July.
3,000	Macclesfield	100 0	100 0 0 pd.	60 0 0	-	
250	Melton Mowbray	100 0	-	200 0 0	9 0 0	July.
130	Nutbrook	109 0	-	-	6 2 0	
52	Oakham	130 0	-	32 0 0	2 0 0	May.
1,786	Oxford	100 0	-	500 0 0	32 0 0	Mar. Sept.
2,400	Peak Forest	100 0	48 0 0	65 0 0	3 0 0	June, Dec.
2,520	Portsmouth and Arundel	50 0	50 0 0	10 0 0	-	
21,418	Regent's	100 0	33 16 8	18 0 0	0 13 6	July.
5,669	Rochdale	100 0	85 0 0	70 0 0	4 0 0	May.
200	Stroudwater	150 0	-	480 0 0	23 0 0	May, Nov.
533	Swansea	100 0	-	200 0 0	15 0 0	November.
350	Tavistock	100 0	-	105 0 0	-	
4,805	Thames and Medway	100 0	30 4 3	4 0 0		
3,344	Ditto New	3 10	2 15 0 pd.	-	-	
—	Ditto 1st Loan	-	56 0 0	-	2 10 0	
—	Ditto 2d Loan	-	40 0 0	-	2 0 0	
—	Ditto 3d Loan	-	100 0 0	-	5 0 0	
—	Ditto 4th Loan	-	100 0 0	-	5 0 0	June.
1,150	Thames and Severn, New	-	-	30 0 0	1 10 0	June.
1,300	Ditto Original	-	-	25 0 0	1 10 0	Jan. July.
905	Wey and Arun	110 0	110 0 0	32 0 0	-	May.
20,000	Wilts and Berks	-	-	5 0 0	0 4 0	June.
126	Wisbeach	105 0	105 0 0	40 0 0	-	February.
6,000	Worcester and Birmingham	-	-	87 10 0	3 0 0	February.
800	Wyrley and Essington	125 0	-	115 0 0	6 0 0	February.

14   *Table of canal share prices. In December 1824 Lord Selsey said that the company's shares had fallen to their lowest point but in 1832 the £50 shares of the Portsmouth & Arundel Canal were only quoted at £10.*

plight. Not only had the company borrowed £40,000 from the Government, which had to be repaid in yearly instalments together with interest at four per cent, but it owed 'various other persons a considerable amount, which debts the present funds of the company were wholly inadequate to discharge'. Furthermore, he continued, the annual expenditure, including the interest and instalments to Government, greatly exceeded its income.* Lastly, he had to remind his audience that the canal was in many respects incomplete.[12]

However, he was able to add that, in spite of all 'the adverse circumstances with which they had had to contend, from the incomplete and defective condition in which the contractors had left the canal and, notwithstanding the prejudice and opposition which has existed and still existed against it, the tolls had greatly increased within the last year'. The committee now expected that the tolls, when all the canal's defects had been remedied, would amount to at least £5,000 p.a., which would give a clear profit of over £1,000 p.a. However, this supposition depended on the company being able to raise at least £20,000 by making a further call of £10 a share. It was proposed that while this would not be compulsory, those who obliged were to be favoured as an inducement with a dividend of up to five per cent while those who refrained were to be denied a share of the profits until all the company's debts had been discharged.

The management committee, and Lord Egremont in particular, were decidedly in favour of the proposal to make a further call on each share as 'the best means of promoting its prosperity and as the only one, in fact, which can save it from ruin, and make it ultimately productive'. The committee also observed that, although the company's shares 'were now at the lowest point of depreciation', nothing would more effectually increase their value than the knowledge that the proprietors were raising the money themselves. The meeting thereupon resolved that the committee should apply to Parliament for power to raise up to £50,000 to discharge the debts of the company and complete the navigation.

Meantime one of the problems to be resolved was 'the incomplete and defective condition' in which the contractors had left the canal. In July, less than ten weeks after the official opening, the contractors had given notice that they were 'under the disagreeable necessity of suspending the works remaining to be done for want of necessary funds'. The company, however, had refused to pay what was asked on the grounds that the canal had not been properly completed, to which the contractors riposted, 'but in what respect they complain they do not inform us'. As all the works were, or should have been, executed under Hollinsworth's superintendence and he had not at any time asked them to redo any of the work, Dyson & Thornton claimed it was fair to presume that all had been executed to the engineer's satisfaction. 'It is not to the fanciful objections of any one or more of the committee that the contractors are bound to listen but to the objections of the Company's Engineer and him only.'

Dyson & Thornton's statement of claim ran to 30 folio pages setting out their grievances at not being properly remunerated and defending the

---

* Lord Egremont had guaranteed the loan from Government of £40,000 which had to be repaid by annual instalments of £2,000 with interest at four per cent. These charges had amounted to £2,064 in 1824 which Lord Egremont had paid.

allegations made by the company as to the reasons for non-payment. The total claimed was an astonishing £96,842 9s. 2d.[13]

What is evident is that after the execution of the contract 'not only were many alterations made in the work mentioned', such as the decision to abandon building the new channel round Thorney Island, but new contracts were entered into for other and additional works and other parts of the works thereby contracted were abandoned. 'So great were the alterations made between original works and those afterwards executed by the direction of the Committee of Management that the original contract might almost be considered as having been abandoned; indeed part of it was actually annulled.'

The main alterations and additions to those that were included in the original contract were:

   (i) The widening and deepening of the Chichester Canal.
  (ii) The construction of Southgate Basin and the new road to the city for which no fixed price was agreed.
 (iii) The boating of earth from the excavation of Southgate basin to form the embankment at Bersted Valley.
  (iv) The enlargement of the Portsea Ship Canal.

In addition there was work ordered by Hollinsworth at a cost of £9,669 which had not been sanctioned by the committee.

The canal company's grounds for non-payment was poor workmanship. An attempt to settle this impasse by hoping that Hollinsworth (now engineer to the Bridgewater & Taunton canal) and Thomas Telford could resolve the dispute came to nothing. Not until February 1824 did the company agree to hold a special meeting at Portsmouth Town Hall to consider the expediency of submitting the matter to arbitration.[14]

Until the hearing the company was uncertain as to its outcome, as well they might be, seeing how the contractors had had to carry out many alterations and additions not specified in the original contract without agreement being made nor fixed price settled. And so in December 1824 the management committee, while admitting a debt of about £1,200, thought they had made a most ample allowance to meet the claim 'by setting aside £5,000 which to them appears an extravagant addition'.[15] The contractors on the other hand regarded the company's actions as 'most iniquitous and scandalous' and that if they persisted in their case 'a more base, unprincipled and shameful attempt to cheat and defraud was never made by any individual or body of men'. An analysis of the amounts claimed by the contractors shows how Rennie's original estimates were exceeded. In addition to incurring £55,430 as per contract, over £5,000 was spent on enlarging and deepening the Chichester Canal, £6,000 on excavating Southgate Basin and forming the new road to the city, an extra £5,300 on additional work to the barge canal and over £18,000 on enlarging the Portsea Canal.

The failure of the company to pay the contractors regularly obliged them to borrow money and it was also claimed that the company retained more money than that to which it was entitled and that payments made by the company were not always in cash but by dated bills which the contractors were obliged to get discounted by their bankers. It appears that the contractors were eventually awarded £7,600 but of this sum only £4,570 had been paid by 1836 (see page 135).[16]

There were two possible developments considered in 1825 which might have improved the canal company's prospects. In January a prospectus was issued to form the Portsmouth Commercial Dock Company with a capital of £100,000 to excavate 'the great morass' near Southsea Castle and develop Langstone Harbour as a commercial port.* The proposed site was from the Bathing-House Rooms to Lumps Fort. 'It had long been considered an object of first importance to convey heavy goods between London and Portsmouth' speedily and safely, and it was presumed that the proposed docks would be regarded by the proprietors of the existing canal as an 'appendage which cannot fail to contribute largely to the success of their undertaking'.[17] The second was the Grand Imperial Ship Canal project whose prospectus was issued in March (see Chapter XI). Neither scheme progressed.

However, in the same year the first serious threat to inland water transport appeared on the horizon. Although the initial attempt to obtain an Act for building the Liverpool & Manchester railway was defeated, the Bill was supported in the House of Commons by William Huskisson, now MP for Liverpool and a government minister. He claimed it was his duty to back the railroad irrespective of his personal interest in canals and would have done so had he still been the Member for Chichester.[18] 'He had no preference except that which was connected with increasing facility, despatch and economy in removing merchandize from one place to another.'[19] In September the opening of the Stockton and Darlington railway proved the practicable use of steam locomotives for goods traffic, but it was not until 1830 that the railways came to be regarded as a revolutionary form of transport.

---

* The scheme was revived in both 1846, when the Rennies were listed as the engineers, and again in 1901 by Colonel Holbrook.

VIII

THE HAYLING ISLAND BRIDGE
1823-1824

The wadeways linking Hayling and Thorney Islands – the navigation company decides to dredge a new cut north of Hayling – the island's inhabitants petition for a bridge from shore to shore – the navigation company agrees to contribute towards the cost – Hayling Island Bridge Act – opening celebrations.

The line of navigation between Chichester Harbour and Milton was initially planned to pass to the north of Thorney and Hayling islands. Both these islands were connected to the mainland by wadeways, or hard surface tracts through the mud, which could normally be used by horse-drawn carts and pedestrians at low tide. Bridges were therefore required under the Act to be built over the new channel to be dredged through the wadeways, to the depth of low water at spring tides and wide enough for the tug and its train of barges to pass. To save costs the company decided to avoid building one bridge by rerouting the dredged channel to the south of Thorney Island. This option was not feasible for Hayling Island so plans were made to excavate a channel through the wadeway and build a bridge. Hollinsworth drew the plans and specification and work was begun in January 1822. By May the piles had been driven and the timber for the upper work of the bridge prepared ready for fixing.[1]

However, the bridge would only have spanned the new cut through the wadeway leaving either side of the channel still subject to the tides. Clearly this was an unsatisfactory situation so the island's inhabitants, being unable to persuade the company to build a bridge from shore to shore, decided to petition Parliament for a Bill to build such a bridge. The canal company in its turn agreed to contribute the sum their bridge would have cost: £3,080 as well as £500 for being absolved from future maintenance costs.

The Hayling Island Bridge Act, which was obtained in May 1823, authorised the building of the bridge and raising the sum of £12,000 in £50 shares (of which £10,080 had already been subscribed) and the toll rates to be levied. The names of the subscribers included Vice Admiral Halkett and Edward Casher. The preamble referred to the perils of the crossing:

Whereas for the space of twelve hours out of every twenty four, there is no direct communication between the mainland and Hayling Island in the County of Southampton (except by boat) owing to the passage commonly known by the name of the Wadeway, which runs in a very uneven, unequal and circuitous manner from Langstone Harbour to Hayling Island aforesaid, being overflowed by the sea: And whereas, from the violence of the winds and sea, the passage, called the Wadeway, is frequently covered by the tide the whole twenty four hours together, and boats are often totally prevented from crossing the said harbour, by reason whereof any communication between the mainland and Hayling Island becomes impracticable, and great inconvenience, difficulty and loss are thereby occasioned, and the lives of His Majesty's subjects are much endangered.

The Act also prohibited any conveyance to be available for hire on land or sea within one thousand yards of the bridge, which was intended to prevent local fishermen carrying passengers and goods from Langstone, Bedhampton quay or Pook Lane at less cost than the bridge toll. The bridge was described in 1826 as being 'handsomely and substantially built on piles of African Oak and other timber. It is one of the finest structures of the kind in the kingdom; it measures in length three hundred and twenty yards, and is twenty four feet wide. Its centre is composed of a swing, or swivel, bridge covering an aperture of forty feet, to admit the passage of vessels. The entrance of this aperture; or rather chasm, is protected on each side by additional and projecting piles.'[2]

The causeway on either side of the swing bridge was faced with stone and line by an ornamental post and fence. The headroom in the New Cut beneath the bridge was ten feet at high water so the bridge had only to be swung for the steam tug and coasters passing between Chichester and Langstone harbours. The bridge was opened on Wednesday, 8 September 1824. The weather was cloudy and unpropitious but it was recorded that from an early hour the local inhabitants began preparing for the occasion with 'a hilarity and unanimity seldom before manifested'. By 12 o'clock almost a hundred vehicles consisting mainly of gentlemen's carriages 'filled with all the fashion and beauty of the neighbourhood' had assembled at the east end of Havant. Meanwhile the Duke of Norfolk, having landed at Portsmouth from his 'beautiful' yacht, had driven through the town to Warblington House where he was received by the owner, William Padwick, and Sir George Staunton, MP, who was the Lord of the Manor and owned Leigh Park on the island. Mr Padwick and Sir George then led the procession on horseback followed by the duke in his carriage and four other gentlemen. On arrival at Havant the *Hampshire Telegraph*'s correspondent reported that the party was joined by a number of post chaises, gigs, a long line of waggons

decorated with evergreens and ribbon, and filled by rustics in their holiday suits. Here the party now proceeded by a pair of the King's Colours, borne by two Waterloo men, the band belonging to the Portsmouth Division of the Royal Marines, and another pair of colours. The band struck up a lively tune, and the cavalcade in this order proceeded down the East and South Streets of

Map 5 *Langstone Harbour. Although the 'new Cut' had been made in 1822 as part of the London to Portsmouth navigation, it continued to be so designated, as this 1907 survey shows.*

Silvester & Cº sc:.27, Strand London.

15   *View of the Hayling Island Trestle Road Bridge, 1826.*

Langstone, and from thence over the bridge and causeway, into Hayling Island. On arriving here his Grace alighted, and accompanied by Sir G Staunton, Mr Padwick, and other Gentlemen, took a survey of the works, when he was pleased to express his high approbation of their construction. At this time the scene was particularly animating and interesting: the bridge, causeway, and approaches, which are near a mile in length, were completely covered in their whole extent assemblage on horseback and a foot.[3]

The steam tug *Egremont* also played a part in the celebrations. The canal company's management committee had boarded its 'principal barge' at Milton and had then been towed round Langstone Harbour, heading a colourful procession of boats decked out in all their finery and were as usual entertained by a band on board.

In the evening several members of the committee, including Lord Egremont, Admiral Halkett and John Snook, were among 60 guests who attended the celebratory dinner at the *Bear Inn* in Havant. After appropriate toasts had been proposed and speeches delivered, the evening was enlivened by the marine band and a company of glee singers.[4]

The agreement which the navigation company had concluded with the Langstone (Hayling Island) Bridge Company proved advantageous to both parties since the former was no longer requested to maintain the bridge and the latter could collect a toll which would provide for this responsibility while also providing a public facility for the island's residents.*

---

* The sturdy road bridge was acquired in 1851 under the Hayling Bridge & Causeway Company (Railway to Havant) Act which confirmed the provisions of the 1823 Navigation Act. The timber structure was later to be saddled with a maximum weight limit of 6¼ tons, further reduced to 5 tons, in 1954. Two years later it was replaced by the current pre-stressed concrete feature. In April 1960 the Hampshire County Council declared the bridge free of tolls. The railway bridge, which had been constructed in 1867, was demolished in 1966.

IX

THE STEAM-PACKET, SIR FRANCIS DRAKE
1822-1829

Formation of company to operate a packet service between Portsmouth and
Plymouth – prospectus published (1822) – over £4,000 subscribed – Lord
Egremont a leading shareholder – the *Drake*'s maiden voyage (1823) – promoted
in unison with fly waggon and barge services to London – promising start
– encounters competition from the *Brunswick* – abandons the Portsmouth service
– attempts to sell the *Drake* at a fixed price fail – offers excursions round the
Eddystone lighthouse – carries voters to a Cornish by-election – advertised for
sale without reserve (1829).

It was not until 1815 that the first British steamers ventured to sea. In that
year the 75-ton *Argyle* put in at Portsmouth where so great was the interest
that an Admiralty court-martial suspended its sitting to watch the first arrival
of a steam-propelled vessel. In 1817 the Admiralty commissioned a steam
packet, the *Regent*, which had been designed by Marc Isambard Brunel and
the steam-packet *Britannic* commenced running between Portsmouth and
the Isle of Wight. Nevertheless, the steamers of the period continued to rely
mainly on sail, primarily because the furnaces consumed a great quantity
of fuel and the space for coal bunkers was limited. Indeed, experience was
soon to show that, in order to secure economy, vessels needed to be built
larger and with more powerful engines.

From 1819 there was a rapid expansion of the British steam coasting
trade and by 1822 it was recognised that the safety of steam vessels had been
proved 'even in the most tempestuous weather'.[1] In contemplation of the
canal's completion, a company was formed in 1822 to operate a steam packet
service between Portsmouth and the West of England which would operate
in conjunction with the barges travelling to and from the Metropolis.[*] The
company issued a prospectus in April setting out the objects and advantages
of purchasing a 'strong well built vessel of 120 tons burthen, completely
fitted with her tackle, apparel and furniture'. Cabins were to be 'elegantly

---

[*] The Plymouth, Devonport, Portsmouth and Falmouth Steam-Packet Company. Five years earlier the
canal's management committee had envisaged that the waterway would provide 'a rapid and cheap
communication between London and the Western Ports at the same speed as by land but at less
than one sixth of the cost' (*Hampshire Telegraph*, 2 June 1817).

STATEMENT

OF THE PROBABLE COST OF A

STEAM-PACKET,

And the Advantages to be derived from the Employment of Vessels of that description, between PORTSMOUTH and the WESTERN PORTS, on the completion of the Canal from LONDON to ARUNDEL and PORTSMOUTH.

For the purchase of a strong well-built Vessel of 120 Tons burthen, completely fitted with her Tackle, Apparel, and Furniture; and the Cabins elegantly erected for the accommodation of Passengers, at £15 per Ton, with Boats, &c. } £1800

A Steam-Engine of 24-Horse power, and Machinery, complete, } 1 250

£3050

A Vessel of this size will have a capacity for the Stowage of 80 Tons of Merchandize, independent of the space required for the Steam-Machinery, Cabins, &c.

ANNUAL EXPENDITURE.

Insurance, ...	£150	0
Wear and Tear of Engine, Vessel, and Materials, }	250	0
Coals, 1 Chaldron each voyage, say 26 voyages each way, at 32s. }	85	0

Wages, Provisions, &c.

Master, for Wages & Provisions,	75	0
Steward, no Wages or Provisions		
Mate, £3 per month, ...	36	0
Engineer, ...	50	0
2 Seamen, 35s. each per month,	42	0
Provisions for the Mate, Engineer, and 2 Seamen, at 1s. 3d. per day, }	91	5
	294	5
Clerks and Cellar Rent, at Portsmouth and Plymouth, }	100	0
Lights and Harbour Dues, ...	50	0
Extra Expences, ...	26	15
	£956	0

The Vessel being fitted with the lower Masts and Sails of a Schooner, would only use the Engine in Calms, or during light and adverse Winds;—hence the supply of Coals is abundant: a vessel of this description performed the voyage from this Port to Portsmouth, in 24 Hours, against a North-East Wind, and only consumed $1\frac{1}{2}$ Chaldrons.

The Master, who is expected to pay and maintain the Steward, will have the privilege of supplying the Passengers with Provisions and other Refreshments; and therefore it is considered that the Wages allowed for him is very ample.

16 *The prospectus for building a steam-packet on the completion of the Portsmouth & Arundel Canal 1822.*

erected' for 15 passengers. Cargo capacity was to be 80 tons. Fitted with the sails of a schooner, it was intended that the proposed 24 horse-power steam engine would be employed only in calms or light and adverse winds. The estimated cost of the vessel was £3,050. Annual expenditure was expected to be about £950 to be found out of receipts of around £1,450. It was thought that a profit of 16 per cent might be achieved.[2]

The master was to provide the steward who would be responsible for meals and refreshments. The mate, two seamen and an engineer completed the crew. It was calculated that some 8,000 tons of merchandise were brought annually by coaster from Plymouth to London besides goods carried by waggon or coach. It was hoped that up to 40 tons of cargo could be transferred to each of the barges to be exclusively employed on the London service. These were expected to complete the journey in either direction in four days, the steam packet in less than 24 hours, so that goods could be regularly delivered to either port within seven days of their consignment.

The charge for steam packet carriage, barge hire and canal dues was estimated at 35s. a ton which would only exceed the current charge by coaster by 5s. a ton. By waggon, freight cost £13 a ton and the journey was no quicker than by sea. Coach carriage was much faster but was only used for urgently needed goods since the charges worked out at around £28 a ton.

The faster coaches took over 21 hours to cover the 214 miles from Plymouth to London so it was also expected that passengers from Plymouth would prefer the more comfortable accommodation afforded by the packet before boarding a coach at Portsmouth for the nine-hour journey up to the metropolis. However, no mention was made of the delays likely to be encountered at sea in stormy weather nor of the difficulties to be met in obtaining both regular consignments of freight and passengers.

The company was floated with over 50 subscribers, a large proportion of whom were naval officers. Lord Egremont and the steam-engine manufacturers became the largest shareholders, each with five £50 shares. Vice-Admiral Brooking and Sir Charles Burrell, MP held four shares, Vice-Admiral Pellew and Lord Selsey two, while Arun Navigation shareholders William Cutfield of Climping and William Holmes of Arundel had one each.

At the first meeting of the shareholders held at the Town Hall, Plymouth Dock on 3 May 1822 it was reported that £4,350 had been subscribed and that further sums would be sought for the possible building of a second vessel. Meantime it was agreed that it might be advisable to send 'a competent person' to either Liverpool or the Clyde to learn the best plan to adopt and the model steam packet to imitate. The size of vessel was agreed and the amount of subscriptions rose to £4,800; tenders were invited and building began at Plymouth 'on the plan of Sir Robert Sepping's[*] 'diagonal

---

[*] Naval architect who invented machinery called 'Sepping's blocks' for suspending vessels in docks. Surveyor of Navy 1813-32.

17 *View of the entrance to Portsmouth Harbour shortly after the steam-packet* Sir Francis Drake *began operations in 1823.*

framing'. Her length was just over 103 feet, her breadth 18 feet 8 inches and her draught 11 feet. Her bottom was sheathed in stout copper, her engine produced 70 horse-power and her weight was 170 tons – or 50 more than was originally proposed. Named *Sir Francis Drake*, she was described by the committee of management 'as a fine steam schooner' calculated to facilitate the intercourse between Plymouth and Portsmouth.

The *Drake* made her maiden voyage to Portsmouth under the command of James Mill on 9 September 1823. At the same time it was announced that a sister ship, *The Earl of Egremont* with an 80-horse power engine, would shortly be ready for the packet service between Plymouth and the Devonshire ports, but of this vessel no more is heard. Two days later the *Drake* made the return trip and the weekly service had begun operation.[3]

The start of the new steam-packet service prompted carriers Hoare & Stanbury* to introduce a daily (except Sunday) fly waggon service from Cheapside in the city of London to the *Blue Post Inn* at Portsmouth in 36 hours.[4] No prices were advertised but it was probably three or four times dearer than the weekly service promoted by the Portsmouth Barge Company which offered to convey goods to Portsmouth within seven days and claimed that 'in about ten days goods could be conveyed to Plymouth by steam packet at one quarter of the expense of land carriage'.[5]

The *Drake* was patronised during 1824 in spite of her engine being none too reliable nor her cabins comfortable. Travellers from Plymouth found it more agreeable and less expensive to sail to Portsmouth and take the coach up to London with no great difference in time rather than travel

---

* Hoare & Stanbury had carried on the waggon business founded by the Clark family for more than a century. In 1832 Hoare offered for sale the half-share in the partnership (*Hampshire Telegraph*, 1 October 1832).

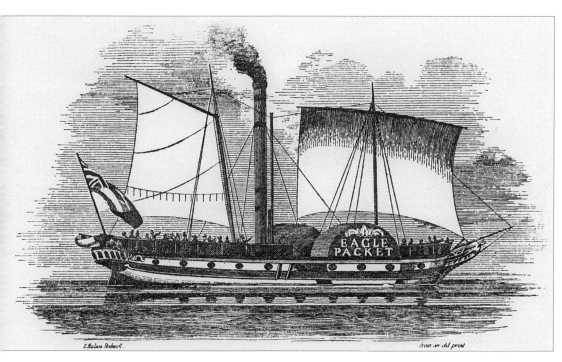

18 *The steam-packet* Eagle, *sailing between London and Margate, was a contemporary of the* Sir Francis Drake *when the latter began operation between Portsmouth and Plymouth in 1823.*

LONDON & PORTSMOUTH FLY WAGONS.

HOARE & STANBURY beg to inform the Inhabitants and Trade in general of PLYMOUTH, PLYMOUTH DOCK, TAVISTOCK, DARTMOUTH, TORBAY, TEIGNMOUTH, and their Vicinity, that, in connection with the *Sir Francis Drake* Steam Vessel, they will CONVEY GOODS of every description to and from those places, with great facility, by their FLY WAGGONS, which leave the White Hart and Ship Inns, Borough, and Blossoms' Inn, Lawrence-lane, Cheapside, London, every day (Sunday excepted), at five o'clock in the afternoon, and arrive at the Blue Posts Inn, Portsmouth, in thirty-six hours, being only one day on the road (the only every-day conveyance of this kind to and from London and Portsmouth); from which Inn they return every day at the same hour (Sunday excepted), and arrive at the above Inns, London, in the same time.

Any application to Mr. BLEWETT, Agent, Exchange, Plymouth, will be duly attended to.

19 *The commencement of the* Sir Francis Drake *steam-packet service between Portsmouth and Plymouth encouraged land carriers such as Hoare & Stanbury to introduce a fly waggon service in 1823 from London to connect with the packet at Portsmouth.*

by road the whole distance. Although the coach to London awaited the arrival of the packet, no special freight or passenger rates were promoted for those planning to use both modes of carriage.

In January 1825 the *Drake* owners announced that 'the greatest exertions are now using under the direction of the ablest engineers, to render her machinery the most complete and efficient; and that the accommodations on board will be made as commodious and comfortable as possible'.[6] However, a new steam-packet – the *Brunswick* of 250 tons and 100 horse-power – was nearing completion and early in 1825 commenced running weekly in competition with the *Drake*. She was advertised as being supplied with 'Captain Mills Patent Paddles by which the back-water and tremulous motion, so much complained of in steam vessels, are avoided'.

The *Brunswick*, larger by 80 tons and faster, proved a formidable adversary and the *Drake* was soon forced out of contention. In October they attempted to sell the *Drake* 'but were unable to find a purchaser at an acceptable price'.

The year 1826 was not a good one for the *Drake*'s shareholders. James Mill, the steamer's captain, changed ships and became commander of the *Brunswick* which was now advertised as having already established herself as a superior vessel for 'extraordinary dispatch and for the elegance and convenience of her accommodation'. More irksome tidings related to the revelation that the company secretary, Mr Blewett, had also defected to her rival.

The *Drake* responded to the competition by reducing her fares. Thomas Russell, the new secretary who had succeeded Blewett after his dismissal in May, reported that receipts for the first three months were considerably down on what had been received the previous May due to competition from a vessel 'of superior power, speed and accommodation'. What, however, was more alarming for the shareholders was the injury done to the company by 'the election of members to the committee of persons largely interested in, or collaterally connected, with a rival vessel' (i.e. the *Brunswick*) whose owners had thus been enabled to anticipate and detect whatever measures the committee had contemplated to improve the company's profitability.[*] Furthermore the company was suffering from 'the severe pressure of the commercial distress which has tended in no small degree to lessen the number of travellers of every description'.

Another piece of disappointing news was that Brunton's patent Fire Regulators had proved 'by repeated and costly experience, utterly unsuited to a sea-going vessel'. The fire regulators having been discarded, the boilers were now more powerful and it was hoped that with moderate care they would last the current season. The cabins had also proved unsatisfactory and had

---

[*] William Eastlake and Vice-Admirals Sir Israel Pellew and James Brooking were all Brunswick Committee members in 1826 and 1827 as well as *Drake* shareholders.

20   *Notice of the sale of the*
Sir Francis Drake *by the*
candle *1829.*

STEAM PACKET.
FOR UNRESERVED SALE, BY THE CANDLE.
FOR SALE by PUBLIC AUCTION, without reserve, at the Steam Packet Wharf, Stonehouse, near Plymouth, on Thursday, the 2nd April next, at three o'clock in the afternoon.—The faithfully, and substantially built STEAM-PACKET SIR FRANCIS DRAKE; length, 103 feet 8 inches: breadth, 18 feet 8 inches; depth, 11 feet: about 170 tons, Builders' measure, and 80 horse power, with her Masts, Yards, and Spars, Boats, Anchors, and Cables, Machinery, &c. as they now lay on board, alongside the aforesaid Wharf.

This superior Sea Boat was built in this Port with the best materials and workmanship, under the inspection of an officer of his Majesty's Dock-yard, on the plan of Sir Robert Seppings' diagonal framing, &c. and is copper fastened, and sheathed with stout copper. Her Masts and Spars are complete for a Schooner, and are together with the Hull and Store, in most excellent condition. She can be equipped for sea at a trifling expense. The Engines, on the principle of Bolton and Watt, are in an efficient state for immediate use.

The spare Stores, Launch, Coals, &c. will also be disposed of by Auction, without reserve, to close the concerns of the Company, the day after the sale of the Vessel, commencing at eleven o'clock in the morning.

For viewing, &c. apply to Mr. Russell, at the Commercial Inn; or to Mr. Stumbles, at the said Wharf, Stonehouse; or to

J. E. BLEWETT, Broker.

EXCHANGE, PLYMOUTH, 9th March, 1829.

now been repainted and refitted so as to hold out a reasonable hope that the nuisance complained of last season 'will not again be experienced'.

More bad news emerged that the company had not been able to procure from Blewett a final settlement of the accounts for the previous season 'nor recover his debts' on account of sundry private transactions charged to the company. Mr Blewett responded forcibly to these 'malicious accusations' which were finally settled by an arbitrator who awarded him three-quarters of the payment claimed for his services from October 1825 to January 1826 and ordered him to pay £1 11s. of the sum claimed by the proprietors of the *Drake* who also had to pay the arbitration expenses. Blewett continued to act for the *Brunswick* whose chairman, William Eastlake, moved a resolution that he be given ten guineas for 'his zealous conduct to the duties of his office'.[7]

It was reported on 18 December 1827, at the last meeting for which minutes are available, that, in spite of the *Drake* making a profit after expenses of £275, the company was still in debt to the tune of over £500.

New boilers had cost £718 and further attempts to sell the vessel at less than half her original cost had failed. The problem was that the *Brunswick* had taken the lion's share of the Portsmouth traffic and the Irish packet boats the Falmouth to London business, 'thereby shutting out the line of coast previously occupied by the *Drake*, for which she was expressly built and would have returned a great profit'.

The *Drake* committee had, therefore, to decide whether to operate in 1828 a weekly service from Devonport to Guernsey and from Guernsey to Portsmouth or to run against the Brunswick to Portsmouth. To operate both these services a further call of £5 a share was necessary to pay their bankers, but Admiral Halkett was 'decidedly of opinion that no further call should be made'.[8] Six others including Lord Selsey and Holmes thought likewise but nonetheless £480 was subscribed, new boilers were installed and the *Drake* continued in service. In March 1828 a reduced fare from Portsmouth to Plymouth, and from that latter port to Guernsey, was advertised.

In the autumn the shareholders decided enough was enough, and on 2 April 1829 the *Sir Francis Drake* was put up for auction, 'FOR UNRESERVED SALE BY THE CANDLE' at the Steam Packet Wharf, Stonehouse, Plymouth.[9] Purchased by the owners of the *Brunswick*, 'the established favourite and powerful steam packet', the *Drake* was now forced to wait on the arrival of her rival from Portsmouth before sailing for Fowey and Falmouth.[*]

---

[*] The *Drake* continued in service until 1837 or later. In November 1836 she was used to tow the new wooden floating bridge from the builder's yard at Stonehouse to Southampton for use on the river Itchen.

X

The Failure of the Portsea Ship Canal
1822-1826

Canal entrance blocked by silt (1822) – closed for six months – complaints of
salt water polluting wells – further closure for repairs – public meetings held
– claims for compensation – dangerous bridges – Lord Selsey rebuts the unjust
attacks upon the company's character – no money available to remedy the evil
– canal remains closed – attempts to obtain a new Act postponed – Portsmouth
Barge Company goes into liquidation – sale of barges at Chichester – auction of
the company store at Halfway Houses – Lord Egremont relinquishes his interest
in the navigation (1826)

The story of the Portsea Canal is a sorry saga. Within a few weeks of its
opening in September 1822 disaster struck. A severe storm caused the
dredged channel, from the Convict's Watering Place to the sea lock at
Milton, to be blocked by silt. Nor was it possible to clear it quickly. Because
of the limited winter daylight and the fact that the channel could only be
dredged at low water spring tides, it was not until the beginning of May
1823 that the canal could be reopened.* When it was, a great show was
made of the fact that three colliers, of from 150 to 230 tons burthen, had
entered the canal and discharged their cargoes at Halfway Houses. Another
vessel was said to be preparing to do the same.

The company had again to attempt to refute the prejudices 'excited by
interested persons' and Lord Selsey felt bound to tell the shareholders that
the masters of those vessels had 'unanimously approved the canal as safe
and convenient and that two of them had voluntarily left written statements
to that effect to encourage others engaged in the same trade'.[1] From these
remarks it was evident that not every merchant agreed.

During 1824 there had been a growing number of complaints about
the island's drinking supplies being polluted by salt water and it became
increasingly certain that the canal was the cause. Because of the gravelly
nature of the ground the contractors had been required to give both
the bed and sides of the excavated channel a watertight lining three feet
thick. It soon proved unlikely that this had been satisfactorily achieved.

---

* The 470-yard channel was required to be dredged to four feet below the low water mark (Report of
  the Committee of Management, 21 May 1822).

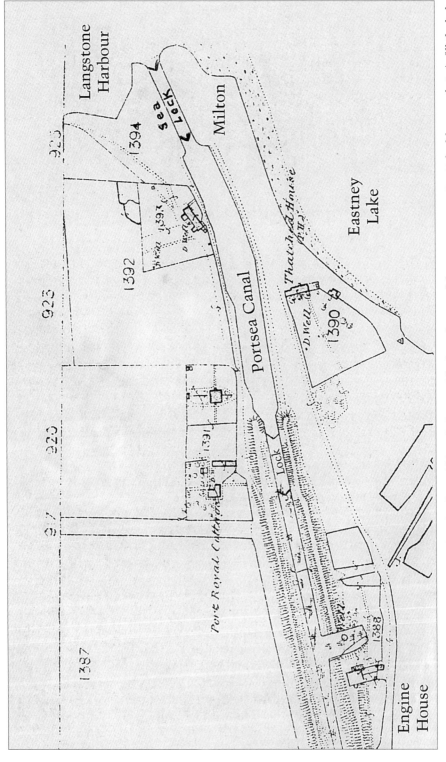

MAP 6 *The entrance to the Portsea Canal, 1870. Although the canal had not been used for 40 years, no attempt had been made to infill the bed between Fratton and the sea.*

PORTSMOUTH AND ARUNDEL CANAL.

THE Public are informed, that the Water being drawn off from a part of the Portsea Line, in order to effect some necessary Repairs, arrangements have been made; that all Goods sent by the Portsmouth and Arundel Barge Company, will be landed at a Wharf near Fratton Bridge, without delay, or any extra expence.—PORTSMOUTH, *Nov.* 13.

21 *It was this announcement in the* Hampshire Telegraph *in November 1824 of the partial closure of the canal which spelt the doom of the Portsea Canal. No funds were available to carry out repairs and the contractors Dyson & Thornton refused to carry out further work unless their bills were paid.*

In April the Portsea Island Waterworks Company lodged a complaint and demanded that immediate steps be taken to remedy the evil. The contractors told Edgecombe that they were unaware whether 'the evil' complained of by Mr Allen, the water company's agent, existed, but that if it did 'we cannot but observe that same would long since have been remedied if the company had paid the amount that is due to us under our contract; therefore the existence of such evil (if it exists at all) does not lay with us, but as the company and ourselves materially differ in their, and our, view of the case, they may perhaps not agree with us in what we have stated and as we have no wish to put the company to any inconvenience, we now state that we have not any objection to their doing what they may consider to be necessary to remedy the evil complained of by Mr Allen.'[2]

This unfortunate state of affairs had arisen partly as a result of the contractors' skimping the puddling of the canal bed and banks but also because the backwash and overflowing tide, which had occurred in 1822, had seriously damaged the lining of the banks. Hollinsworth had failed to have the original work properly superintended nor had he ensured that weaknesses were effectively remedied; however, the management committee, while determining that the draught of the canal should be increased from five to ten feet, and then to 12 feet, had not thought it necessary to specify any additional measures to prevent such an occurrence since clay three feet thick if properly puddled was impervious to leakage. The fact that the contractors had only required an extra £200 to deepen the 2½ miles of canal by two feet should, however, in itself have given rise to concern.[*]

---

[*] The committee were only too well aware of the need to make the bed water-tight. In their report in May 1821 they had referred to the 'open gravelly quality of the ground for a considerable extent and the need for a lining three feet thick along both bottom and sides to prevent the water escaping when the canal is filled. This requirement making it necessary for the work to be done in short lengths as the excavation proceeds caused much delay'.

OLD TOWN-HALL, PORTSMOUTH.

NOTICE is hereby given,—That a special
GENERAL MEETING of the Portsmouth,
Portsea, Gosport, Arundel, and West of England
FLY BARGE COMPANY, will be held on Friday
next, the 12th day of May, at eleven o'clock in the
forenoon, at the Old Town-Hall, Portsmouth, agree-
ably to the 25th Article of the Company's Deed, to
confirm a Resolution entered into this day by the Proprietors convened for that purpose,—" That the Company be dissolved; and other special affairs."
J. M. HOFFMEISTER,
5th May, 1826.   Honorary Secretary.

22   *The winding up notice of the Fly Barge Company.*

Matters were made worse by the dispute between the company and the contractors who were charged with not completing the works to a satisfactory standard and failing to complete the work in the stipulated period of 30 months. The contractors retorted that all the works had been 'under the superintendence and inspection of Mr Hollingsworth [*sic*]' who had not required any of their work to be re-executed. No agreement being reached, the contractors advised the company on 14 July 1823 that they were 'under the disagreeable necessity of suspending the works remaining to be done for want of the necessary funds for that purpose'. Not until February 1824 did the company agree to submit the dispute to arbitration and the result was still awaited when the proprietors met in December. By then the upper part of the canal had been drained and the Portsmouth Barge Company had announced on 13 November that all goods would be landed at a wharf near Fratton Bridge 'without delay or any extra expense'.[3] As, however, there was no money available to carry out the repairs, the closure was the canal's death sentence.

Thirty-six gentlemen attended a meeting at the Beneficial Society's Hall in Portsea on 3 December 1824 to decide how to obtain redress. Among the audience, anxious to learn what would happen when the canal was refilled with water, were Daniel Howard, the Mayor of Portsmouth, and solicitor John Shugar, who was clerk to the trustees of the Portsmouth-Sheet Bridge Turnpike. William Deacon took the chair and observed that 'much was to be apprehended from the effects of salt water in the canal, under circumstances which appeared, from what had recently happened to the Farlington Water Works, not improbable, and which might materially affect the supply of the town with pure water, and that viewing the place as a great Naval and Military station, and considering its vast population, the subject assumed even a National importance.'[4] The meeting then agreed a number of resolutions which were published in the local press.

TO BARGE PROPRIETORS, &c.

TO be SOLD by AUCTION, by Mr. J. N. ROBINSON, on Monday the 21st August 1826, at the Canal Wharf, Chichester, at noon.—Three BARGES, the *Portsea*, *Portsmouth*, and *Southampton*, each about 69ft. in length, 13ft. in breadth, and 40 Tons burthen, have been built within the last three years, are well found in all necessary stores, and well adapted for inland navigation, now lying at the Canal Basin, Chichester, where they may be seen by applying to Mr. Purchase, Clerk at the Wharf.

For further particulars, apply to the Auctioneer, at his Office, opposite the Custom-House, Portsmouth.

23-4 *In 1826 the future of the Portsea Canal was bleak. In May the Portsmouth Fly Barge Company went into voluntary liquidation, in August the Portsmouth Barge Company put up for sale at Chichester its fleet and in October the contents of the barge company's store at Halfway Houses were sold.*

BARGE COMPANY'S STORE, CANAL BASIN, HALFWAY-HOUSES.

TO be SOLD by AUCTION, by Mr. J. PUSHMAN, Jun. (to clear the Premises), on Tuesday, 17th of October, 1826, at ten o'clock in the forenoon,—A variety of useful ARTICLES, comprising a quantity of Turner's blacking, in bottles; about a cwt. stone blue, china, glass, and earthenware, an assortment of useful timber and plank, spars, barge poles, sails, ropes, and sundry other articles, which may be viewed on the morning of sale, by application to Mr. Bonamy, on the Premises; or the Auctioneer, St. Thomas's-street, Portsmouth.

This action infuriated the canal company's management committee who called a special general meeting at the Old Town Hall on 21 December. Lord Selsey moved that the resolutions entered into by the local residents were 'an unjust and unfounded attack upon the character and conduct of the company' since it must have been known to several who were present that in various instances redress had been granted to those who had complained to the management committee and that in other cases the committee had informed them of the reasons which had obliged them to defer a decision until the cause of the damage had been established. His lordship greatly regretted that the owners and occupiers of property, instead of supporting an enterprise which had already nearly halved the cost of coastal freight, should view the company 'with feelings of such marked hostility and dislike'. Lastly Lord Selsey stressed the point that they 'would not allow themselves to be dictated to by any set of individuals, however respectable … nor be deterred by their threats from pursuing such measures as they shall deem fitting'.[5]

However, the wording of the company's counter resolutions also contained the proviso that their readiness to pay compensation might be deferred until 'the peculiar circumstances of the company would permit'. Since the company had just announced its intention of applying to Parliament to raise more capital for completing the canal 'either by a loan or a call on the proprietors for a further sum' or in some other way, it was clearly in no position to pay any claims.

The day after Boxing Day William Deacon chaired a meeting of the 'Committee for obtaining compensation' and reported that the company had declined a conference on the subject. Those present strongly rebutted Lord Selsey's response and stressed that they felt 'the liveliest interest in the welfare of the place and whatever tends to its prosperity, and that they were not opposed to the canal', only to 'withstand the evils which it has produced' and to prevent 'the continuance of a local calamity'. Deacon went on to say that they were not surprised by the resolutions passed at the recent meeting of the canal proprietors seeing that 'the same plausible mode of representation had been used to promote the canal speculation'. However, they found it difficult to conceive how a public company could consider themselves at liberty to injure the property of others 'without having it in their power, according to their own declaration, to make compensation'.[6]

In February 1825 the company petitioned the House of Commons for a further Act to enable the navigation to be completed. The directors announced that they hoped to raise £50,000 either by a voluntary call of £10 a share or by 'a loan, mortgage, bonds or additional shares'; but that if none of these modes of raising money should succeed, the company sought power to sell the entire property to any party by resolution at a general meeting. It was revealed that besides the £40,000 mortgage, £122,200 of the initial capital of £126,000 had been raised and expended, the difference of £3,800 owing from defaulter or bankrupt shareholders.[7] The Bill received a first reading in the House of Commons on 18 March but before the second reading took place petitions had been lodged against the Bill by property owners in Portsea demanding compensation 'for damage due to their springs and wells' and by the inhabitants of Portsea and Portsmouth to compel the company 'to render the bridges over the canal more safe and convenient'.

The Bill was read a second time on 18 April but on 30 May Mr Curtain, on behalf of the parliamentary committee to which the Bill had been referred, reported that they had found the 'allegations to be true and had made several amendments to the bill from which it was clear that the

We have sincere satisfaction in being enabled to communicate to those persons who are interested in the success of the Portsmouth and Arundel Canal, the particulars of a munificent gift offered to the Proprietors by the Patron of the undertaking, the Earl of Egremont, being no less than the voluntary surrender to the Company of the whole of his Lordship's shares, which cost him 15,750*l.* his Lordship engaging at the same time, for the payment of the debt due from the Company to Government, for which he heretofore gave his guarantee, and abandoning his claim on the Company for its future reimbursements. The sole condition required on the part of his Lordship from the Proprietors is, that they shall cause the Canal to be rendered complete and efficient, as originally contemplated.

25 *The* Hampshire Telegraph *reports (18 September 1826) 'Lord Egremont's munificent gift' to the company of his shareholding which cost him £15,750 as well as the abandonment of his claim for the repayment of the £40,000 loan. Rousseaux's wholesale price index indicates that the 1995 equivalent purchasing power of Egremont's £55,750 outlay in 1825 would have been £3.3 million.*

26 *The western shore of Langstone Harbour, looking east in 1967. Two lines of caravans mark the filled-in bed of the Portsea Canal where there are still traces of an embankment on each side.*

27   *A closer view of the canal at Milton, 1967. The former pump engine house can be recognised by its twin gabled slate roof in the centre of the picture and to the right of a cluster of houses.*

bill could proceed no further'. The company, acting on Lord Egremont's advice, decided that the Government should be approached to see if they would be prepared to take an interest in this 'waterway of great national importance'.

By now the Portsea Canal was moribund. During 1826 no attempt was made to put the waterway back into order. There is no record of any traffic to Fratton Bridge but on 14 April the *Fly* took five tons of 'old household goods' to London and on 18 August the *Fly* is listed as carrying 15 tons of bullion from Portsmouth, but from which wharf is not recorded. The next load of gold and silver in October was dispatched from Chichester. Meanwhile the Portsmouth Barge Company was still operating ten barges between Chichester and the Thames, albeit at a loss. However in April 1826 its fleet carried only 332½ tons to Guildford and beyond. In May this figure had fallen to 222 tons. On 12 May the Portsmouth Barge company shareholders met at the Old Town Hall and resolved to go into liquidation. In August the three barges, the *Portsea, Portsmouth* and *Southampton* lying in Southgate Basin, were sold.[8] In October the barge company disposed of the contents of its warehouse at Halfway Houses. Included in the sale were barge poles, ropes, sails, earthenware, china, glass, bottles of Turner's blacking and an assortment of timber and plank together with all the sundry paraphernalia of the barging trade.[9]

The company's position was now grave. It lacked the financial resources to pay its creditors and parts of the navigation were in a miserable state of repair. It was at this point that Lord Egremont decided that the only way the company could be saved from being put into liquidation was for him to abandon his financial interest. In September the *Hampshire Telegraph* detailed the particulars of his lordship's 'munificent gift' being no less than the voluntary surrender of all his shares (which had cost £15,750), an undertaking to pay the debt due to the Government and his abandoning any claim for its future reimbursement. His sole condition was that the proprietors should cause the canal to be rendered 'complete and efficient'.[10] To all intents and purposes the Portsea Canal was now a dead duck.

XI

JOHN RENNIE'S REPORT
1827

Lord Egremont's proposal to the Admiralty – the Lord High Admiral invites John
Rennie to examine the state of the canal – Rennie's terms of reference – visits
the canal in July and August 1827 – estimates the cost of repairs – proposes
direct access to Portsmouth Harbour via Portsbridge – considers how further
capital might be raised and likely profitability – writes to Lord Selsey – the
Grand Imperial Ship Canal project.

During 1827 there was virtually no traffic between London and the
Portsmouth & Arundel Canal. The only bullion traffic was 40 tons of
money loaded at Littlehampton in May and, on 31 May, 18 tons of money
was recorded as coming from Portsmouth, probably being loaded at Milton.
The Wey Navigation ledgers record only three barge loads to Portsmouth.
There were two consignments of wine totalling 17 tons in the *Fly* for Edward
Casher, and Moor Wilkins carried 25 tons of stall goods in *Charlotte* for
the Portsmouth Fair at the end of June. The trade to Chichester was no
better. The Arundel Barge company and Richard Isemonger delivered less
than one hundred tons of groceries. Not only was the Portsea Canal closed
but the barge canal at Ford was in a very imperfect state, inadequately
watered, poorly fenced and reedy. The management committee, frustrated
at every turn, finally agreed that their only recourse was to try to persuade
the Admiralty, and thereby the Government, to take responsibility for
completing the navigation. This seemed an unlikely prospect.

However, it so happened that now was as favourable an opportunity to
approach the Government as was likely to occur. The death of HRH the
Duke of York in January 1827 had left the Duke of Clarence, the third
son of George III and brother of George IV, heir to the throne. William
FitzClarence had served in the Navy until 1790 and was then formally
promoted through the successive ranks to that of Admiral of the Fleet
in 1811. In June 1814 he had commanded the fleet at Spithead when
it was reviewed by the Prince Regent and the Allied Sovereigns. George
Canning had succeeded Lord Liverpool as Prime Minister in February
1827 and since Lord Melville, the First Sea Lord, now refused to continue
to serve in the Cabinet, he decided to revive the post of Lord High

28 *Proposals for a ship canal to link London and Portsmouth surfaced in 1825 with the announcement that a survey was to be made by the Rennie brothers, John and George. (Hampshire Telegraph, 18 July 1825)*

SHIP CANAL FROM LONDON TO PORTSMOUTH.

A Proposal for a SHIP CANAL from LONDON to PORTSMOUTH, capable of conveying Line of Battle Ships and the largest Merchantmen, having been submitted to several Noblemen and Gentlemen, and the preliminary opinions of eminent Engineers having been expressed in terms so favourable as to warrant the recommendation, that a detailed Survey, under the direction of the Committee of Management hereinafter named, be forthwith made by Messrs. RENNIE, with or without other professional assistance, as the Committee may determine, in order to ascertain, with the utmost attainable precision, the amount of the probable expense, and the most eligible of the several suggested Lines, the foundation of a Company has been laid for the conduct of so important a national object.

The rough estimates of this work give reason to believe that the expence will be within Five Millions Sterling, and the official returns and calculations prepared by the originators of the measure, and carefully examined and reported upon by several gentlemen of the highest eminence in the commercial and maritime affairs of this country, induce the belief that even upon this large capital, although the whole should be required, there would be a reasonable return in time of peace, with the prospect of a very great increase in time of war, by a levy (upon those vessels which will have an unquestionable interest in using the Canal) of from 2s. 6d. per ton upwards, according to their tonnage.

In order therefore to defray the requisite Survey, and other necessary expences, Messrs. Cockburn and Company, Whitehall, London, will receive applications (directed to Charles Dance, Esq. the Secretary), for 5,000 subscriptions of 1*l.* each, with power of adding to that number. These applications will be taken into consideration, and appropriated by the Committee of Management, *and every such Subscription of 1L will entitle the accepted Subscriber to take up Ten Shares of* 100*l. each* (making up 50,000 or more such Shares), *if the Subscribers, when the completion of the Survey may have furnished full information, shall decide to claim those Shares.* To facilitate that decision, the result of the Survey, which will probably occupy several weeks, will be reported to the Subscribers on the earliest possible day after its termination, at a Meeting of which general notice will be given.

For deciding upon the applications of gentlemen desirous to subscribe, for directing the investigation of the plan, for defraying the expences incurred and to be incurred, and for the other purposes of the undertaking, the following Noblemen and Gentlemen have undertaken to be the Provisional Committee of Management, three of whom will be Trustees of Deposits:—

The Lord Viscount Palmerston, M.P. Vice-Admiral Sir George Cockburn, G.C.B. M.P. Capt. Sir Jahleel Brenton, Bart. R.N. K.C.B. Thos. Wilson, Esq. M.P. William Manning, Esq. M.P. Horace Twiss, Esq. M.P.

Solicitors to the Provisional Committee—Messrs. Freshfield, Kaye, and Freshfield, New Bank-buildings.

CHARLES DANCE, Esq. Secretary.

Admiral and offer it to the Duke of Clarence. The duke was pleased to accept. However, although in nominal command of the navy, he was to be given no individual authority since he had to consult a council of six members headed by Vice Admiral Sir George Cockburn (1772-1853), whom he positively disliked. Furthermore John Croker, the Navy Secretary, was Cockburn's friend. In practice, though, HRH wanted to be his own man and often took it upon himself to act on his own initiative. He knew both Egremont and Rennie well. His eldest son by Mrs Jordan, George Fitz Clarence (created Earl of Munster in 1830) had married Egremont's daughter Mary Wyndham. And HRH had only that summer discussed with Rennie the improvements being made to Plymouth Harbour; furthermore his regular visits to Portsmouth would certainly have made him aware of the Portsea Canal. It was possible, therefore, that he would view the resurgence of the Portsmouth & Arundel Navigation more encouragingly than the other members of the council.[*]

There was also a precedent for Government to promote and construct canals of national importance. The purpose in building the Portsmouth & Arundel was little different from that which prompted the Government to build the Caledonian Canal.[†] As an added inducement Lord Egremont had advised William Huskisson,[‡] who was now Treasurer of the Navy as well as President of the Board of Trade, that he would give the Government his shareholding if they would assist in completing the navigation.[1]

Huskisson referred the matter to the Lord High Admiral who in July 'desired' John Rennie[§] to examine minutely the state of the Portsmouth Canal and to estimate the expense of putting the whole into complete repair. In addition he was to find out what part of the original plan remained to

[*] It so happened that on 2 August HRH, during his first visit to Portsmouth as Lord High Admiral, dined as the guest of the mayor and corporation at the Green Row Rooms. The mayor was none other than attorney Daniel Howard, one of those seriously aggrieved by the canal company's failure to remedy the damage caused by salt water polluting the water supply (*Hampshire Telegraph*, 6 December 1824).

[†] This waterway authorised by Act of Parliament in 1803 avoided the navigational hazards of the Pentland Firth and would have saved shipping from deprecations by French privateers. Although construction had begun in 1804, it would not be opened until 1822 by which time the collapse of the Baltic timber trade, the end of the Napoleonic wars and the development of steam navigation had caused public enthusiasm to decline. Telford had originally estimated the cost at about £350,000, William Jessop increased the figure to £474,500 in 1804 but over £900,000 had been expended by the time of the opening. Government had also promoted the construction of the Royal Military Canal in 1804 but this was built primarily as a defence against invasion.

[‡] Huskisson, who ten years earlier had sought financial aid from the Government for building the navigation, had not long ago spoken in the House of Commons (March 1825) in support of the first Liverpool & Manchester Railway Bill, not as a minister, but as the Member for Liverpool. Although a shareholder, he favoured any proposition whether by land or water which would benefit the country's commerce. Huskisson received fatal injuries at the opening of the Liverpool & Manchester Railway in September 1830.

[§] John Rennie (1794-1874) was the second son of John Rennie (senior). After his father's death in 1821, he continued to work on several of his harbour projects and was appointed engineer for the rebuilding of London Bridge in 1824. He was knighted on its completion in 1831.

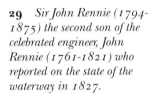

29 *Sir John Rennie (1794-1875) the second son of the celebrated engineer, John Rennie (1761-1821) who reported on the state of the waterway in 1827.*

be completed and whether in the light of such examination it was advisable for the Government to accept Lord Egremont's gift and become principal shareholders in the canal.

Rennie spent three months acting upon these instructions which from the 'tedious and intricate nature of the subject necessarily occupied a good deal of time'. His report dated 4 October 1827[*] included some surprising revelations and confirmed that the contractors had made a nonsense of the work. Firstly, there was the need completely to reline the banks and re-puddle the bed of the Portsea Canal at an estimated cost of over £11,000 'due to the very defective manner in which it has been executed as it is incapable of holding water'. Nevertheless, the bridges, buildings, engine-house and locks were well executed; only the seven swivel bridges needed replanking and the culverts were in need of some repair. Alternatively, if the canal was made capable of accommodating vessels drawing only five feet instead of 12, Rennie thought the cost of renovation would be halved. The experienced engineer doubted whether deepening the canal to provide additional land water to save working the steam engine was a feasible proposition; the engine was regarded as being the only legitimate means of supply. As to what was the best plan for completing this line, he felt that since so much money had already been expended, it would be better, if completed at all, to complete it as a ship canal rather than to reduce it to a five-feet canal. Alternatively, he suggested the most proper course might be 'to leave it alone for the present until increasing trade and communication should render it advisable'.

[*] A copy is deposited in the archives of the Institution of Civil Engineers.

The 13 miles of tidal navigation was said to be generally navigable at low water spring tides except at the wadeways at Hayling and Thorney islands which required 2,200 yards of dredging to a depth of 18 inches at a cost of £2,090. Rennie felt that this section of the waterway was unlikely to cause delays to traffic 'except in the case of very extraordinary storms'.

However, the whole section of the canal between Salterns and Ford was 'still in a very imperfect state'; for much of its length it had not been puddled and, having been cut through porous soil, it was not watertight. Since the steam engine at Ford had to supply all the water for this section, except for about eight locks a day from the adjoining streams, the engineer had had the banks cut through in about thirty different places and had found them mostly defective. To remedy this evil the sides and bottom needed to be puddled for 'about two thirds of the whole line'. Furthermore, the tow-paths were in a poor state and in many parts required to be formed again and the fencing and hedges were wanting for much of the line, but Rennie excluded them from his estimate 'until more prosperous circumstances'. Even so, over £20,000 was needed to put this section into sound working order.

At Ford the steam engine, pumps and buildings were well constructed and in good repair. Only a boiler was waiting to be replaced. Rennie went on to observe, of what the management committee was only too well aware, that it would be very desirable to find a water supply to obviate using the engine. When his father's report had been written in January 1816 it was thought that a steam engine would be required to supply the line with water. Now he went on to point out that, even if a reservoir could be made to receive the water from a copious stream near Chichester, it would only be able to supply two locks a day which was less than was currently being lost though leakage. Again, he felt this was a matter best left until trade increased.

Rennie next considered the communication between Portsmouth and Langstone Harbour through Portsbridge Creek. The original plan had envisaged a lock at each end of the Cosham Cut to ensure that it was navigable at high water neap tides. However, to avoid the cost of the locks, the existing tideway could be deepened down to low water with a 24-feet bottom and, by replacing Portsbridge with a double swivel bridge, the tideway would be rendered navigable from one-third flood to two-thirds ebb 'which would be the same as the Thorney and Hayling Wadeways'. The cost of doing this was put at £6,159.

Rennie estimated the expense of completing the line of navigation, but excluding the Portsea Canal, to be £28,333. However, Fowler had calculated that the canal company was still in debt to the tune of £20,894 after deducting the sum (£40,000) liquidated by Lord Egremont. So, the fact of the matter was that nearly £50,000 would be required. To raise this sum Rennie suggested the creation of additional shares offered initially to the old proprietors and, in the event of their refusal, to the Government.

All profits to be equally divided but – and this was something which would not have appealed to the Treasury – should the profits not equal the disbursements, the deficiency was to be made good by the Government.

On the question as to whether it would be prudent for the Government to become the principal shareholder, Rennie made the figures as favourable as possible by listing the revenue received since the opening of the Chichester Canal in May 1822. From £669 in 1823 it had risen to £1,010 in 1826 of which rather more than half was from Arundel to Chichester and the Salterns, 40 per cent from Salterns to Chichester but only £17 from traffic between Salterns and Ford. The total tonnage carried in 1826 was 13,351 tons. No revenue had been derived from the Portsea Canal because it was his understanding that this section had never been completed.*

Rennie considered, after taking into account the gradual increase in revenue which it was claimed was in mid-1827 still exceeding that of the previous year, that it was difficult to determine what the future revenue would be if the whole was placed in a perfect state of repair. The tolls currently collected were barely sufficient to work the steam engine at Ford and to carry out necessary repairs. However, he thought it would be fair to presume that its income would probably be increased five fold within a reasonable period and in time of war a large additional income would arise.

Rennie referred to the original calculations based on the Customs and Excise returns of goods passing coastways by land between Portsmouth, Chichester, Arundel and London in 1816 which totalled 75,259 tons and which at 5s. 7d. per ton would have produced an annual revenue of £21,010. The only way now to make the canal profitable was to make the cut by Portsbridge and so provide direct access to Portsmouth Harbour. Even so, he would not count on a greater return than £5,500 per annum. £176,314 had already been spent, £28,333 was still needed and there were outstanding debts amounting to £20,894. The likely revenue would thus barely provide a return of 2½ per cent on the total sum of over £225,000. When the cost of collecting the revenue, working the steam engines and keeping the canal in repair was deducted, the profit would barely exceed £4,000 and Rennie considered that a return of 1¾ per cent on the capital expended for a work of this kind was too little.

If, therefore, the Government was to enter into this concern, it would probably be necessary to advance £25,000 towards the £49,227 required to complete the canal and pay off its debtors. The Government, however, would not derive any greater advantage from this than the other proprietors unless it was allowed free transit for their naval and military stores and, if this was permitted, the profitability of the concern would be still further reduced.

* Tolls and wharfage charges would, however, have been collected between 1823 and 1825 (see pages 60 and 77) but no figures were available from Fowler.

REPORTS

ON THE

GRAND SHIP CANAL

FROM

LONDON

TO

ARUNDEL BAY AND PORTSMOUTH,

WITH AN ABSTRACT OF

MESSRS RENNIE AND GILES'S REPORT THEREON.

ALSO AN ESTIMATE OF THE PROBABLE EXPENSE AND REVENUE,
WITH PLAN AND SECTION OF THE APPROVED LINE OF
CANAL, A MEMORIAL TO THE LORDS COMMIS-
SIONERS OF THE TREASURY, AND AN
OUTLINE OF THE PROPOSED ACT
OF PARLIAMENT, WITH
THE NAMES OF THE
COMMISSIONERS.

DEDICATED TO ALEXANDER BARING, ESQ., M.P.
&c.   &c.   &c.

By N. W. CUNDY, Esq.,

ARCHITECT AND CIVIL ENGINEER.

LONDON:

SOLD BY THOMAS EGERTON, CHARING-CROSS; F. C. and J. RIVINGTON,
ST. PAUL'S CHURCH-YARD; SMITH, ELDER, AND CO. AND J. M.
RICHARDSON CORNHILL; GEORGE HERBERT, CHEAPSIDE; J.
RIDGWAY, PICCADILLY; C. CHAPPLE, PALL-MALL; BOOTH,
DUKE STREET, PORTLAND PLACE; LLOYD, HARLEY STREET.
SOLD ALSO AT DORKING, ARUNDEL, CHICHESTER, BRIGHTON, SOUTH-
AMPTON, AND PORTSMOUTH, AND BY ALL OTHER BOOKSELLERS
IN ENGLAND.

MDCCCXXVII.
Price, 10s. 6d.

30   *The title page of Nicholas Cundy's reports on the Grand Imperial Ship Canal published in 1827.*

Rennie concluded his report in fine style:

> Taking an impartial review of the whole of the circumstances connected with this important question and estimating in its fullest extent the munificent and princely offer of the Earl of Egremont and regretting most sincerely the unfortunate state of the proprietors, and that such a great work should remain unfinished, nevertheless judging from the actual state of the concern and looking prospectively towards its improvements, we are of opinion that the prospects of advantage to be derived are not of a nature sufficiently encouraging to induce the Government to embark in the concern with a view of deriving profit; if however they are content to make common cause with the rest of the proprietors of a great assistance by way of loan at a low rate of interest, we think that the money would be well bestowed in a national point of view towards the completion of this great undertaking.

Lord Selsey requested a copy of Rennie's report. The engineer wrote to him more than six weeks later stating that 'he had learnt that there would be no objection from a high official quarter' if he communicated to his lordship the extent, nature and estimate of the repairs which he thought necessary. His letter did no more than summarise his findings, emphasising that the first and most important measure was to make a navigable cut through Portsbridge Creek. Secondly, that Thorney Wadeway should be deepened and, thirdly, that the Ford section should be made watertight. Rennie could offer little prospect of supplying the canal with water without the steam engine. His only comment about the Portsea Canal was that it should be left alone entirely for the present and he suggested that Fowler was better able to advise Lord Selsey about the debts. Rennie ended his letter by saying that when the additional money had been raised he would have great pleasure in finding proper persons to execute the work.[2]

It was clear that no help could be expected from the Government. The advent of steam power and 12 years of peace with France made the possible benefits of Lord Egremont's offer less sustainable, and the Caledonian Canal's subsequent chequered history rather confirms the Government's decision not to participate in the future of the Portsmouth & Arundel Canal. In November, Fowler advised his lordship that Dyson & Thornton had served a writ at the canal office.

While the canal's future was under such active consideration, the company's shares were the subject of some speculation. A grandiose scheme was afoot. Since 1825 there had been talk of a grand ship canal.[3] In March the Rennies (George and John) had put forward a scheme to link the Thames at Deptford with Portsmouth via Guildford: 300 feet wide, 24 feet deep, 86 miles in length, its cost was estimated at £7 million. There were other proposals. Nicholas Cundy suggested a more direct route via Dorking and James Elmes a tide-level canal. A provisional committee was formed, which included Lord Palmerston, the Secretary for War, to study the project. In May the Wey & Arun Junction Canal Company had, at its annual meeting, regretted the drop in tolls 'which may be attributed to the failure of the Portsmouth Canal' but hoped that that line of canal be restored or a new one made.[4] In the autumn of 1827 Cundy published his own reports and a prospectus inviting the public to subscribe three-quarters of the equity capital of £4 million. However, on 15 October the Rennie brothers announced the results of the survey of five different lines and decided that the line via Guildford and Pulborough would be decidedly the best, 'having the least height, the easiest route and the best supply of water for the lockage'. They estimated the cost at £6½ million. On 22 November *The Times* published the full story of 'The Portsmouth Canal from its inception' which concluded with the announcement that it was impossible to raise the immense sum of money required.[5]

In spite of this lambast Cundy petitioned the House of Commons for leave to bring in a Bill on 15 February 1828. Mention was made of the intention to 'grant remunerations' to the various inland navigations likely to be affected including the Portsmouth & Arundel. The petition was referred to Committee and lost. Even so, land was still being advertised, hopefully, in 1829 as being on the exact line of the intended Grand Ship Canal.[6]

The year 1827 closed with the news that the brig *Spring* from Bombay, which had been wrecked at Pagham during the late heavy gales, had become a complete wreck and that the beach from Bognor to Selsey was strewn with timber. The greater part of her cargo had been saved and was waiting to be brought to Chichester to be sent in barges by canal to London.[7] An unexpected bonus for the canal company, which was probably delayed as it was announced the following week that 'incessant rains and general bursting of the springs' had caused the river Lavant in Chichester to overflow its banks and that most of the houses in its vicinity had one to three feet of water in their cellars. Navigation on the Arun had also been halted by the floods in the neighbourhood of Stopham Bridge and Pulborough.[8]

XII

THE FOURTH ACT OF PARLIAMENT
1828

Petition for Bill – Act granted (May 1828) – its main provisions – publication of *Chronicles of Portsmouth* (1828) – water-borne goods for the annual Free Mart fair.

After many frustrating delays the company was at last able to petition Parliament for a fourth Act. The petition was brought to the House of Commons in 1828, the Bill was read twice and referred to committee where it was examined before being sent to the Lords where it completed its passage without amendment. On 23 May the Bill received the Royal Assent.

The Preamble stated that £122,403 12s. 2d. of the original capital of £126,000 had been raised and £40,000 borrowed, but that, even so, the sums raised were insufficient to complete and enlarge the canal by reason whereof it was in an unfinished state and many parts had from disuse fallen into decay 'for want of the necessary funds for keeping the same in repair and will soon be in danger of becoming useless'. Additionally, debts had been incurred which the company had no means of discharging.

The new Act authorised the raising of up to £50,000 in new £25 shares (Section III) or, if unable to do so, by mortgage of the undertaking (XIII); alternatively the proprietors could grant annuities out of the company's revenue (XIV) and how this was to be done was disclosed in sections XV to XVIII. Since the original subscribers had lost most of their capital few were prepared to invest more, so that, although some proprietors still believed in the canal's future possibilities, the committee of management were well aware that there had to be some special inducement to encourage speculators to subscribe for the new £25 shares. What was offered was not particularly generous but it proved to be just enough to restart the waterway.

The Act authorised an annual dividend of up to 6 per cent on the new shares for ten years 'from the date following the canal being declared to be in a fit state for purposes of navigation' (VIII). Any default in this payment during the ten-year period had to be remedied before a dividend could be paid on the original £50 shares. Furthermore, if after ten years the profits were insufficient to pay 5 per cent, the holders of the new shares were to preferred (Section XI).

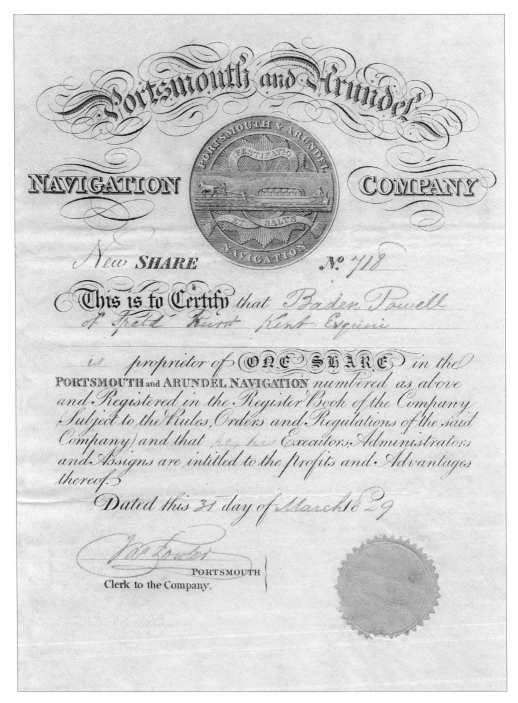

31 *New share certificates were issued in 1829 to those subscribing £25. Neither the old nor new shares paid a dividend although, when the company went into liquidation in 1888, holders of the old received double the amount paid to holders of the new. The company's motto, Festinatio et Salus, speed and safety, proved somewhat incongruous.*

PORTSMOUTH AND ARUNDEL NAVIGATION.

I hereby certify that the first Installment of Five Pounds per Share, on *Five* shares of the new Subscription of Twenty-five Pounds per share Established by Act 9. Geo. 4 Ses. 1828 has been paid by *Baden Powell Esq*

Shares at £5 per Share *5*   £. *25*

Clerk to the Company.

---

32   *Receipt for the payment of the first instalment of £5 per share paid by a member of the Baden-Powell family from Speldhurst in Kent who had subscribed for five of the new £25 shares issued under the 1828 Act.*

The management committee was further empowered to buy up any shares offered for sale by any proprietor, such shares to be either merged in the undertaking or transferred to the clerk in trust for the company and which could later be sold for the benefit of the company (XII).

It is clear that commercial interest in canal speculation had abated during the decade after the passing of the original Act. Although railways were not yet regarded as serious competitors to water transport, the improvement in the reliability of steam power for coastal vessels clearly lessened the commercial prospects of the Portsmouth & Arundel Navigation – except in the unlikely event of a revival of war with France.

Members of the management committee had either to hold at least ten new shares or five old shares. Any subscriber, who acted as a member of the committee of management who was not so qualified, was liable for a £10 fine for every illegal act performed which act would become null and void (IV). This suggests that hitherto some committee members had ceased to hold shares while still serving on the committee.

The earlier petition against the Bill by the inhabitants of Portsea was taken into account. Justices of the Peace were now empowered to determine what bridges were to repaired (XXVI). The committee of management had hitherto been uncertain as to the extent of its powers under the original Act. Various clauses were included in the new Act to clarify the position. It appears that over 100 of the original shares had never been fully paid up, causing the company to fail to raise £3,606 of the authorised capital. Subscribers for the new shares who did not pay their £5 calls could now be sued in court for debt (V). The proceedings in actions for the recovery of unpaid calls were further simplified (VI). Shares on which calls had been unpaid could be forfeited and either cancelled or sold by public auction (XXIII) and shares of deceased proprietors, whose calls had not been fully paid, could be sold after the executor of the estate had sworn that there were insufficient assets to discharge the debt (XXIV).

The new Act also contained features which one would have expected to have been included in the earlier Acts especially as such requirements were often set out in other canal Acts which the legal draftsmen would have had to hand. For instance, every proprietor was to be sent a copy of the annual audited accounts (XX)* and power was sought to remove the company's servants in cases of misbehaviour and to obtain possession of their houses (XXVIII). Curiously, in view of the hitherto lackadaisical management, it was agreed that only three, instead of five, members of the committee were needed to constitute a quorum because it had previously been 'difficult, and sometimes impossible to assemble' sufficient members. The only exception to this was when a vacancy on the committee had to be filled, cheques had to be signed or seals affixed to deeds (XXV). Presumably as a result of local concern, the Act also repealed the company's power to obtain water from within 2,000 yards of the line of navigation which had not hitherto been utilised (II).

One of the surprising feature of the Portsmouth & Arundel Canal Navigation is the fact that, although its birth and completion were the scenes of great rejoicing and much publicity in the Hampshire and Sussex newspapers, its failure passed almost unrecorded. Local historians gave it scant attention. For instance, take the publication in 1828 of the *Chronicles of Portsmouth; the History, Antiquities and Present State of every Public Edifice of the Towns of Portsmouth, Portsea, Gosport, Southsea*. This 248-page volume was written by Henry and Julian Slight, whose references to the Portsea Canal, quoted below, form less than half a page:

> A Canal has been formed across the Island, commencing from a lock in Langstone Haven (where is also a large steam-engine for filling it with salt water) and terminates in a basin at Halfway-Houses. It was opened with much formality a few years ago; a collier, several barges and a steam-vessel passing along it. From various circumstances it is however now in disuse, though during the period of its existence, the mercantile conveniences were of the greatest utility to the towns and neighbourhood.[1]

Assuming that this passage was written only a year or so before the book was published, it is interesting that they should mention that the canal was filled with salt water, curious that they gave no details of the 'various circumstances' referring to its current disuse and that they should feel bound to state that, during its existence, it was of the greatest utility to the neighbourhood when no barge had ventured upon its waters since 1825.

The annual Portsmouth Free Mart Fair was a tremendous to-do which lasted a fortnight. The fair was officially opened on 9 July when the town sergeants hung a wooden hand or gauntlet from a public building in the High Street at midnight in the presence of a large and boisterous crowd. However, what had originated as an occasion for serious trade by the 1800s had become

---

* It is curious that in spite of diligent research no copies of the annual accounts after 1831 have been discovered.

transformed into little more than an annual festival of merry-making. As John Webb related, 'Menageries, circuses, waxworks, theatres, booths containing all manner of freaks and oddities, and roundabouts, swings and other simple amusements were packed closely together on Grand Parade'.[2]

Most of the paraphernalia was brought to the city by cart or waggon but every year from 1827 onwards (possibly earlier but no record exists) a barge left Guildford Wharf laden with what were termed 'fair goods'. These comprised some 20 tons of stalls, hurdy-gurdies, roundabouts and swings as well as tawdry bric-a-brac and wares to sell or offer as prizes. From 1827 to 1830 it was barge-master Moor Wilkins of Guildford who took *Charlotte* to Portsmouth and, since the Portsea Canal was not in use, the goods were unloaded at Milton and moved by waggon to Grand Parade. In 1830 Charles Smart took over this delivery with the *Eagle*.

After 15 hectic days the stall-holders collected their unsold wares, took down their huts and canopies and loaded the showmen's waggons which rumbled out of the city and across Portsbridge to Portsdown Hill. Here they unpacked and set up their stalls in preparation for the three-day Portsdown Fair which began on 26 July. Not until the beginning of August were the articles which had come down from Guildford sometimes returned by barge. In 1828 the *Charlotte* was 3¾ tons lighter, in 1829 4½ tons heavier, on her return passage to Guildford.

The popularity of the Free Mart Fair fluctuated. The press gangs in 1803, when the town gates were closed and potential seamen rounded up, caused many able-bodied young men to give the event a miss. In later years the congestion the fair caused in the heart of the city brought much criticism and the *Hampshire Telegraph* drew attention to the noise, the increase in crime and the insobriety which the fair created. The poor were said to pawn their possessions in order to be able to participate in the revelry, and seamen to desert their ships. The Vauxhalls, where dancing and drinking went on into the early hours, were blamed for much of the licentious behaviour. By the mid-1840s few of the more articulate townspeople had much to say in the fair's favour, and in 1847 it was held for the last time. Despite the rumbustious scenes which had once attended it, in later years the Free Mart was often recalled nostalgically by those who could recall the excitement it had engendered. The Portsdown Fair, held close by where Fort Widley now stands, ceased in 1862 when the right to hold it was revoked under the 1860 Defence Act.

A local guide published in 1828 referred to Arundel's

> busy little river and the various canals with which the river is connected opening a direct communication with the metropolis on the one hand, and with Portsmouth and the numerous towns and villages in the intermediate space, afford immense advantages to its inhabitants and render it a place of considerable commerce.[3]

Arundel was, and indeed remained, a flourishing port throughout most of the 19th century.

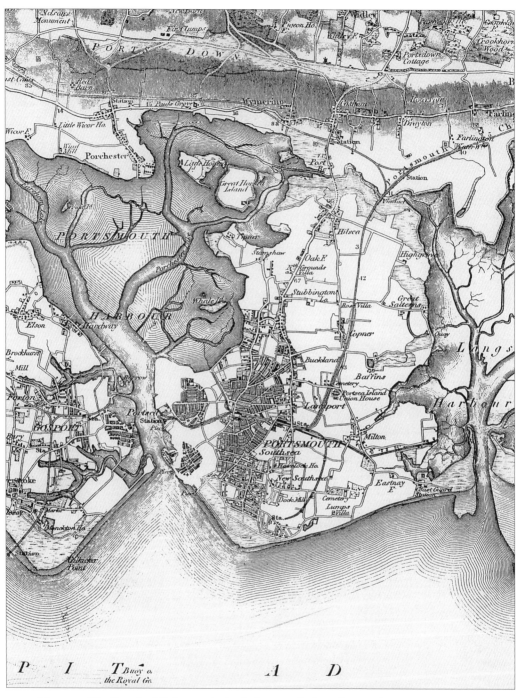

MAP 7 *The Board of Ordnance insisted that vessels from Portscreek entering Portsmouth Harbour must not pass between the gunpowder magazine on Great Horsea Island and Tipner but had to sail north of Little Horsea Island through Porchester Lake. (1816 survey, revised 1893.) Fort Cumberland not shown for reasons of national defence.*

XIII

THE COMPLETION OF THE NAVIGATION
1829-1830

Additional capital raised – announcement that work was to begin on Portsbridge creek – the Board of Ordnance is taken by surprise – Portscreek straightened to provide direct access to Portsmouth Harbour 1830 – Tipner gunpowder magazine presents a difficulty – representative committee formed (1829) – efforts made to obtain reciprocal toll reductions with the connecting navigations – petition sent to the Thames Commissioners – local toll concessions agreed (1830) – carriers unwilling to restart Portsmouth trade – John Williams retires as Comptroller of Customs (1830) – annual general meeting (1831) – repairs completed to the Sussex line.

The management's immediate task was to set about trying to raise the fresh capital authorised by the new Act. No easy task considering that in most merchants' opinion there was less need for the navigation than hitherto. Britain was at peace, highways were being improved and steam power had reduced the risk of shipwreck by the coastal route.

The first of five calls of £5 were made in the summer upon each of the new shares, the last in February 1830. In view of the problems which had arisen, it was perhaps surprising that a little over £20,000 was raised. It was hoped to start at once on putting the navigation back into order. In September 1828 Lord Selsey announced that £5,000 had already been received and that as soon as £7,000 had been subscribed, work would begin.[*] Of this sum £1,500 would be spent on repairing the Sussex line of the canal.[1] The next step was to begin work on straightening and rendering Portscreek navigable and to build a new bridge at Portsbridge Fort. However, this announcement caused a flurry of creditors to demand payment of bills long due which the company did its best to meet.

In April 1829 the company placed advertisements in the local press seeking 'navigators and masons' to undertake the work.[2] No one was more confounded to read this announcement than William Spencer, the Storekeeper at Portsmouth Dockyard, whose responsibilities included that

---

[*] Twenty years later Sir Charles Burrell's son, coming across certificates for eight new shares, lamented: 'These I subscribed for at the desire of Lord Selsey – but which by mismanagement of the canal across freshes of the sea, have not paid any interest and probably never will' (Burrell MSS XXI/H/1, 2 October 1848 WSRO).

PORTSMOUTH & ARUNDEL NAVIGATION.
To Navigators and Masons.

SUCH Persons as may be desirous of undertaking the WORK required to be performed in Deepening and rendering Navigable the CREEK from PORTSMOUTH to LANGSTON HARBOUR, and for Erecting a NEW BRIDGE, in lieu of the present Road Bridge at Portsbridge Fort, may see the Plans and Specifications at the Office of Mr. T. E. Owen, Portsmouth, who will afford the necessary information regarding the Contract. Separate Proposals may be offered for the Excavating and Building the Bridge.

The Proposals to be sent, sealed up, at the office of the Portsmouth and Arundel Canal Company, 22, Lombard-street, Portsmouth, on or before Tuesday, the 21st April, 1829.   JAMES FOWLER,
                                                    Clerk to the Company.
CANAL OFFICE, PORTSMOUTH, }
            31st March, 1829.   }

33 *It was this advertisement in the* Hampshire Telegraph *on Monday 13 April 1829 which caused William Spenser, the Storekeeper (and Land Agent), hastily to put pen to paper and inform the Board of Ordnance that he had not been advised of the matter. The Board replied that neither had they, so work by the canal company had to be postponed until the following year.*

of being the Board of Ordnance's land agent. He at once wrote to Richard Byham, the Board's Secretary, enquiring why he had not been informed. The Board calmly replied that 'they were pleased to express their surprise and regret that their attention had not been drawn to the matter by any of their officers, military or civil'. Spencer proceeded to Hilsea where he found that work had already commenced and thereupon informed the commander 'who I was and that as I had not received any instructions to allow any such work to be commenced, warned him to proceed at his peril'.[3]

It is incredible that 11 months after the Act had been passed, Spencer had now to draw the Board's attention to clauses in the 1828 Act which not only allowed the canal company to pass through the Board's land at Wymering and Widley but included clauses, introduced into the Bill by Portsmouth Corporation, which allowed the Corporation to levy tolls upon any article landed in Wymering and Widley as if they were goods landed at the Town Quay.

A hasty round of consultations followed. The commanding Royal Engineer (CRE) South-West District, Lt Colonel J.F. Burgoyne, agreed that the clauses relating to wharfage dues were most objectionable since they allowed no exemption in favour of Government and that it would be burdensome for the tenants of Ordnance property in the neighbourhood of Hilsea and Portsbridge. The upshot was that it was agreed that, rather than obtain

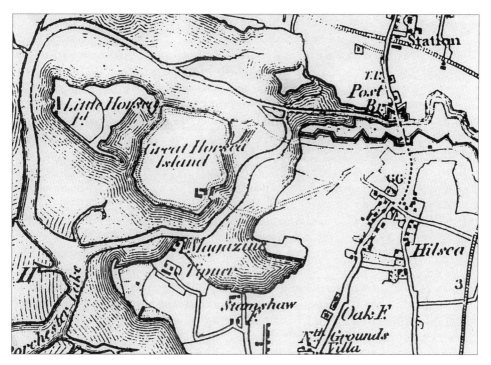

MAP 8 *An enlarged plan of the channel which had to be dug from Portsbridge round Little Horsea Island in 1830 to avoid the risk of sparks from steam boats igniting the powder magazines on Great Horsea Island and at Tipner. The additional dredging cost the company £950.*

Parliamentary sanction to repeal the clauses, Portsmouth corporation would not attempt to enforce them.

It was not only the Board of Ordnance who remained ignorant. The trustees of the London Road turnpike (Portsmouth to Sheet Bridge) were chastised by the local paper for being 'highly negligent' of their duty in not watching the canal Act through Parliament and raising objections to the clause which allowed the P & A to pull down and raise Portsbridge five feet over sixty feet. The editor felt that the resultant lack of visibility could lead to a carriage, driven at speed up the single lane, colliding with an oncoming vehicle.[4]

The task of dredging a bargeway from Portsbridge to the Town Quay also presented problems not foreseen when the Act was passed. Colonel Burgoyne discussed the matter with Admiral Halkett. No difficulty was envisaged over the company taking the Board's land when straightening the channel through the creek, but beyond Portsbridge the shortest route was to pass between Tipner and Great Horsea Island. However, the Director of the Royal Laboratory, A.S. Frazer, felt that there might be a danger to the gunpowder magazine at Tipner and the adjoining Bull Dog floating magazine if steam vessels, such as the *Egremont*, were allowed to use this channel. The Surveyor General reported that the magazine, which could

34   *A mud dredger at work in Portsmouth Harbour, 1829. The canal company had to spend nearly £1,000 dredging a new channel to meet the Board of Ordnance's objections. Etching by E.W. Cooke.*

hold 10,000 barrels of gunpowder, had been erected at considerable expense 'with a view to perfect security. As boats laden with powder constantly passed up and down across the channel almost daily', the proposed routing gave grounds for anxiety.

James Smith, the Assistant Solicitor to the Board of Ordnance, was therefore instructed to write to Fowler, the company's clerk, drawing attention to the potential danger if the new dredged navigation were to pass close to the magazine. The canal company advised the Board that if this passage was made to the north of Great Horsea Island it would be both a costly measure and more circuitous. Smith was unsympathetic and told Fowler 'these are inconveniences which the Honourable Board cannot prevent'.

However, while General Mann was requested to instruct Colonel Burgogne to appraise Fowler of the Board's determination, Burgogne went out of his way to advise the Board that the canal company had 'in every instance submitted to any expressed desire of the Ordnance notwithstanding the inconvenience and expense it might put them to'. The CRE went on to suggest that the Horsea Island munition works might be moved to Stamshaw where a small magazine to hold 1,500 barrels could be built for the current service of the powder works. The Master General concurred with the CRE's suggestion but minuted, 'The expense of such an alteration stands in the way of making such a proposition at present'.

> ## CANAL OFFICE, PORTSMOUTH,
> ### 16th October, 1829.
> NOTICE is hereby given,—That Tenders will be received at this Office, directed to the Committee of Management of the Portsmouth and Arundel Navigation, on or before Tuesday the 27th Instant, for the ADDING of WINGS, and other REPAIRS, to the Company's Steam-Vessel *Egremont*, now lying on blocks at Milton.—Plans and Specifications of the Alterations to be made may be seen at the Office.
> ### JAMES FOWLER, Clerk to the Company.

35 *While the Portsea Canal was closed, repairs to the tug* Egremont *were carried out in the basin between the lower and upper sea lock at Milton.*

Colonel Burgoyne continued to plead the canal company's case by drawing attention to the lack of draught in the upper part of the harbour but in November the canal's management committee reluctantly agreed to make their navigation into Portsmouth Harbour between Little Horsea Island and Portchester Castle.[5] However, it was the company's hope that some allowance would be made for the inconvenience and added expenses to which they were put. However, no compensation was paid. The dredging of the new channel occasioned an additional cost of £950[6] – a sum almost as great as the navigation's total revenue for the year. And so it must have appeared to the canal's shareholders that the misfortunes of the company would never end. Yet some optimism may have been engendered by the news in October that the tug *Egremont*, which had been lying on blocks at Milton since being taken out of service two years before, was going to be given 'wings'[*] while other repairs were carried out.[7]

The closure of the Portsea Canal caused an unexpected expense to a local carrier in September 1829. The frigate *Druid* had arrived at Portsmouth from South America with 1.3 million dollars and the contractor, having engaged to deliver the cargo to the Bank of England, decided to send the bullion to Arundel in the coaster *Elizabeth* for forwarding by barge. However, he had overlooked the need to pay port duties at Arundel. The Collector of Dues[†] had to seize a barrel of gold as security for the sum due of £787 10s. od. and at an emergency meeting of the harbour commissioners it was decided that the gold should be removed to the Banking House of Messrs Hopkins & Co in Arundel until the sum was paid.[8]

It was not until 1829 that representatives of the management committees of the five navigations linking Portsmouth and Weybridge met to decide

---

[*] Lateral projections added to improve stability.

[†] The 1817 Act empowered the Borough of Portsmouth to collect dues on goods landed at Halfway Houses.

on a common approach to the problems of restarting trade between the
two ports. The first meeting was held on 13 October at the *White Hart*
in Guildford at which each navigation was asked to consider lowering
its tolls on through-traffic to the lowest amount possible. The *ad hoc*
committee of representatives of each navigation comprised: William Cutfield
and Richard Seward (Arun Navigation), Lord Selsey, Cartwright, Edward
Casher and George Palmer (Portsmouth & Arundel), James Mangles and
William Newland (Wey & Arun Junction and Godalming Navigation),
and Charles Hodgson (Wey Navigation). However the stumbling block
proved to be the refusal by the Thames Navigation Committee to abate the
tolls which they levied on barges entering or leaving the Wey Navigation.
In November Palmer and Hodgson petitioned the Thames Navigation
Committee requesting that 'the present mode of charging tonnage on
the River Thames' be changed as it is a 'very great obstacle to increasing
trade'.* A reduction of one moiety 'for the number of tons on board at the
time of passing' was suggested in the belief that 'a very extended increase
in revenue would arise'. Because of the circuitous line of navigation and
the extra time required, it was impressed on the Thames Committee that
only 'by an extreme moderation in the charges for tonnage' could road
and coastal traffic be attracted. It was also pointed out that the lowering
of many of the hills and general improvements of roads between London
and Portsmouth mitigated against trade as it enabled carriers to take
heavier loads with fewer horses.

As the Thames Navigation Committee did not even acknowledge the
petition, Hodgson wrote again on 10 December pressing for a reply. Stephen
Leach, the clerk to the Thames Navigation, replied the following day apologising
for 'a press of business rather more than usual' which had prevented the
Committee attending to the petition but that it would be considered in the
New Year when they would probably be requested to attend.

Early in the New Year Hodgson is writing to J.S. Langton, joint owner
of the Wey Navigation, saying that he has been uneasy at not receiving any
reply to his last letter fearing that Langton's illness may have worsened,
stating that he has made little progress with the projected canal club and
that it would be prudent to refrain from sending out any more circulars
until he has received any corrections to the draft letter he has prepared.
'You will see by the foregoing proceedings that I have had, and still have,
a good deal of extra work to do lately as all the gentlemen who meet, only
give their attention and assent any proposition, without writing one line
or suggesting a single resolution.'[9]

There is little doubt that Hodgson was a zealous and energetic servant
of both the Wey Navigation and of the Co-ordinating Committee of the

---

* The Thames Navigation Act, 1777 (17 Geo. III *c*.18) empowered the City of London to levy tolls
  between London and Weybridge of 3d. a ton. These tolls were increased in 1812 to 7½d. a ton in
  addition to the lock charges at Teddington, Molesey and Sunbury of 3d. per ton. Barges passing
  from the Wey Navigation to and from London had therefore to pay 1s. 4½d. a ton.

Inland Navigations

BETWEEN THE

River Thames & Portsmouth.

ALL Barge Owners, Merchants, and **Traders** in general, are hereby informed that the **Completion** of the **Navigation** into **PORTSMOUTH HARBOUR,** and from thence to **PORTSMOUTH QUAY** is rapidly proceeding, and will be **quite finished** and **open** for **Barges** of every description, prior to the **Fifteenth** of **April** next; in the meanwhile the various Trustees, Commissioners, and Committees of Management, are using their utmost endeavours by general Improvement of the whole Line, and by extreme **Moderation** in the **Charges** for **Tonnage,** to offer every Inducement to the **Owners** of **Barges,** to start with **Punctuality,** proceed with **Despatch,** and convey every Description of Lading on such **reasonable Terms,** as shall encourage all **Merchants** and **Traders** to freight their **Barges,** instead of risking the **Delay** and **Uncertainty** of Conveyance by **Coasting Vessels,** or the expensive mode of **Carriage** by **Waggons.** To promote which objects, and enable **Barge-masters** immediately to calculate their probable Expenses, that they may decide without doubt upon the **Price** per **Ton,** at which they can afford to convey every Description of Lading whatever ;

NOTICE IS HEREBY GIVEN,

THAT from the 15th day of April next, until the 15th day of April, 1831, the Trustees, Commissioners, and Committees of Management of the undermentioned **Inland Navigations** will only charge the following very **reduced Rates** of **Tonnage.**

From the River THAMES direct to PORTSMOUTH,

FOR TALLOW, SUGAR, PORTER, AND HEMP.

	s	D
The River Wey Navigation	1	4
The Godalming Navigation	0	2
The Wey and Arun Junction Canal	0	9
The River Arun Navigation	0	3
The Portsmouth and Arundel Navigation	0	9

Total...... 3 . 3 per Ton

FOR ALL OTHER LADING WHATEVER.

	s	D
The River Wey Navigation	2	8
The Godalming Navigation	0	7½
The Wey and Arun Junction Canal	3	6
The River Arun Navigation	1	0
The Portsmouth and Arundel Navigation	4	0

Total...... 11 . 9½ per Ton

From PORTSMOUTH into the RIVER THAMES,

FOR EVERY DESCRIPTION OF LADING WHATEVER.

	s	D
The Portsmouth and Arundel Navigation	4	0
The River Arun Navigation	1	0
The Wey and Arun Junction Canal	2	3
The Godalming Navigation	0	7½
The River Wey Navigation	2	8

Total...... 10 . 6½ per Ton

C. O. HODGSON,

Agent for the Wey Navigation, and Honorary Treasurer and Secretary to the above mentioned Inland Navigations.

RIVER WEY NAVIGATION OFFICE,
Guildford, 25th March, 1830.

N. B. All applications relative to Wharfs and Water-side Warehouses of every description throughout the whole Line, to be addressed as above, post paid.

36 *Notice of completion of the navigation into Portsmouth Harbour and of toll reductions between the River Thames and Portsmouth, 1830.*

PORTSMOUTH AND ARUNDEL CANAL.

TONNAGE RATES.

	s. d.		s. d.
For all Dung, Ashes, Chalk, Lime, Lime-stone, Marl and Manure .... }	0 3	per Ton, per Mile.	0 2
For all Chalk, Marl, Lime, Lime-stone, except when used for Manure, and for all other Goods, Wares, Merchandize and Things......................... }	0 6	ditto. ditto.	0 4
For every Empty Boat, Barge or Vessel passing through any Lock on the said Canals, or either of them .. }	1 6	each, per Lock.	1 6
For every Passenger in the same, not employed as Navigators therein .... }	0 2	ditto, per Mile.	0 2
For every Package not exceeding Two Hundred Weight and addressed to different Persons........ }	0 1½	ditto. ditto.	0 1

Wharfage Rates may also be demanded for Goods shipped or landed in the said Lines, viz. Four-pence per Ton for the first Ten Days, and Three Half-pence per Ton for every subsequent Day they remain.

Fractions of a Ton and of a Mile to be taken as the Quarters therein, and of a Quarter as a Quarter.

Naval Stores to be exempted from One-sixth of the Rates.

The Company are authorized to demand for all Vessels using Portsbridge Creek, the Tonnage Rates in the Second Column above.

King's Stores are free from the Rates of Portsbridge Creek, and Revenue Boats may enter the Canals Toll Free.

37 *The 1830 tonnage rates included those for passengers and cargoes using Portsbridge Creek.*

Inland Navigations of which he was styled Honorary Treasurer and Secretary. On one occasion in August 1829 he had organised an all-day excursion cruise from Guildford with 40 of the local gentry on board in an attempt to draw public attention to the practicability of operating passenger boats between London and Portsmouth. Two horses towed the barge *Portmore*, four musicians played and according to Hodgson 'everybody seemed determined to be happy and expressed their thanks to the proprietors of the navigation for thus enabling them to do that which they had never before had the opportunity of doing'. In February he drafted an announcement that the navigation between London and Chichester had been repaired, was now navigable and 'perfectly free from all impediments whatsoever'; the completion of the navigation into Portsmouth Harbour was now 'rapidly proceeding'.

At length the London & Portsmouth Committee agreed reduced rates of tonnage in March 1830 which would allow tallow, sugar, porter and hemp to be carried to Portsmouth for 2s. 3d. and other goods at 11s. 9½d. a ton instead of 13s. 6d. From Portsmouth the charge was to be 10s. 6½d. a ton on all freight. The announcement made in the local newspapers was headed 'INLAND NAVIGATIONS between the RIVER THAMES and PORTSMOUTH' and informed all barge owners, merchants and traders in

Cheap and Safe Conveyance (by Canal) to and from
Portsmouth to London.

SEWARD and CO.'S BARGES leave Randall
and Co.'s Queenhithe Wharf, Upper Thames
Street, punctually twice a week (loaded or not) for
Portsmouth and Vicinities, and will continue regularly
to do so, on every succeeding Wednesday and Saturday.
The utmost care and attention will be paid to every
description of Goods forwarded either to or from London, by this Conveyance.—AGENT
THOS. BONAMY,
30, Lombard Street, Portsmouth.

38 *In the autumn of 1830 Seward's barges were advertised as departing
Queenhithe Wharf twice a week and the Portsmouth Fly Barge from Brooks's
Wharf (Hampshire Telegraph, 20 September 1830). However no carrier at
Portsmouth wished to carry on the trade and only 92 tons of cargo passed from
the Thames to the Portsmouth and Arundel during 1830.*

general that 'the completion of the navigation into Portsmouth Harbour
and from thence to Portsmouth Quay was rapidly proceeding' and would
be open by 15 April. In the meantime the 'various trustees, commissioners
and committees of management' were using their utmost endeavours by
general improvement of the whole line to offer every inducement to barge
masters to start with punctuality, proceed with dispatch and convey every
description of lading on such terms as to encourage all merchants to send
their freight by barge and so avoid the delay and uncertainty of coasting
vessels or the expense of carriage by waggons.[10] Seward & Company's barges
were advertised as departing from Queenhithe punctually twice a week for
Portsmouth whether loaded or not.[11]

Rumours of a new ship canal being planned from London to Portsmouth
continued during 1829. A prospectus for the George the Fourth Canal was
circulated proposing a waterway from the Thames at Deptford through
Epsom and Odiham for ships of 700 tons burthen. A branch canal, to be
named the Wellington, for vessels of 400 tons, was to run to Bristol from a
large basin to be built at Odiham. It was suggested that £8 million should
be raised in £100 shares of which £6 million was to be subscribed by the
counties through which the canal was to pass.[12] Such grandiose schemes
were generally ignored by the public at large but it did not stop notices of
land being auctioned at Portsmouth to claim their added worth by being
on the line of the 'intended Grand Ship Canal'.[13]

Although the Portsea Canal had been drained, until Rennie's report
had been studied and a fourth Act of Parliament obtained, no action
could be taken to sell off the company's surplus properties. Now in June
1829 ten lots were advertised for sale by auction at the *King's Arms Inn*

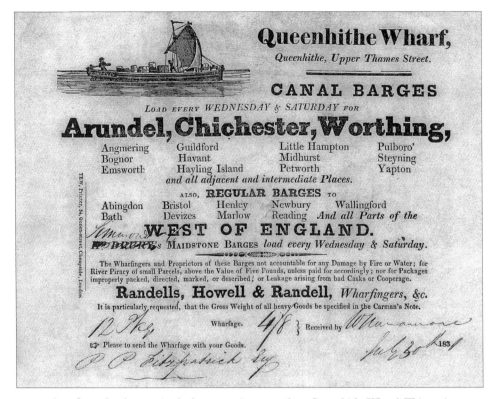

39 *An 1830 wharfage receipt for barge consignments from Queenhithe Wharf. This notice was reprinted in similar format between 1830 and 1840. Seward and Co.'s name is sometimes legible on the barge vignette and, whereas this item lists Hayling Island, those in 1833 and later omit it but in 1840 include Amberley.*

in Portsea.[14] However, at least three lots were unsold and the cottages formerly occupied by the bridge keepers at Green Lane, Hill Lane and Milton were re-offered the following year.[15] In the meantime work on filling up the giant basin at Halfway Houses had been proceeding so that by June 1831 Edward Casher was able to announce that the work was nearly completed[16] and that the adjoining land and that near the end of Surrey Street was up for sale.[17]

In June 1830 it was learnt that John Williams, the Comptroller of Customs at Portsmouth and initial promoter of the navigation, had retired after more than fifty years' service and been granted a substantial pension of £430 p.a. The *Hampshire Telegraph* commented that this circumstance was a matter of some satisfaction since it afforded evidence that the customs commissioners had found no truth in the allegations of fraud relating to the principal officers at Portsmouth. These charges had been investigated by a lengthy enquiry before the Surveyor General's Department.[18]

The same month the Portsmouth correspondent of the *Hampshire Telegraph* reported that trade was 'becoming very brisk. The barges are going regularly, and well loaded …

About twenty tons of marble ex Asia 84* from the Mediterranean, for his Majesty at Windsor and above forty tons of gold and silver, for the Bank of England have, with other goods been sent by this conveyance from this Port within the week.

However, this promising snippet was a trifle misleading for, in spite of the toll concessions and the concerted effort to restart traffic, the company's results for 1830 were sadly disappointing. Toll receipts of £1,028 exceeded expenditure by only £41 and there was of course no cash available to pay a dividend on the new preference shares. Indeed, only four barges had reached London in the latter half of 1830. Although there was little Portsmouth traffic, trade from London to Chichester was on the increase and it was claimed that the tolls collected on the Chichester Canal were sufficient to pay the management charges and current repairs. Improvements had also been made at Southgate Basin where a new warehouse and an additional crane had been established. Another hopeful sign was the establishment of a pitched corn market in Arundel which had been instigated by the local farmers wishing to make greater use of the excellent facilities at that town and Chichester for the conveyance 'particularly by water' of all sorts of grain, to all parts of the Kingdom. The market opened on 8 March 1831 and dealt in barley, beans, flour, oats, pease and wheat.[19] In anticipation of the opening of a similar market in Chichester the company was prompted to reduce the toll on grain to one shilling per load each way.

In September, Egremont was distressed to learn of the tragic death of William Huskisson at the opening of the Liverpool & Manchester Railway. They had shared a common interest in the improvement of transport for the benefit of trade. Although a shareholder in other canals, besides the Portsmouth & Arundel, Huskisson realised their limitations; in 1825 he had supported the railroad bills in the House of Commons irrespective of his personal interest and would have done so had he still been the Member for Chichester.[20] Egremont generously contributed £50 to the memorial fund set up to erect his statue in Chichester Cathedral.[21]

The opening of the Liverpool & Manchester Railway prompted a rush of schemes to build new lines. In October the prospectus for a Southampton, London & Branch Railway repeated the benefits offered in the prospectus for the Portsmouth & Arundel Canal 13 years before. It was hoped to raise £1,000,000 but Southampton had to wait a further ten years before direct railway communication to London was achieved. Railway competition remained but a distant thought.

---

* The 84-gun *Asia* was a three-decker man-of-war paid off on 18 June 1830. She had previously taken part in the battle of Navarino.

XIV

'Our Last Gasp'
1831-1833

George Palmer – The Portsmouth Lighter Company reconstituted – London
traffic restarted (1831) – Palmer summarises the problems facing the company
(1832) – his efforts to extend the period of toll concessions – the Corporation of
London remains unsympathetic – Palmer threatens to resign – Admiral Halkett
disagrees with Palmer's actions – the company ceases to operate its own fleet.

By late 1829 George Palmer had become the largest shareholder.[1] He was
now to play a leading role in the company's affairs. All that is known of
Palmer is what can be deduced from his correspondence as his name does
not appear in any of the extant company reports. The nature of his own
business is not mentioned but he had 'much experience in canals', was
familiar with the work of the Thames Navigation Committee and was on
speaking terms with its chairman Sir Chapman Marshall. In spite of that,
his efforts to persuade the Thames Navigation Committee to waive tolls
on the Portsmouth traffic were to no avail.

In the autumn of 1831 the navigation company hired three barges – the
Portsmouth, Portsea and *Southampton* – to form the nucleus of the reconstituted
Portsmouth Lighter Company. These were advertised as fly barges departing
Brook's Wharf in Upper Thames Street every Saturday whether loaded or
not. A barge was also to leave the Town Quay in Portsmouth in the reverse
direction every Saturday 'and will continue to do so without fail'.[2] With
these George Palmer managed to restart the London traffic, but although
goods were transported virtually toll-free to London with a freight charge
payable solely to the carrier, no more than eight cargoes reached the
Thames during the ten weeks before Christmas; and whereas 189 tons
were brought back to Portsmouth, the Hampshire merchants could be
encouraged to ship only 22 tons to London. This latter amount was shared
among six barges.

Efforts to extend the period of toll relief continued and the joint-owners
of the Wey Navigation finally agreed to charge only a nominal 7½d. per ton
on all goods except bullion. However, the Thames Navigation Committee
of the City of London remained adamant in their refusal to grant any
toll concessions. Nevertheless, Palmer did not give up. His petition to the

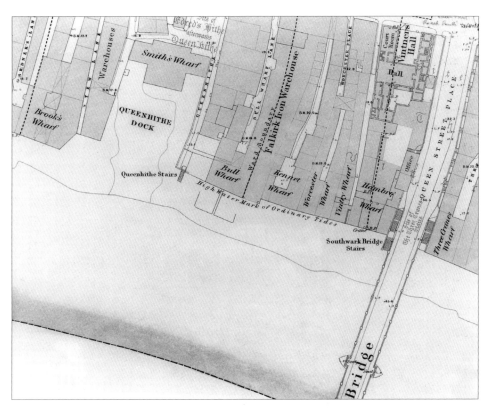

MAP 9   *The wharves by Southwark Bridge, 1875. In the 1830s barges bound for Arundel, Chichester and Portsmouth were loaded at Brook's Wharf, Upper Thames Street. Seward & Co operated a twice-weekly service from Randell's Wharf as did the Arundel Lighter Company from Bull Wharf. Richard Isemonger's barges left Chichester every Monday for Three Cranes Wharf.*

City's Navigation Committee leading proprietors of the other navigations in the spring of 1832, and his letters written in a vivid staccato style, reveal clearly enough the problems he had to face. Although feeling 'considerable difficulty in asking a boon of the Honourable Committee', wrote Palmer, 'peculiar circumstances require peculiar aid'. 'The Portsmouth & Arundel Canal Company', he wrote, 'has strenuously endeavoured to induce carriers to embark in this trade – it has been decidedly unsuccessful, – not a man would venture upon it, and it my earnest solicitation, the committee has hired and started Barges, in order to try what can be done.'[3]

A letter dated 4 April 1832, addressed to William Newland, management committee member of the Wey & Arun Junction Canal Company, recounted the problems which had beset the Portsmouth & Arundel. Undaunted, Palmer wrote,

> My exertions shall not cease and when duly supported as I am persuaded they will be by you and all those connected on the line, I feel confident of success, tho' many circumstances have occurred to throw a damp on the trade, but winter and floods are now over.

REGULAR CONVEYANCE by the **FLY BARGES** on the **CANAL** to and from **LON.DON** and **PORTSMOUTH**.

Fly Barges will start every **Saturday** (whether loaded or not), and proceed with dispatch from Brooks' Wharf, Upper Thames-street, London, for Portsmouth, Portsea, Gosport, and the Isle of Wight, and forward Goods, &c. by Steam Packets, or otherwise, from Portsmouth Harbour for Southampton, Plymouth, Guernsey, Jersey, &c. free of Wharfage and Booking in London.

A Barge will leave the Town Quay, Portsmouth, for Brooks' Wharf, London, every Saturday, and continue to do so without fail.

Agent, Mr. JOSEPH PUSHMAN,
Oyster-street, Portsmouth.
Of whom every information may be had.

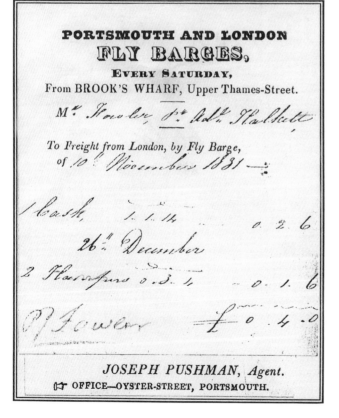

PORTSMOUTH AND LONDON
FLY BARGES,
EVERY SATURDAY,
From BROOK'S WHARF, Upper Thames-Street.

Mr. Fowler, pr. Adl. Halket

To Freight from London, by Fly Barge,
of 10ᵗʰ November 1831—

1 Cask, 1.1.14 . . . . 0. 2. 6
26ᵗʰ December
2 Hampers 0. 3. 4 . . . 0. 1. 6
P Fowler . . . £ 0. 4. 0

JOSEPH PUSHMAN, Agent.
☞ OFFICE—OYSTER-STREET, PORTSMOUTH.

40 *Announcement of the resumption of the fly barge service 'whether loaded or not' between London and Portsmouth in November 1831. Even so, only 296 tons passed through the canal from the Thames in 1831.*

41 *Portsmouth and London Fly Barge invoice issued to Mr Fowler, the clerk, in respect of a cask and two Christmas hampers for Admiral Halkett.*

No. 311. BASINGSTOKE CANAL NAVIGATION.

TIME TICKET of the FLY BARGE ___*Andover*___

DATE.	PLACE.	TIME OF		SIGNATURES.
		ARRIVAL.	DEPARTURE.	
1830 11 Novo.	Thames Lock, Weybridge,	½ past Eight o'clock at Night	o'clock Morning 12th	J Mathews ___ Lock-keeper.
	Woodham Lock, ...			Lock-keeper.
	Frimley Lock, ...			Lock-keeper.
	Farnham Road Wharf, ..			Wharfinger.
	Odiham Wharf, ...			Wharfinger.
	Basingstoke Wharf, ...			Chief Clerk B. C. N.

I CERTIFY, that in my judgment, the above-named Barge may _____ safely proceed this Night up the Locks on the
Basingstoke Canal.   Woodham Lock, the   of   183

_____Lock-keeper.

REMARKS.

42   *Contemporary time ticket for a fly barge on the Basingstoke Canal 1830.*

I am considered to sanguine – but I will be sanguine while I can see such a population to be supplied – dispatch and cheapness are wanting and if well regulated must command a trade – Impositions have been practiced by the Master of the Barges –

The Barges hired were not adapted to the trade – tho' others more suitable could not be had – a new one is built by one of my friends and he will build another as soon as we find what improvements can be made – 'The tunnel [Hardham] has been an impediment – but the new Barges will pass where others cannot – 'I wish for two barges a week[d] – if goods come a day after the time or if there happens to be a few more than can be taken on board they are obliged to wait a week – thus there is great delay – but when once they can go twice a week – they will find goods come faster. The hired Barges are so constructed that they could not carry according to the Register – Several floods have taken place and cause delay and a check to trade –

The report of cholera has operated against business –

The Steamer's boiler is worn out – there must be a new one[*] – It is true that the vessel's back is broken – We are obliged to hire until arrangements are made – I have got rid of Fowler[†] – he has been sadly negligent – The Office is moved to 18 Lombard Street, Portsmouth – Edgcombe is elected in his stead – I would give you more particulars – but really I am tired tho' I seldom feel fatigue.[5]

A second and longer letter followed the next day addressed to the committee of the Wey & Arun Junction Canal thanking them for allowing

[*] The tug had been re-registered in 1825 and refitted in 1829.
[†] The clerk appointed to succeed Jackson Williams in 1824.

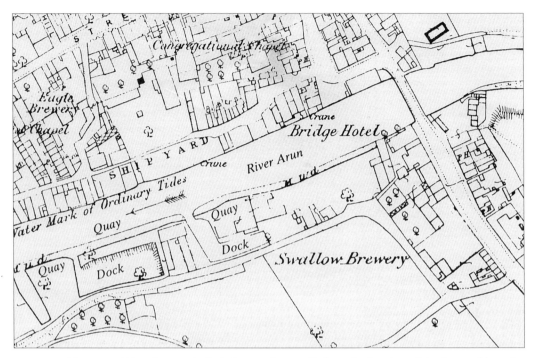

MAP 10   *The 1875 25-inch Ordnance Survey discloses the location of the former shipyard, quays and docks at Arundel.*

the London-Portsmouth barges to pass toll free and requesting a six-month extension. Palmer admitted that the difficulties they had encountered could not have been guarded against in the infancy of a trade 'commenced by parties not practically acquainted with its details'. The vital need for a back-carriage was stressed. So difficult was this to obtain that a man had even been sent over to France to try to arrange the import of eggs. In this the company were successful and on 12 April the *Southampton* carried the first of many consignments to London. Palmer had also decided not to wait for the committee's answer to his earlier letter since,

> I conceive that I cannot be defeated by you – indeed my conviction has gone so far, that I have been tempted to an evasion, in my conversation today with the Chairman of the Thames Navigation Committee by saying that a free passage was granted by all the Navigations on the line – it is true that it has been granted tho' not a matter of fact that it will be granted for another six months – however, I have ventured to imply as much, believing it to be your best policy to back my representations and knowing that unless the aid is given, the trade must cease.

As a result of Palmer's efforts, the quantity of goods transported between the two ports rose to some 2,000 tons in 1832. Two-thirds of this traffic emerged from London, however, and consisted almost entirely of groceries for the Fleet. The struggle to find a back cargo persisted, as the following list of the very wide range of items carried up to London in 1832 reveals:

	Tons
Eggs	254
Rags	89
Flour	79
Soldiers' baggage	58
Old lead	35
Bullion	32
Empty casks	28
Burr stones	21
Fruit	17
Planks	13
Old canvas	12
Old cable	8
Beer or porter	6
Wine	5
Acorns	1
Sundries	12
	670

Every fourth barge, however, left empty and the average load per barge of eight tons up and 16 tons down was clearly uneconomic.[6] Although the Chichester section of the canal was making a profit, receipts were insufficient to cover the cost of maintaining the canal, let alone meet the payment of interest on the preference shares. The canal's finances were tottering. The failure of trade led to further recriminations between members of the committee and divided opinions amongst the shareholders. On 11 April 1833, shortly before the annual meeting, Palmer wrote to James Mangles, deputy chairman of the Wey & Arun about the P & A's position:

> My intentions have been to induce every proprietor to know the real state of the concern in which his property is embarked and to urge some decided steps to be taken; I have also wished to show that the undertaking was feasible and to justify myself for being sanguine in my expectation.

43 *Richard Isemonger & Son were well known timber and coal merchants at Littlehampton who operated a fleet of four barges carrying a wide variety of cargo between London and Chichester.*

PORTSMOUTH AND ARUNDEL NAVIGATION.

REPORT of the COMMITTEE of MANAGEMENT to the Proprietors of the Portsmouth and Arundel Navigation, at their Adjourned General Meeting, held at the Old Town Hall, Portsmouth, on Tuesday the 7th of June, 1831, in pursuance of directions contained in the Act.

My Lords and Gentlemen,

The General Meeting intended to be held on the 17th ult. was adjourned to this day, to ensure a more full attendance. They have much pleasure in reporting that all the Works have been completed in the most satisfactory manner, as the Repairs on the Sussex Line of Canal have proved substantial, and it is confidently expected that the Steam Engine which was retained for occasional supply of water in case of need, will not henceforth be required, as the present natural supplies will prove sufficient for an extensive trade, the Company not having yet had occasion to resort to the water from a mill which they purchased, in order to command a sufficiency in the driest seasons.

The Warehouse and additional Crane at the Basin at Chichester are completed, which will afford much facility to the trade; extra expences have been incurred in gravelling, and in the erection of a fence; this part is now compact and complete, and will not require any material repair for many years.

The new cut at Portsbridge having rendered the Basin at the Halfway-houses unnecessary, it has been nearly filled up, and the ground is now for sale, which will tend to liquidate the debt, agreeable to the prospects held out, when it was proposed to raise the sum of 20,000l. for that and other purposes then stated.

The Committee regret that at the time they were raising this sum they did not extend it somewhat further when they had the means, as the purchase of the Mill and Stream was not then contemplated, and by a general decline in the value of property the sales have not equalled the valuation; in addition to which they were put to extra expence, at the request of the Ordnance Board, who wished them to avoid going near the Gunpowder Magazine at Tipner, and which occasioned an extra expence of 950l., as referred to in their report of last year; had not these circumstances occurred the balance of property now in hand for sale, would have nearly met the demands against the Company, and it would have been free from any charge; and considering generally that expenses in works of this nature so frequently exceed the estimates, they congratulate themselves in having kept very nearly, although not entirely, within that compass which they contemplated in the outset in renovating this concern, yet they feel satisfaction in having kept so near to the boundary of their estimates. Although the opening from London Bridge into the Harbour of Portsmouth was thus made so complete, no Carrier has yet presented himself to start Barges for the conveyance of goods.

The Trade from London to Chichester has been on the advance, and while your Committee lament that they cannot yet report a trade to Portsmouth, they have the satisfaction of stating that the trade to Chichester alone, after paying all the charges for management and current repairs, realises a small surplus.

I am,
My Lords and Gentlemen,
Your obedient and humble Servant,

(Signed)   EDWARD CASHER,
                                                                    Chairman.

44 *Extract from the company's management committee's report in June 1831. Once again the previous meeting had had to be adjourned for want of a quorum.*

The optimistic director was not entirely discouraged and continued:

> On looking calmly over what I have written upon the subject, I cannot but feel a
> satisfaction that it was taken up on good grounds and that however unfortunately
> things have turned out, there was and still is a fair prospect, tho' certainly not
> so good as I at first contemplated.

Although the largest shareholder, he was by now tired of the wrangling and
complaints of the committee and intended resigning at the next general
meeting 'unless a more liberal course is taken' and 'rather than be any
longer a galley slave to the company'. Palmer claimed that the Wey & Arun
Committee had been blind to their own interest, for 'the Wey & Arun depends
for success on a trade from London to Portsmouth, without this it never can
be anything but a poor concern, with it, it may be made a rich one'.

In conclusion he added,

> I have had too much experience in canals to be daunted. I have exerted myself
> by day and by night. I have sacrificed my own business frequently to attend to
> the affairs of the company and I can now retreat with honour. I only wish that
> every proprietor will take the trouble to making themselves masters of the actual
> state of things and either prosecute or abandon the concern altogether. I will
> neither drive a starved horse nor whip a skeleton.[7]

On the other hand, Admiral Halkett, in a letter to Mangles, disagreed that
Palmer had not met with the assistance which his exertion merited and
that the committee had still to learn how he could have received more
pecuniary assistance.

PORTSMOUTH AND ARUNDEL NAVIGATION.

ABSTRACT of ACCOUNT for the Year beginning 1st May, 1830, and ending 30th April, 1831 :—

Dr.	£ s. d.	Cr.	£ s. d.
To Balance 30th April, 1830	310 3 11	To Paid to Sub-Committee here, to finish the Works on this Line	807 14 9
Instalments received as per Cash Book	497 13 11	To Sub-Committee at Chichester, to finish the Works on that Line	229 3 0
Cash from Trustees of Turnpike Road	250 0 0	Tythes	6 1 0
Tolls received	1028 7 3	Repairs, &c. for Steam Vessel	43 19 1
Rents	258 18 9	Law Expenses	130 0 0
Received for Land Sold	546 0 0	For Surveying, &c. Mr. Owen	50 0 0
		Office Rent	41 0 0
		Printing, Stationery, &c.	37 3 4
		Insurance from Fire	3 18 9
		Rates and Taxes	67 11 2
		For sundry Works on the Portsea Line	145 10 10
		Ditto on Sussex Line	142 9 2
		Salaries, Wages, Postage, and Travelling Expenses	323 3 0
		Paid Admiral Halkett—Land sold	546 0 0
		Ditto on account Rents	193 13 9
		Mr. Newland—Interest	52 0 0
		Balance in Treasurer's hands	38 16 11
	2891 3 9		2891 3 9

45 *The last known published accounts of the company, 1831.*

46 *Southwark Bridge and St Saviour's Church viewed in 1834 from Brook's Wharf by Queenhithe. The London & Portsmouth fly barges departed from this wharf twice a week in the 1830s. The bridge was replaced in 1920, St Saviour's having become Southwark Cathedral in 1905.*

Besides Palmer, the most active members of the management committee remained Halkett, Lord Selsey and Edward Casher. However, by now it is clear that disagreements had arisen between Palmer and the admiral. Palmer, writing to James Mangles, expressed the view that while the Wey & Arun Committee had been blind to their own interest, Sir Peter remained determined to have his pound of flesh. This comment referred to the admiral's wish to receive the interest due to him on the £3,000 loan in consols he gave the company in March 1823: 'I do receive', he wrote, 'five per cent for debt due to me and if the company had not most willingly offered deeds to me for that amount, it would not have had my money.'

Halkett attributed the company's failure to the want of men of business upon the committee and offered to give up his shares to enable 'efficient' Portsmouth men to join the committee if Palmer would do the same. The latter, however, feared that if Sir Peter nominated the committee it would be too much under his control. Halkett's letter to James Mangles on 29 April was possibly his last comment on the business:

> It is to be regretted that Mr Palmer did not sooner acquaint you as a member of the committee that he was not supported ... I cordially wish that Mr Palmer, yourself, and others in Town engaged in the concern would endeavour to recommend an efficient committee. Many men of business unoccupied in

> ## TWICE A WEEK.
> ### REGULAR CONVEYANCE BY CANAL BETWEEN LONDON AND PORTSMOUTH.
>
> THE Public are respectfully informed, that from the great increase of Trade, it has been resolved to employ ADDITIONAL BARGES for the CONVEYANCE of GOODS between LONDON and PORTSMOUTH, and Places adjacent, and that a Fly Barge will regularly, every Wednesday and Saturday, leave Brook's Wharf, Upper Thames-street, London, and proceed with dispatch to the Town Quay, Portsmouth.
>
> Goods, &c. for the Isle of Wight, Southampton, Lymington, Poole, Plymouth, all parts of the West of England, Guernsey, Jersey, &c. will be immediately forwarded by Steam Packets or otherwise. No charge for wharfage or bookage in London.
>
> A BARGE will also regularly every Wednesday and Saturday leave the Town Quay, Portsmouth, for Brook's Wharf, London, for the Conveyance of Goods, &c.
>
> Every information may be obtained on application to Mr. Joseph Pushman, Agent, Oyster-street, Portsmouth.

47   *The opening of Portsbridge Creek enabled barges to convey goods from the Thames directly into Portsmouth Harbour* (Hampshire Telegraph, *16 April 1832*).

Portsmouth would materially assist ... it is most desirable to have you and Mr Palmer present [at the General Meeting in May] and any other gentleman with knowledge in such affairs, or we will be at our last gasp.[8]

However, Palmer wrote to Mangles the next day commenting, 'as to the men of business at Portsmouth, I am sorry to say to you that privately and confidentially that I think one of them at least who might assist us a good deal, is a very wavering man and to use a vulgar expression I think he earwigs the Admiral. I allude to Mr Casher, He is a man I can never make out.'[9] Not a happy situation. The committee was indeed fast running out of breath in their efforts to attract fresh traffic. Meanwhile Mason, the wharfinger, had told Palmer that the barge trade was going on favourably.

In August the company still claimed that trade was 'fast improving and that there was every prospect of it being made a lucrative business'; however, for reasons which it said would be fully explained (on application to the clerk), it was now intending to dispose of the carrying business.[10] Apparently, and perhaps not surprisingly, no interest was shown in this proposition and in December Joseph Pushman, a ship's chandler, who had been acting as agent for the company since October 1831, announced that he would be operating the four barges on his own account and that the twice-weekly service to London would continue as usual.[11]

XV

THE THAMES TRAFFIC DIES AWAY
1834-1840

The company's lax management – its share prices – gradual decline in the
London-Portsmouth trade – demolition of Yapton House (1836) – death of Lord
Egremont (1837) – carriage of soldiers' baggage to Gosport – toll concessions
discontinued (1838) – bullion traffic ceases – the tug *Egremont* broken up (1840)
– Portsmouth's poor commercial facilities.

At this point we are left in the dark as to the actions of the management
committee and whether the enigmatic Palmer continued to exert every effort
to promote trade. No company reports or minute books have survived after
1831[*] and newspaper references are negligible. During the hearing of the
winding-up petition in 1888 Thomas Edgcombe junior related how after
the early 1820s management committee meetings were often adjourned
for want of a quorum (even though only three members were required
after 1828) with no business done.

Indeed some idea of the lax way the company's affairs were run in
the 1830s can be judged by its abstruse actions. For example, in 1830
the Board of Ordnance had granted a lease for a piece of land on which
to erect a wharf at Portsbridge. But after paying the annual rent of £2
for nine years, Edgcombe explained why the company had not made the
wharf. 'The land has been entirely useless', he wrote, 'since it could only
be approached by vessels with standing masts from Portsmouth Harbour
and by a very circuitous course.' However, he continued, the wharf would
be of great benefit if it was formed on the east side of the bridge and
on the south side of the cut near the turnpike road. More extraordinary
was the company's failure to pay for the land needed for widening and
straightening the Portsbridge channel. The Board of Ordnance both in
1831 and 1836 had extended the time for completion and payment of the
£210 consideration on payment of £10 p.a. interest. Even so, the company
had paid no interest after 1839 and in 1847 the Board's solicitor stated
that, although innumerable applications had been made to settle their
claim, the company had replied that they had no funds of any description.

[*] The company's minute books were produced by the clerk at the High Court hearing in 1888.

48 *Queenhithe viewed from Southwark Bridge, 1851. The* Hampshire Telegraph *reported in June 1823 that the Portsmouth & Arundel Navigation Company's fly barge reached Queenhithe from Portsmouth in 2 days 16 hours and made the return journey in 2 days 20 hours. It was pointed out that these times could be improved since there had been a delay in getting horses and some had to be used which had previously done their day's work.*

Edgcombe stated that an attempt been made compulsorily to wind up the company, 'but no proceedings had been had recently for the want of funds'.[1] Nevertheless, the Board's adviser did not regard its claims hopeless as some portion of the land 'will be required for a railroad'.[2]

The price of the company's shares had followed a downward path since the initial flotation in 1817. During 1824 Admiral Halkett, whose 40 shares had cost £2,000, now brought an additional 12 for £3. At the end of 1824 Lord Selsey stated they were at 'the lowest point of depreciation'[3] and the failure of the proposal to raise additional capital left them almost valueless. The scheme to build the Grand Imperial Ship Canal and the passage of the fourth Act of Parliament gave rise later to some speculation in the share price. Nevertheless, the figures listed by London stockbrokers and printed

KIPSTONE BANK WINDMILL,
HUNSTON, near CHICHESTER, SUSSEX.
PARTICULARS of an excellent FREEHOLD SMOCK WINDMILL, in full trade, in a flourishing part of the country, within easy distances of some of the best markets in England; contiguous to the Mill is a very comfortable brick built RESIDENCE, with about half an Acre of rich Garden and Orchard Ground, with excellent Stabling, Cart House, Piggeries, &c. situate at Kipstone Bank, in the parish of Hunston, to be SOLD by AUCTION, by Mr. HENRY SALTER, at the Anchor Inn, Chichester, on Tuesday, the 20th of March, 1832, at four o'clock in the afternoon, by direction of the Proprietor, and under such Conditions as shall be then produced, (unless previously disposed of by Private Contract, of which due notice will be given.)—The Mill is worked by two pair of French Stones, and all the tackle as well as the frabric is in good repair, the exterior of which has lately been newly canvassed and pitched.

The House is very substantially built and extremely well situated for the person occupying the Mill, and consists of one parlour, kitchen, washhouse, cellar, and five bed rooms.—This valuable Freehold Property is within a quarter of a mile of the Portsmouth, Chichester, and Arundel Canal, and adjoins the road leading from Chichester to Selsey, and only three miles distant from the former place; the Corn Market of which is unrivalled by any in Europe.

Further particulars may be known of Mr. Richard Salter, Solicitor, Arundel; Mr. Edmund Dash, Slindon; and of the Auctioneer, Arundel.

49 *The waterway continued to be quoted as a benefit for would-be purchasers of property in the vicinity; for instance in March 1832 Kipson (Kipstone) Bank Windmill was so advertised for sale. The large ten-sided smock mill had been built in 1801 with a beehive cap. Two pairs of French burrs were powered by shuttered sweeps. The mill remained in use until 1915 and was pulled down in 1919.*

from time to time in the provincial press were only a general guide as few dealings took place. The price of the £50 shares between 1832 and 1834 was around £10.[4]

The 1830s were the hey-day of water transport in Great Britain. Every year saw barge traffic increasing on the Wey, the Wey & Arun Junction and the Arun Navigation. Parry, writing in 1833, mentions that Arundel was 'enlivened by its river which is the means of considerable traffic in coals and corn between London and the Mediterranean. Ships of 150 tons drawing 16 feet of water come up as far as the bridge.'[5] Yet unfortunately there was little waterborne traffic approaching the entrance locks to the Portsmouth & Arundel Canal at Ford.

The only records of barge traffic are to be found in the lock-keeper's journal at Weybridge and the wharfinger's accounts at Guildford. These show a gradual decline in the London-Chichester-Portsmouth trade. Whereas, in 1833, 1,500 tons was moved down from the Thames and 1,000 tons

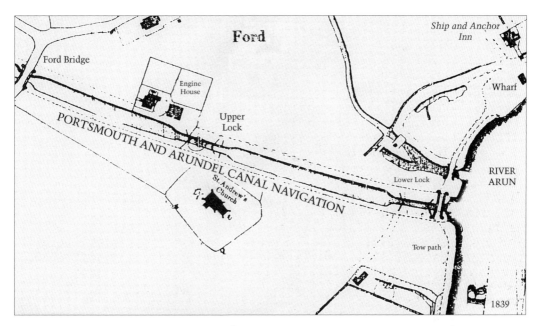

MAP 11   *The entrance to the Portsmouth & Arundel Canal at Ford as it appeared in 1839.*

carried up, the tonnages for each subsequent year became less and less (see Appendix D). By 1838, the total had fallen to 750 tons.

The ledger entries reveal some curious cargoes such as the delivery of old rope, hemp and glue shreds to Queenhithe. In 1835 the *Trout* carried 13 tons of cattle up to Smithfield and one wonders why there were not more cargoes of that nature since it would surely have been the most practical mode of taking them to the London market. Presumably, the prices fetched were little or no more than what would have been obtained at Chichester.

An unexpected boost to traffic on the barge canal occurred in the summer of 1836 when the owners of Yapton House decided to raze the building and sell the materials by auction.[6] The manor house had formerly been the residence of the Edmundes family to whom it was sold by Henry Fitzalan in 1571. It was greatly extended and rebuilt by George White in 1800. White, who took the surname Thomas on the death of his uncle in 1788, died in 1821 without male issue. A settlement made in 1829 empowered the trustees to demolish the building and not to rebuild it.[7] However, the mansion was let for six years (*Hampshire Telegraph*, 1 June 1829) and it was only after his daughter Frances Crosbie's death in March 1835 that it was decided to raze the buildings.[*] Horsfield described the mansion, whose park extended to the canal banks, as 'a handsome structure of considerable size, pleasantly enclosed in a paddock'.[8]

---

[*] Frances was married to Lt-General John Gustavus Crosbie of Donnington who died in 1843.

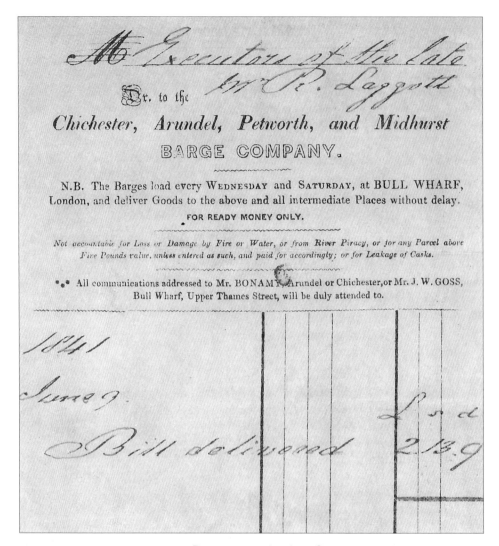

50　*Barge company invoice, 1841.*

The sale particulars drew attention to the 'great facility' which the canal offered for the disposal of the 200 lots. All the buildings were to be taken down and removed by the purchasers at their expense. The total size was prodigious. The 'noble mansion' occupied almost 5,000 square feet and contained a large quantity of plain tiling, about three tons of sheet and stack pipe lead, an extensive and winter cut oak timber roof, coping stones and cornices, porticos, about 70 noble modern sashes and frames with moulded inside shutters and architraves, a sweep front of six handsome windows and fittings, about 40 six-panel doors, 10,000-foot run of oak joists; there were 20 sets of marble jambs and chimney pieces, 50 oak beams 12 inches square, moulded surfaces, dados, yellow batten and deal floor boards in good condition. The noble main staircase with its mahogany handrail, back staircases, stone and brick paving, 600,000 bricks, all were included as was the extensive brick stabling with two lofts and groom's room. In addition, a fine range of outbuildings included the brew-house, bake-house, byres and cart sheds. Also in the sale to complete the utter dismemberment of the estate were all the cisterns, wells, pipes, garden walls (852 feet long and 11 feet high) and the five-foot high 560-foot-long ha-ha with its 14-inch brick walls.* Such vast quantities of paraphernalia must have filled 20 or more barges, but the names of the purchasers are not known nor the destinations to which these items were consigned.

In November 1837, the 3rd Earl of Egremont died at the age of 85. His eldest son, Colonel George Wyndham (1789-1869), inherited Petworth House, the Rother Navigation and his father's shareholdings in the Arun Navigation and the Wey & Arun Junction Canal companies. The earl had already voluntarily surrendered in September 1826 his 315 shares in the Portsmouth & Arundel Navigation Company and paid the company's debt of £40,000 to the Government. Indeed his total investment in, and loans to, the company could not have been less than £56,000, an investment that never paid a dividend.[†]

The canal was to play a small part in the despatch of the British Expedition to Canada in 1838. The previous autumn disturbances between the British and French settlers in Quebec caused the Government to despatch in the New Year two Guards battalions (Grenadiers and Coldstream) totalling 1,600 men under the command of Major-General James MacDonell to assist the Governor in restoring order. It was decided to send the officers' heavy baggage from Wellington Barracks in Birdcage Walk by water to Gosport. Lieutenant Hope was put in charge of a detachment of 32 troops to supervise the journey. The trunks, boxes and miscellaneous effects were carted to Westminster Pier where the Portsmouth Lighter Company's barges *Rapid* and *Quicksilver* were loaded. At Guildford the cargo was weighed and totalled 38½ tons. Some days later, after passing through the Arun Navigation and the Portsmouth & Arundel Canal, the two barges reached Gosport. Here the baggage was transferred to the vessel *Apollo* and the man-of-war *Inconsistant*. These vessels set sail on 17 April and made landfall at Quebec on 11 May 1838. By that time the rebellion was over.[9]

Each year now saw a gradual decline in traffic passing from Portsmouth Harbour to Arundel and up through the Wey & Arun Junction Canal to the Thames. Barges after 1837 were often listed as being empty or loaded with only a few tons of butter, corn, rags or sundries. Although the bullion traffic continued spasmodically until March 1838, it was rare for more

---

* When visited in 2002 the only surviving remains were the walled garden on the west and north-west and possibly an 18th-century dovecote to the south-east.

† The equivalent purchasing power in 1998 of £3.3 million. (House of Commons Library Economic Policy and Statistics: Inflation: the value of the pound, 1750-1998.)

than two consignments a year to pass to the Bank of England after 1826 (see Appendix E). At the end of September 1838 the toll concessions granted by the inter-connecting navigations on through-traffic ceased and brought to a close the Portsmouth to London traffic through Portsbridge Creek. In July 1840 the *Quicksilver* passed through Ford Locks bringing 14 tons of furniture up to London and in September the *Trout*, carrying six tons of groceries, became the last barge to leave Three Cranes Wharf. The registration of the tug *Egremont* was also cancelled in 1840 when the vessel was broken up.[10]

Between 1823 and 1840 only 22,715 tons of cargo had passed from the Thames to the Portsmouth & Arundel Canal, a far cry from the annual expectation of 80,000 tons. The estimates of trade made in 1816 had assumed that merchants would be willing to use a waterway which would avoid the risks of shipwreck and prove to be both quicker and cheaper. However, the advent of steam power, peace with France, the extensive lockage, water shortages, floods in the Arun Valley, all mitigated against success. And there was another reason why the navigation failed. Portsmouth was essentially a naval base with limited commercial facilities. The number of mercantile vessels registered in 1831 was only 184 whose tonnage totalled 8,484. As late as 1836 the Committee for Improvement of Trade and Fishery complained of

> the almost total want of wharf or quay room for landing and shipping merchandize, there being no accommodation at the present quay on ordinary tides for even one vessel drawing more than 6 or 7 feet of water, and room only for two or three of that draught; indeed Portsmouth, although the first naval port of the kingdom, has less accommodation for mercantile business in the form of wharfs and docks than any other place in the English Channel, however insignificant its pretension.[11]

Consequently, goods had to be put into lighters instead of being landed directly, leading to delay, damage and loss, particularly of perishable groceries. The lack of a dry dock for repairs also made many ships avoid the port altogether.

Finden, writing in 1838 in his *Views of Ports and Harbours*, stated, 'As a commercial town Portsmouth does not rank very high'. In 1839, the town clerk noted that no significant addition had been made to the Town Quay (only 250 feet long) in the past 150 years, and that the Camber on the west side of the town opposite Gosport was 'as it had been for several centuries, an extensive bed of mud in the midst of the buildings of the Town, by which it is nearly surrounded on all sides, into which the principal sewers of the Town discharge themselves'.

Pigot's *Directory of Sussex*, 1839, mentioned the fact that the canal passed through the village of Yapton and commented 'but it is of little advantage to the inhabitants, this being an agricultural district'. Yet only twenty years earlier one of the reasons strongly advanced for building the canal was that it would improve agriculture.

XVI

THE ARRIVAL OF THE RAILWAY
1840-1865

The advent of rail transport – opposition to its development in Hampshire and
Sussex – the railway reaches Gosport (1841) – passing of Act for the Shoreham
to Chichester line (1844) – Thornton *v* the Portsmouth & Arundel Navigation
Company (1845) – the Board of Ordnance fails to obtain payment for land taken
by the company – part of the Portsea Canal used for a railway track – opening
of Portsmouth station (1847) – decline of barge traffic – fear of war with France
– Arthur Perceval's proposition to the Admiralty (1852) – his offer ignored – the
barge canal no longer navigable (1856) – the Bognor Railway Act (1861).

The railway age was now fast approaching. As early as 1825 there had been
various proposals to form a London to Portsmouth railroad with collateral
branches but they had come to nothing. It was not until the opening of
the London to Southampton line in 1835 that the first trains reached
Hampshire. The navigation company was now well aware that the bed of
the Portsea Canal might prove of value for any railway line to Portsmouth.
However, no record of their negotiations with the railway companies survives.
What is known is that the attempt by the London & Southampton Railway
to promote the Portsmouth Junction Railway from Bishopstoke (Eastleigh)
was opposed by the citizens of Portsmouth who secured the Bill's defeat
at its second reading in the House of Commons in 1838. However, when
the Portsmouth people tried to form their own independent company
to build a line from London via Dorking, they failed to raise the capital
of £1.5 million. Critics of the scheme doubted whether a new line could
be justified, especially as a group of influential landowners including the
Duke of Norfolk and Colonel George Wyndham (Lord Egremont's eldest
son) had signed a paper expressing their determination to oppose the
projected railway from Portsmouth to London by way of Chichester, Arundel
and Horsham 'as we consider such a project to be wholly uncalled for,
originating in speculation and infringing the rights of private property,
without any equivalent public advantage'.[1]

May 1840 saw the opening of the first railway in Sussex and marked
the end of the canal era. Southampton had been reached in 1839 and
a branch line opened to Gosport in 1841. Henceforth, the barge had to

51 *Barques from north-east England regularly came up to Arundel to discharge cargoes at the Co-operative Society's wharf to which the vessel at left is moored in this 1870s view.*

give precedence to the truck in much the same way as the stagecoach was being usurped by the railway carriage. However, while the railways secured unquestionable superiority for passenger traffic, the waterways possessed certain positive advantages over any form of land carriage; nevertheless, lacking as they did uniformity in width, depth, and gauge of locks, the navigations were ill-equipped to meet rail competition as a whole. Even in so short a distance as between Guildford and Chichester, locks of six different dimensions had been built, so that only barges able to enter the smallest chambers could pass.

The canal proprietors did what they could to oppose the flood of railway Bills. In some cases not even a formal protest was made, so inevitable was the Bill's success; a few navigations seized their last chance of financial gain either by accepting compensation as the price for withdrawing opposition or by concluding an advantageous sale to the newly formed railway companies. Sometimes a victory could be achieved and the railway Bill would be thrown out, but this was seldom due to the persuasions of the navigation companies but rather because either the line chosen was not considered the best or because the opposition from the landowners was too powerful. Rarely could canals successfully compete against railways on equal terms.

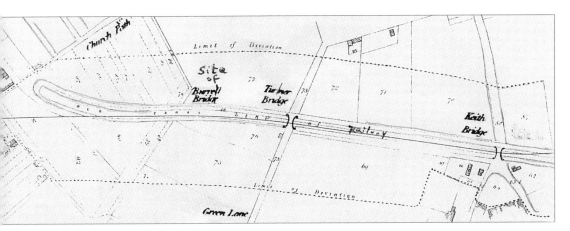

MAP 12   *Both the London & South Western Railway in 1840 and the London, Brighton & South Coast Railway in 1844 deposited plans showing the intended use of the bed of the disused canal from Keith Bridge, Fratton to Burrell Bridge before swinging west to the site of the present main-line station. The Act was passed in 1845. The L & S W R and L B & S C R agreed to share the line into Portsmouth which was opened in June 1847. Burrell Bridge stood at the end of Upper Arundel Street near Railway View. Keith Bridge is now the site of Fratton Bridge. Green Lane is now Somers Road.*

Several companies, the Portsmouth & Arundel and the Thames & Severn included, ran their own boats out of sheer desperation and without parliamentary approval. No prosecutions followed, but the Act as it stood made the quotation of through-rates for long distance carriage a complicated and discouraging procedure. Once the Act for the competitor railway had been passed, the navigation might sing its swan song and spend two or three profitable years carrying the materials for the building of its usurper. Once this windfall had been gathered, however, it was seldom long before expenditure swallowed up revenue.

The development of railways, as with the canals, was a slow and rather haphazard process. Several private Bills had often to be promoted before an Act could be obtained, and more than one Act granted before a line was built – no fewer than four attempts being made and three Acts passed between 1846 and 1861 before a railway reached Bognor in 1864.

The majority of traders and townspeople favoured the plan to extend the railway from Shoreham to Chichester. Even so there were no fewer than 20 petitions lodged against the Brighton & Chichester Railway Bill when it was brought to the House of Commons. Although the waterway from Ford to Chichester would be directly affected, the Portsmouth & Arundel Navigation Company had little traffic to lose and no money to meet the legal costs. Furthermore, since the railway did not interfere with any part of its property, it had no grounds for compensation.

The efforts made by the Arun Navigation company to oppose the bill are recounted in *London's Lost Route to the Sea* (see Bibliography). Although Colonel Wyndham took an active interest in the Arun Navigation,

52 *Arundel remained a busy port until the early 1920s. This painting by Stuart Lloyd in 1899 shows the barge* Speedwell *of Arundel laden with timber; also three coasters including the* Alice *of London and the* May *of Milton. One of the dock entrances is visible at the bottom right.*

53 *Eighteenth-century flint and stone warehouse in Arun Street, Arundel in 1970 shortly before its demolition.*

54 *In spite of determined opposition from the Arun Navigation Proprietors, the London &*
Brighton Railway Company obtained its Act in 1844 to build a line from Shoreham to Chichester
which involved building a single-track drawbridge across the Arun at Ford. The telescopic
bridge had a 60-foot opening which took two men and a boy at least five minutes to open (ILN
14 November 1846). Delays in opening the bridge to river traffic led to claims for compensation.
In 1858 a hold-up to the tug towing the brigantine Arun *caused the railway company to be*
fined £10.

he replied to the Commissioners of the Port of Arundel's enquiry on
14 March 1844: 'I have no idea of taking measures alone to oppose this
bill, although I object to it very much and have returned myself dissentient.'
During the House of Lords Committee hearing in June 1844, it was stated
that the Portsmouth & Arundel Canal had fallen into semi-disuse and was
used on average perhaps once a week. The promoters gave evidence that
2,320 tons were carried annually by barge between London and Arundel[*]
at a cost of 28s. a ton in 'uncertain time' and that a further tenth of this
amount passed by road. To counsel's question during the committee hearing
as to whether there was any doubt that the traffic on the canal would be
transferred to the railway, witness replied that the railway would take away
much of the Arun's traffic, not only on grounds of expense but because
'there is great delay occasioned every now and then from impediments in
the navigation. If you take the average of the year, there is a stoppage of
six or seven weeks annually and they never can get any goods down under
from 27s. to 37s. per ton.' A Bognor ironmonger said it took three weeks
or more to get goods down from London by water carriage at a cost of
31s. 8d. a ton which was, he admitted, less than half the cost of carting
them. A Littlehampton grocer said that timber imported from the Baltic

[*] Seven-year average (1836-43).

55 *Ford Lock looking toward Arundel as it appeared about 1855. The Ford section of the Portsmouth & Arundel Canal had become virtually disused since the opening of the Shoreham to Chichester Railway in 1846 and according to Stanton, the lock-keeper at Bramley, had not been used since 1856.*

was then taken by barge to London for 27s. a ton compared with 50s. by waggon; although it was expected that the cost by rail would be only 17s. a ton. The only other occasion when the Portsmouth & Arundel Canal was mentioned was the comment by the Duke of Richmond's steward that the occupation bridges over the waterway were a great inconvenience both to the public and farmers alike and that an extra horse had to be used to draw loaded waggons over them. The railway would, he claimed, be of great benefit since it took five days to drive cattle to London from Chichester and the 18,000 cattle sent annually to Smithfield became slimmer by a stone on the journey.[2]

The railway company obtained its Act in July at a price. At Ford, where the line was to cross the river Arun to the north of the entrance to the canal, the Admiralty had given its approval only if the timber drawbridge provided the least obstruction to the ebb and flow of the tide, that no work would be done above high water mark without their consent and that lights would be hung on both approaches from sunset to sunrise. The Arun Navigation, having failed to secure any financial compensation, secured the right to keep the bridge open for 90 minutes before and after high water – except for ten and four minutes, before and after respectively, the passage of trains. If a barge was detained for longer than 20 minutes a £10 fine was to be imposed. Although the bridge carried only a single track, the 63-ft opening section, designed by John Rastrick, had the widest movable span constructed at that date.*

The contractors' accounts had not been settled 20 years after the navigation had been opened. Dyson & Thornton had been awarded £7,600 at the first arbitration hearing and, by 1836, £4,570 had been paid by the company when the partnership had been dissolved. Thornton brought his case against the company in April 1845 for the balance of £3,030, which was secured by mortgage of the canal tolls, and sought the appointment of a receiver. George Palmer, still one of the management committee, claimed demurrer – a pleading which, while admitting the facts, demands that the plaintiff is legally entitled to relief. Palmer was apparently the mortgagee and Thornton offered to pay what might be due upon this and sought foreclosure.

Mr Rolt, in support of the demurrer, submitted, under the clause of the Act, that the company had no power to mortgage their tolls for a debt which existed at the time, and in favour of any particular creditor, that the deed of mortgage had not strictly followed the form given in the Act, only that the power by the mortgage deed was merely to hold the tolls and rates as a security until repayment, and that the present Bill sought to narrow the time intended to be given for discharging the debt.

His Honour, without calling upon Mr Wood and Mr R.T. Fisher, who appeared in support of the Bill, decided that the general demurrer could not be sustained. As to any defect in the instrument creating the mortgage, such an objection could not be allowed as coming from the company. There was some little doubt whether all the parties were before the court, as to which he would take time to consider.[3] Whether Thornton ever received the balance due to him is uncertain and there is no mention of the matter when the company went into liquidation 40 years later.

The opening of the railway from Shoreham to Chichester on 8 June 1846 greatly reduced the barge trade between Arundel and Chichester but not entirely. As there was no rail link to Arundel (until 1863) and all goods destined to the town had to be carted from Ford Station, there was a small amount of local traffic carrying farm produce, coal, sand, chalk, manure and building materials along the canal. The expense of operating the engine house at Ford (£20 a day), however, caused pumping to be abandoned sometime in the 1840s, possibly much earlier,† since the canal's

---

* In 1862 a double-track 'lift-and-roll' iron drawbridge replaced the timber bridge to meet the heavier traffic requirements imposed by the railway from Hardham junction to Ford, opened in 1863. The bridge, designed by Jacomb-Hood, had a centre span 90 feet long although the navigation passage was in fact reduced to 40 feet.

† In June 1831 Edward Casher confidently expected that the steam engine would not henceforth be required 'as the present natural supplies will prove sufficient for an extensive trade'.

56   *The bridge carrying the Arundel-Climping road over the canal at Ford photographed in 1933. It was demolished in 1936. The roof of the engineer's house can be glimpsed to the left of the bridge.*

natural water supply was normally adequate for the small amount of traffic. However, it was the company's failure to maintain the locks at Ford which finally made the canal impassable.

The canal had fallen into semi-disuse before the opening of the railway to Chichester, for it was stated to a parliamentary committee that this part was used on average perhaps once a week.[4] In March 1846 John Rastrick, engineer of the London & Brighton Railway, reported that the navigation was 'very little used' and that a proposed railway from Chichester to Bognor intended using part of the canal for their line. It was, however, his intention to span the waterway near Woodgate by a 25-foot bridge 12 feet above the water level.[5]

The extension of the railway to Portsmouth was delayed while three companies sought to obtain parliamentary powers for diverging lines. Eventually the London & South-Eastern and the London & South-Western jointly agreed to finance and construct the line into Portsmouth using some 500 yards of the Portsea Canal bed and tow-path from Fratton Bridge to a point some 400 yards from the site of the former basin at Halfway Houses. During the parliamentary proceedings in June 1845 reference was also made to the waterway (the Portsbridge cut) being both deserted and abandoned.[6] The railway line was eventually opened on 14 June 1847.

The navigation company ceased to hold regular annual general meetings after 1845, although they were formally advertised in the local press.

Management committee meetings stopped being held in 1847, which I would regard as being the last year when the Ford-Hunston section was commercially used. The last entry in the Wey Navigation ledgers is dated 29 December 1847 and refers to the passage of two pleasure boats at Thames Lock, Weybridge bound for Portsmouth. Certainly no tolls for this section appear to have been collected after this date. After the general meeting held in May 1851, the last took place on 26 June 1855 and consequently no committee of management could be elected thereafter.

During the committee stage of the Direct London & Portsmouth Railway Bill, 1845, Mr Humphrey Brown, a traffic estimator, stated that 12,000 tons of merchandise passed between Portsmouth and Godalming and intermediate places by barge.[7]

This estimate might lead one to believe that the Portsmouth & Arundel Canal still carried a fair amount of traffic. However, the canal was not mentioned by name and Brown admitted that the source of this information was solely the ledgers at Stonebridge Wharf, Shalford and at Godalming. During further cross-examination, he stated that 'goods went direct from Portsmouth to Godalming every day by water.' I doubt, and so did counsel for a rival railway company petitioning against the Bill, whether this was true. The amount of cargo carried by water between the places situated on this route probably totalled this figure – 2,905 tons being carried by the Arundel Lighter Company alone beyond Guildford and back in 1844 – but the bulk of any traffic originating at Portsmouth came by coaster to Arundel and then up the Arun Navigation by barge, or by road to Godalming.

One last and rather forlorn attempt to maintain the inland water link between London and Portsmouth was made by the Hon. and Rev. Arthur Perceval[*] (1799-1853) who in 1852 was chairman of both the Wey & Arun Junction Canal and the Portsmouth & Arundel Canal companies. In May of that year he sent a memorandum to the Admiralty setting out the 'importance of having at all times safe and cheap conveyance between London and Portsmouth'.[8]

The reason for this dispatch undoubtedly reflected the growing unease in Britain of the increasing ambition of Prince Louis Napoleon, nephew of the former emperor. In 1848 Prince Louis had been elected President of the French Republic and in December 1851 he had staged a *coup d'état* which resulted in him being elected president for ten years – and later for life.

In Britain events in France had revived anxiety as to the state of the national defences. The army, as always after a long period of peace, was

[*] The chairman had been chaplain to King George IV, King William IV and Queen Victoria. He was also vicar of Little Bookham in Surrey, a kinsman of the Egmont family, as was Spencer Perceval who was assassinated by Bellingham in the House of Commons in 1812. An indenture dated 4 March 1851 records that Perceval paid the estate of the Rev. H.H. Wood £180 for seven shares or 'assignments' in the Godalming Navigation. He was also an active shareholder in the Basingstoke Canal (q.v. *London's Lost Route to Basingstoke* (1968), p.122).

unprepared for war. It was said that the aged Duke of Wellington, Lord Warden of the Cinque Ports and still Britain's Commander-in-Chief, could not sleep at night for thinking of the defenceless state of the coast. The navy, too, was not in good shape with the greater part of the battle fleet laid up and the change-over from sail to steam going far from smoothly.

On becoming prime minister in February 1852 Lord Derby had told the Queen that he meant to proceed as speedily as possible to improve the defences of the country.[9] Within a few months the Militia Bill had been passed by an immense majority and the Queen approved the prime minister's recommendation that a substantial surplus should be provided for in the May Budget 'in case of unforeseen difficulties with Foreign Powers'. *Punch* recorded that with the establishment of the first rifle club 'a very laudable feeling is growing in the hearts of thousands of the British people – the feeling for rifle practice'.[10]

Perceval headed his paper, 'On the Public Advantage derivable from maintaining in efficiency the inland navigation between London and Portsmouth'. The main tenor of his argument was that in time of war coastal traffic was liable to be intercepted by enemy steamers and that rail traffic 'being so completely at the mercy of any evil disposed person, no vigilance can render it secure'.

> With the view of securing safe and cheap conveyance at all times between London and Portsmouth the inland navigation which, leaving the Thames at Weybridge, passes by Guildford and Arundel Harbour [*sic*], was carried into Chichester, Langston and Portsmouth Harbours, and into the Island of Portsea soon after the close of the last war.
>
> By reason of the fraudulent conduct of the contractor, in not properly puddling the line of the canal from Ford in Arundel Harbour [*sic*] to the Salterns in Chichester Harbour, this line has never been efficient, the canal not retaining water enough for the purpose of efficient navigation. The Company have no funds to undertake a work of such magnitude, and in the present state of their affairs could only raise it, if at all, at great disadvantage.

A fortnight passed and Perceval, not having received any acknowledgement to his note, wrote to the Admiralty Secretary, Augustus Stafford, stating 'As a meeting of the proprietors (annual) of the Portsmouth & Arundel Canal will take place early next week, and I am without tidings from the Board of Admiralty as yet in reply to my communication to them on the subject, I venture to ask whether I may conclude the matter of that communication to be still under their Lordships consideration'.[11]

To this letter there was also no reply. The Admiralty file had already been minuted, 'My lords cannot entertain the proposition'. Could their lordships' views have been coloured by the clerk stating that the writer's last letter, which he enclosed, was about floating semaphores?

One further straw in the wind arose in 1855 which might have benefited the Chichester Canal. The Hayling Island Docks scheme envisaged the reclamation of some 1,000 acres of mud and the building of substantial

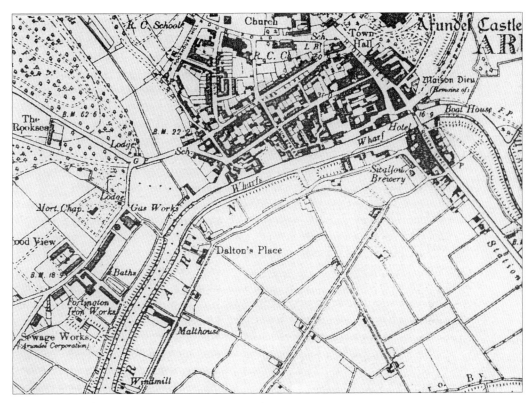

MAP 13   *The six-inch map issued in 1896 reveals the location of some of the main users of the navigation. They included the Arundel Gas Works built in the late 1830s, the Tortington Iron Factory and the Swallow Brewery. The docks on the south bank below the Swallow Brewery were no longer in use.*

wet and dry docks on the western shore opposite the old Milton locks. A public enquiry was held by the Admiralty in Havant at which the promoters, who included William Padwick, of Warblington House, explained how the proposal would convert Langstone Harbour into one of the finest harbours in the land. Local fishermen were the chief objectors but the scheme failed to attract sufficient financial support.

The actual year when the barge canal between Ford and Hunston ceased to be navigable is not known with certainty but it was probably 1856, the year when William Stanton, the wharfinger at Bramley on the Wey & Arun Junction Canal, was quoted as saying that the canal had last been used and which was in 1867 'trodden in by cattle, filled-in in places and quite dry'.[12] The reference in the winding-up petition of 1888 also mentions that this section had not been used for 'thirty years and upwards'[13] while De Salis in his *Chronology of Inland Navigation*, published in 1897, states that it did not fall into disuse until about 1853. Nevertheless, in 1856 the Governors of Christ's Hospital, the owners of the land at Ford, were required by the Commissioners of the Port of Arundel to rebuild the bridge carrying the tow-path over the entrance to the canal. Because the navigation had not been legally abandoned, the railway company, in obtaining its Act for a line from Barnham to Bognor in 1861, was also required by section 40 to build a swing bridge over the 'disused' portion of the canal and that, if 'in the event of the navigation being required for water traffic or if converted into a road or railway', a penalty of £10 would be imposed on every occasion that the swing bridge impeded traffic. A similar clause was included in the Hayling Island Railway Act 1860, which provided for vessels navigating the 'new cut' made by the Portsmouth & Arundel Navigation 'to pass unhindered as reasonably required'. This trestle bridge stood 25 feet above high water when it opened in 1867.

Although sailing barges to Langstone continued to use the new cut through the Hayling Island wadeway, no dredging was carried out by the navigation company after 1838. John Morley, writing in 1987, quotes the story of how in 1854 a farmer attempting a crossing of the wadeway to avoid using the toll bridge had his horse shy and so lost his implements until they were recovered at low tide.[14] Another local resident recalls being told how, about that time, stepping stones were placed in the deeper channels to assist pedestrians. After the London, Brighton & South Coast Railway bought the road bridge in 1878 they also acquired land at the southern end of the wadeway to discourage trespassers.

In the late 19th century the principal trade to Chichester was the carriage of coal and shingle. It was the normal practice to transfer coal from collier brigs moored at Itchenor to smaller sailing barges which could enter the ship canal. These are described by Frank Carr as follows: '... In the waters of Langstone Harbour there were also small barges, known as Langstone barges, flat-bottomed, ketch-rigged, many of them with a sharp or "nip-cat" stern. Others had a transom stern, not unlike a Thames barge. They worked in the confined waters of Langstone, Chichester and Portsmouth Harbours, with an occasional longer voyage to Southampton Water. They had no leeboards, very little sheer and were pole-masted, but fitted with running not steeving bowsprits.'[15] In 1896, of the 471 vessels entering Chichester Harbour, however, only 21 barges were unloaded at the basin.[16]

The closure of the barge canal between Ford and Hunston passed almost unnoticed and unlamented. Many were unaware of the waterway's existence and the few who planned boating expeditions believed, like J.B. Dashwood in July 1867, that it was still in use since it still figured prominently on Sussex maps. However in 1866 the author[*] of an article in the *West Sussex Gazette*, entitled 'Thoughts suggested by A Trip up the Wey & Arun Canal', recalled how his friends remembered the 'glorious doings' at the opening of the Arundel and Chichester Canal, 'and now we live to see the whole property drifted into decay, and sheep and cattle grazing where once the water flowed'.[17]

---

[*] Probably William Mitchell of Arundel, the editor and printer of the *West Sussex Gazette.*

XVII

In Chancery
1888-1896

Petition to wind up the company (1888) – hearing before Mr Justice North – appointment of official liquidator – affidavits submitted by Thomas Edgecombe and others – the hunt for shareholders – a lengthy process – sale of canal bed in Portsea (1891) – distribution made to claimants – winding-up order granted (1896)

For nigh on fifty years the bed of the Portsea Canal from Fratton to Milton was a marshy reed-covered ditch into which every imaginable form of refuse found its way. Complaints of nauseous smells in fine weather were nearly as numerous as those from mothers who feared their toddlers drowning in the rush-dotted pools. The minutes of the Road Works Committee of Portsmouth Borough Council mention in the 1860s and 1870s the urgent need to repair the bridges and that the iron bridge at Milton was in a sorry state. The clerk, like his opposite number at the Board of Ordnance, referred these matters to Thomas Edgecombe whose standard reply was that there were no funds available to carry out the work. When in 1885 further stretches of the bed at Fratton were sold to enable the London & South Western Railway to build a branch line to Southsea, the purchase price of £1,100 had to be lodged in court to the credit of the canal company since no person was authorised to deal with it. Often there was talk of putting the company into liquidation, but the management committee had lost interest in the concern; there was also the problem of what to do with the Chichester Canal which continued in operation.* There was also uncertainty on how to proceed. The Wey & Arun Junction Canal Company had run into difficulties in its attempt to close their navigation in 1868. However, the passing of the Railway & Canal Traffic Act in 1888 appeared to offer an easier solution; even so the Arun Navigation, closed in 1888, had to wait until 1896 before the Board of Trade would issue a warrant of abandonment.

Winding-up the Portsmouth & Arundel Canal Navigation Company was a slow business. It all began when former naval paymaster James Ozzard

---

* The 1888 Board of Trade return shows total receipts of £231 against expenditure of £293. The tonnage carried was 6,001.

57   *The accommodation bridge at Yapton viewed in 1905.*

and two ladies from Southsea, each the holder of five shares, petitioned the High Court of Justice for the company to be put into receivership. The Court of Chancery appointed a Portsmouth chartered accountant, William Edmonds, as the official liquidator.

When the hearing began before Mr Justice North on 4 August 1888 there had been over a dozen petitions submitted to the court.[1] Thomas Smith Edgecombe, who had acted as clerk since the death of his father in 1851, related the history of the navigation and that the company had not held any meeting of the proprietors since 1855. However, all money borrowed on mortgage under the 1828 Act had been discharged by 1858 out of the proceeds of the sale of land. He considered the portion of the canal still in use to have no value and that the cottages and land in Portsea and Sussex had a maximum value of £10,000, 'such estimate being purely speculative'.[*]

Details of how the Chichester Canal had been run emerged during the proceedings. The key figure was Richard Purchase whose father Stephen was employed as a clerk by the company in 1829 and had established his coal business at the basin in 1830. Richard had acted as a manager and wharfinger since 1855 although never formally appointed. Besides collecting the tolls and wharfage dues, he received the rents of the company's cottages.

[*] The actual amount realised by February 1893 was less than £7,000.

58 *Another view of the brick accommodation bridge in 1964. Some years later it collapsed under the weight of farm traffic. The bridle path was moved eastwards and now only rubble and brambles mark the site of the old bridge.*

59 *The sailing barge* Fanny *on the Chichester Canal at Hunston, c.1905.*

With this revenue he paid the wages of the lock keepers, the bridge keeper at Donnington and maintenance workers on the canal. Over the seven-year period 1882-88 the income averaged £53 p.a. which was insufficient to cover the outgoings. The Board of Trade returns for 1888 show that 6,001 tons of coal, gravel, sand and bricks were carried for which tolls of £133 were received and other income amounted to £98, but expenditure of £293 left a deficit of £62.

However, Sir William King, a land valuer at Portsea, reported that the land and buildings of the Chichester Canal produced an annual rent of £80. Along the Ford to Hunston section some rents at Yapton were over ten years in arrears and the engine-house at Ford was partially dismantled and 'quite out of repair'. He recommended that the canal and those cottages, which were occupied rent free by the lock and swing bridge keepers, should be sold.

Edward Arnold, the town clerk of Chichester, disagreed. He swore that this would require the canal to be closed and that the branch was of

CHICHESTER CANAL.

CLASSIFICATION OF MERCHANDISE

FOR THE WHOLE OR ANY PART OF THE CANAL.

MERCHANDISE.	Amounts payable in respect thereof including use of Wharf for a reasonable period.
Sand	6d. per ton.
Coal	6d. „
Timber	9d. „
Slates	6d. „
Bricks	6d. „
Iron	6d. „
Manure	6d. „
Shingle	6d. „
Gas Water in Barrels	6d. „
Tar	6d. „
Coke	6d. „
All other Goods	6d. „

1st January, 1895.

60 *Under the 1888 Railway and Canal Traffic Act, the Board of Trade confirmed in 1894 a Provisional Order to increase canal charges. Consequently in 1895 it was able to approve new toll rates for a range of merchandise on the Chichester Canal.*

great use and value; coal was being regularly discharged at the basin for the Chichester Gas Company. 'I myself frequently see barges being thus unloaded into the company's store.' Others supported this view. George Gatehouse, a brewer and coal merchant who rented four coal yards at the basin, received 1,200 tons of coal annually. Builder John Holt received all his bricks and sand by water, and one of his bargemen, Combe by name, had carried more than 2,000 tons over the years. The chairman of the gas company, Robert Church, brought in 2,500 tons of coal and exported thousands of gallons of gas tar to Chichester Harbour. The railway, he said, was only used in an emergency. A corn merchant, a solicitor, a building contractor and a town councillor all gave evidence as to the usefulness of the canal but it was George Fielder, the city's rate collector, who emphasised how detrimental it would be to the town if the canal was closed. Not only, he said, were quantities of coal, lime and shingle brought up the canal, but it was of great value to the public who have fished and boated in the basin for thirty years.

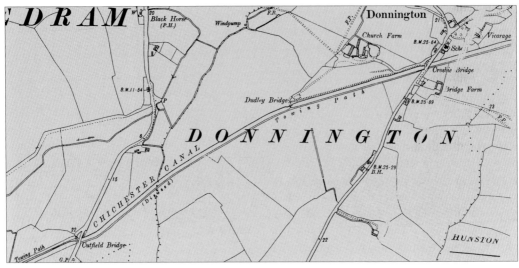

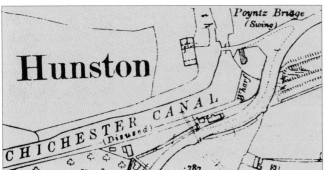

MAP 14   *The swing bridges at Donnington 1933. The earlier ordnance surveys mark the swing bridges without naming them.*

MAP 15   *The Site of Hunston Wharf below Poyntz Bridge, 1909. Earlier editions of the ordnance survey do not mark the wharf which was not constructed until after the entrance to the barge canal had been closed in the 1890s.*

The mayor of Chichester, William Smith, said the waterway kept down rail charges. However, he rather sourly added that, if the company was to be wound up, the canal and any cash should be made over to the Corporation and not to the shareholders 'who have probably not expected anything'. The Corporation were represented by counsel who adduced sufficient evidence that the Chichester portion of the canal was in use for navigation and of value to the inhabitants. Consequently, an agreement was ultimately reached between the petitioners and the Corporation that the latter would withdraw its opposition on condition that the canal and its property was vested in the Corporation 'without the payment of any valuable consideration'.[2] Objection was made to public discussion of the canal company's affairs and nothing further emerged until 1892, with the appearance of the Act to provide for the transfer.

The High Court having agreed that no property forming part of the Chichester Canal should be sold, Edmonds was authorised in August 1889 to sell the navigation company's land in Portsea and between Ford and Hunston. In the first instance he had to negotiate with the adjoining owners whose property abutted on the waterway. However, this was no simple

61 *Sea Lock, Milton at the entrance to the Portsea Canal remains in remarkably good condition although it was built as long ago as 1822 and was rarely used after 1825. The lock, 101 feet long and 23 feet wide, seen here in 1960, is larger than the locks on the Chichester Ship Canal which were only 86 feet long and 18 feet wide.*

task as the ownership was often either in doubt or disputed. Such was the case where the riparian owner had usurped the land forming part of the canal over the past thirty years and now claimed it by having established a prescriptive title, although 'no one in the district could supply reliable information as to length of time'. At Ford, Charles Boniface was renting land which included the canal bed and towing-path whose ownership was claimed by solicitor Richard Holmes of Arundel 'by effusion of time and uninterrupted possession'.

Few sales occurred but the Duke of Richmond purchased 7½ acres in Barnham and Oving in 1890 for £162. In July 1891 over a mile of the disused bed of the Portsea Canal was auctioned at King & King's saleroom in Queen Street. A reserve price was set by the chancery judge on each of the 22 lots. The local paper reported that there was a large attendance at the sale and that the bidding was 'sharp and spirited'. A corner plot at the junction of Upper Arundel Street and Railway View with a 100-foot frontage sold for £185. The timber yard at Fratton Station fetched £590. The bed as far as Milton Bridge was offered in seven lots and bought by Portsmouth Corporation for £1,170. Mr James Goldsmith junior was the

62   *The upper gate of Sea Lock, Milton as viewed in about 1900 with Lime Kiln cottages (on the right). A Portsmouth guide of 1828 states that 'the banks of the canal afford a pleasant walk through the prolific gardens and highly cultivated fields, and which may be continually varied from the number of bridges which intersect it'. The cottages were demolished in the late 1960s.*

main purchaser of the land on the eastern side of the bridge. He obtained seven lots, which included the two cottages by the sea lock at Milton, for £1,110. The total sum realised – £4,440 – was passed to the official liquidator's account.[3]

Meantime the receiver was trying to trace the company's registered shareholders. In the autumn of 1889 he sent out over 600 letters to their last known addresses. The response was no better than might have been expected. No record had been kept of changes of address or ownership since 1855 and many letters were returned via the Dead Letter Office. A number of subscribers had died whose executors, believing the shares to be valueless, took no action; others, either from inertia or ignorance, did not bother to reply.

However the High Court decided that further enquiries should be made and between August 1892 and April 1893, 42 advertisements were placed in ten different newspapers requesting claimants to get in touch with the solicitors, Edgecombe, Cole & Hellyer who were acting for the receiver. Several widows and children of deceased shareholders had great difficulty in proving ownership since the share certificates had either been lost or thrown away. Since there had been no authority to reissue duplicates or to register changes, the High Court agreed to accept a lesser degree of proof.

70, Commercial Road,
Portsmouth,
August, 1895.

In the High Court of Justice,

Chancery Division,

Mr. Justice North.

IN THE MATTER of the Companies Acts, 1862 and 1867,

——— and ———

IN THE MATTER of the Company of Proprietors of the
Portsmouth and Arundel Navigation.

*In pursuance of an Order of the Chief Clerk of Mr. Justice North, dated the
18th day of July, 1895,*

NOTICE IS HEREBY GIVEN that the First and Final Return of
Capital in this matter is now payable at the offices of MESSRS. EDMONDS,
SON & CLOVER, as above, on MONDAY, the 26th day of August, 1895, or on
any subsequent Monday, between the hours of 10 and 4.

Shareholders and Representatives of deceased Shareholders whose
claims have been duly considered by the Chief Clerk and admitted for payment are entitled to the return in accordance with their holdings as under :

On each Original Share of the nominal value of £50,
two pounds eleven shillings and fourpence halfpenny.

On each New Share of the nominal value of £25,
one pound five shillings and eightpence farthing.

You are therefore entitled to £ *10* „ *5* „ *6* being the
amount of the return on

———Original Shares.

8 New Shares.

Upon application for Payment this notice should be produced entire,
together with the Share Certificates, which will be henceforth retained by me.

If you do not attend personally to receive the Return, I shall be obliged if
you will fill up and sign the annexed forms of Receipt and Authority, when a
cheque payable to your order will be handed to your nominee, or, if you so
prefer, sent you by post.

WILLIAM EDMONDS,

Chartered Accountant,

Official Liquidator.

To *Sir Charles Burrell, Baronet.*

63   *Notice of the only payment made to shareholders, 1895.*

64 *The large pound between the lower and upper sea locks at Milton seen here c.1910 was provided to allow craft to moor while awaiting a favourable tide. In 1912 the* Southern Daily Post *printed a nostalgic article on Milton's vanishing canal. 'The locks make at once the most picturesque and most pathetic spectacle in the whole of Portsea Island.'*

After many months it finally emerged that, of the 2,520 old shares and 817 new shares issued, the title to 2,253 old shares and 813 new shares had been established with a reasonable degree of certainty. 267 shares had been forfeited and only the ownership of four new shares could not be traced. The largest shareholders now appeared to be William Glencross of Plymouth holding 60 old and 10 new shares and William Hodge of Devonport with 52 old and 20 new. The descendants of Rear Admiral Sir Howe Popham, C-in-C His Majesty's Ships in Jamaica, claimed a total of 40, the Perceval family 30, and James Mangles, former chairman of the Wey & Arun Junction Canal, 39 shares.

The families of some members of the initial committee of management had retained their holdings. Viscount Sir John Keith who had died in 1823 left 25 shares and the heirs of Admiral Sir Peter Halkett discovered that he had added 20 new shares to his 42 old shares. Among the many others whose whereabouts had to be sought were James Brown, John Snook of Bedhampton and John Williams of Southsea; shareholdings held by the former clerks included George Greetham, Jackson Muspratt Williams and Thomas Edgecombe Snr.

Holders of only new shares included Simeon Warner of Blackheath 60, solicitor William Hellyer 40, barge owner and shipbuilder Richard

TELEPHONE No. 5.

EDMONDS, SON & CLOVER.

TELEGRAPHIC ADDRESS,
"ACCOUNTANTS, PORTSMOUTH."

70, Commercial Road,

Portsmouth,

10th January, 1896.

AND AT 10, ST. HELEN'S PLACE, E.C.

DEAR SIRS,

Portsmouth and Arundel Navigation—IN LIQUIDATION.

With this I send you notice of return of capital payable to you in respect of your claim, which has been considered and admitted by the Chief Clerk of Mr. Justice North.

As I have already pointed out to you, the Chief Clerk having settled the list in July, 1895, of the persons who have proved their claims, objected to make any provision out of the Estate to cover costs for those outstanding ; consequently the expense of proving their title must be borne by the parties advancing the claim.

The inclusive charge of myself and Solicitors, as you were informed, is 5s. per share, which I shall be obliged if you will remit when sending me back the Receipt for the Return and the Share Certificates, in exchange for which a cheque for the amount due shall be sent you.

Yours truly,

WILLIAM EDMONDS,

Official Liquidator.

65   *The official liquidator and the solicitors remember to recoup their costs, 1896.*

Isemonger of Littlehampton and the Rt Hon. William Huskisson. There was no mention of George Palmer, who in the 1830s had claimed to be the largest proprietor, nor of how Lord Egremont's holding of 320 old shares, which he had voluntarily surrendered, had been recorded. The 267 shares listed by the liquidator as rescinded would have presumably included those forfeited for non-payment of calls.

The liquidators also ran into other difficulties. Beneath the barge canal between Ford and Hunston flowed numerous streams from the Downs to the sea. Chief of these was that flowing from Walberton under the railway near Barnham and thence down a depression which the canal crossed by a 25-feet-high embankment. According to the author of an article of unknown origin written in 1891, the Commissioners responsible for the stream opposed the winding-up order until either funds were provided for future repair or until the land had been returned to its original state. The liquidators in an evil hour chose the alternative, little dreaming of the difficulties and dangers ahead. It was a costly matter to move some thousand cubic feet of earth which brought with it a yawning chasm and completely destroyed the public right of way along the towing-path. The solution proposed to this danger was two boards: 'No Road' and 'Trespassers will be Prosecuted'. The Barnham Vestry, however, with considerable public spirit, threw down the glove and forced a bridge to be thrown across the rife. Other parishes were urged to watch vigilantly their own portions of the towing-path since much mischief had already been done and one farmer near Lidsey bridge had been specially daring in his attempted appropriations.

Although the shareholders had never received a dividend, it was now expected that there would be some return of capital out of the money received from the sale of land and the collection of rents. In July 1895, Mr Justice North ordered that each claimant should receive £2 11s. 4½d. for each £50 share and £1 5s. 8¼d. for each £25 share. But this was not quite the end of the matter since the claimants had to wait over five months to learn from the official liquidator that the chief clerk of Mr Justice North had omitted to make provision for the payment of his, and the solicitors' costs, in proving the titles to ownership. So now William Edmonds required that each claimant should be charged five shillings a share, which sum was to be deducted from the cheque which would be sent in exchange for the share certificates. Perhaps in the circumstances it is not surprising that some shareholders ignored the letter and kept their certificates. On 3 November 1896 the Board of Trade finally granted the winding-up order.

XVIII

THE CHICHESTER SHIP CANAL
1892-1928

Chichester Canal Transfer Act (1892) – the Corporation maintains the waterway – Selsey Tramway – Hunston lifting bridge – diminishing traffic – need to replace swing bridges at Donnington and Birdham – angling attractions – commercial traffic ceases (1923) – the canal closed (1928)

The Act for the transfer of the Chichester portion of the navigation received the Royal Assent on 27 June 1892. The Corporation, besides now being responsible for the maintenance, was authorised to acquire up to five acres of land for additional wharves and other improvements. If the running costs exceeded the revenue, the deficit could be recovered from the borough rate. If the loss continued after 1898, the Corporation could abandon the undertaking and sell the land.

The land and buildings which the Corporation acquired by virtue of the Act consisted of the canal from Southgate basin to the Salterns, Canal Road, two houses in Canal Road, various pieces of land, a covered timber store, seven iron swivel bridges and five cottages. The only exception was the coal shed which had been recently erected by the Chichester Gas Company fronting Stockbridge Road.

The cottages had been built not only by both locks but adjacent to the swing bridges at Birdham and Donnington which carried the public highways since it was the occupant's duty to ensure that neither road nor water traffic suffered undue inconvenience. After the 1840s no wages were paid to these men who were allowed to live in the company's cottages rent free on condition that they informed the wharfinger and coal-merchant, Richard Purchase,* if the bridges were not working. In November the city surveyor reported that it would cost £1,000 to put the canal back into working order.[1] Minor repairs and dredging continued periodically but few were the trading vessels which arrived at the basin loaded with timber and coal. The only surviving record of traffic, after the transfer, is to be found

---

* The Purchase family had been coal merchants at Southgate Basin since 1830 and *Kelly's Directory of Sussex* listed Richard Purchase as 'collector of canal dues' in 1852. In the 1870s he was listed as agent to the canal company as well as being a lime burner. The family continued to lease the property around the basin until the early part of the 20th century.

66 *Hunston Bridge was the last of the brick bridges between Ford and the Chichester Ship Canal. Depicted here in 1890 it carried the road to Selsey, now the B2125.*

67 *Oil painting by Walter Malby (1858-92) of the approach to Southgate Basin 1884. The gasometer is discreetly visible.*

68   *The approach to Southgate Basin as it appeared at the turn of the 20th century. The gasometer can be seen beyond the end of the tow-path. The Customs House is to the right of the Cathedral and a barge is being unloaded with the help of a hand-operated crane on the wharf.*

in the Board of Trade Returns required under the Railway & Canal Traffic Act. These show that in 1898 the amount of goods carried had fallen to 704 tons and that toll receipts amounted to only £18.

The rather humdrum activity on the canal was enlivened by the decision to build a light railway from Chichester Station to Selsey. The Hundred of Manhood & Selsey Tramway Company was formed in April 1896. At Hunston a lifting bridge was required to cross the waterway. Five men were needed to open it as fish plates had to be removed before a winch was operated by a windlass. The Chichester Council charged the tramway company £2 p.a. for the use of its bridge. The 7¾-mile line opened on 27 August 1897 and ceased to operate from 19 January 1935. The concrete abutments on the north bank remain the sole reminder of the past.

It was, however, as an angler's retreat that the canal was best known. In 1890 the *Illustrated Sporting & Dramatic News* included the canal in its series of drawings of 'Anglers Resorts'.[2] The *Victoria County History* mentions that in 1907 the canal is still open for barges and that the 'four miles of its course is considered one of the best stocked waters in the county'. The contributor, G.F. Salter, detailed the names and weights of the heaviest fish

69   *Southgate Basin viewed from a balloon in the 1920s. Stacks of timber and coal for the gas works can be seen on the north side.*

70   *Circus elephants bathing in Southgate Basin, 1903.*

71   *Tank engine 0-6-0* Sidlesham *crossing the Chichester Ship Canal at Hunston, c.1920.*

72   *The Hundred of Manhood & Selsey Tramway's lifting bridge in operation at Hunston, c.1900. The line from Chichester to Selsey was in use from 1897 until 1935.*

73-4 *Casher Lock, the top lock on the Chichester Ship Canal, in 1890 (courtesy of the RC & HS) and as it appeared in 1954. Edward Casher was a Portsmouth wine merchant, secretary of the Portsmouth Fly Barge Company and a member of the navigation's management committee for over ten years. He was mayor of Portsmouth 1842-3.*

75 *Two sailing barges* Langstone *and* Gladys *lie alongside Langstone Quay, c.1910. These barges were used mainly for transporting sand and gravel from Chichester Harbour to the quay where there were loaded on to horse-drawn carts or railway waggons.*

ranging from carp up to 14 lbs, bream up to 4½ lbs, perch, roach, tench, eels up to 4 lbs – and how a pike of 18½ lbs was once taken. The writer related that 'From Birdham Bridge on the opposite bank to the first lock is a nice stretch of water with a broad bed of rushes on the south side; the holes under the banks on the towing path are noted as the haunts of pike, four brace have been taken in a few hours by dropping the bait over the bank or spinning alongside the rushes. At the lock gate there is a deep hole with from 12 to 14 feet of water where lie big carp and bream. The perch here are large and numerous, and in this reach between locks good

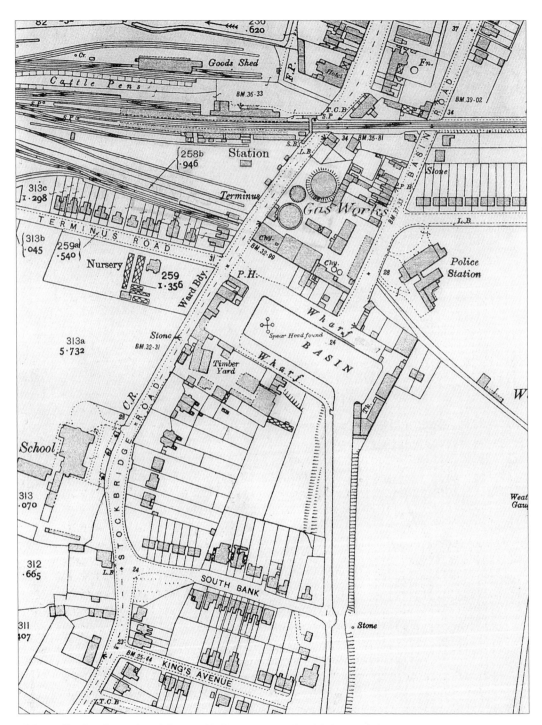

MAP 16 *Southgate Canal Basin, Chichester, 1933. The* Richmond Arms *inn is now shown as a public house and various sheds and buildings now occupy the east end. Opposite the gas works is sited the terminus of the Manhood & Selsey Tramway which was to close two years later.*

76 *In 1867 the Havant to Hayling Island railway was opened which required a swing bridge to allow boat traffic to pass. Approaching vessels were advised by black flag by day, green light at night, that the bridge could be safely opened, and by red flag or light when the bridge was open. The railway line was closed in 1963 and the bridge demolished in 1966.*

tench occur. Pike up to 17½ lbs have been captured. Down the four miles of water, when clear, myriads of fish of all sizes and descriptions may be seen. In fact, it is over-stocked. The city council hold the right over the waterway, but little is done to improve the water for the benefit of anglers.'[3]

By 1914 the canal had ceased to be used for commercial traffic, the last recorded trading activity being the collection of shingle from Chichester Harbour in 1906 when the brothers Combe of Bosham unloaded their sailing barge at Southgate Basin.[4] In that year the road bridges at Donnington and Birdham needed repair and Chichester Rural Council favoured replacing the swing bridges.[5] However, the Corporation was loath to close the navigation and decided that the canal should continue to be kept open for water traffic. The 1924 edition of Ward Lock's *Pictorial and Descriptive Guide to Chichester* mentions that the canal is maintained by the city authorities more for 'recreative' purposes than for commercial traffic; although this was a tourist guide it made no reference to the canal as an attractive feature nor to there being any boats for hire![6] Nevertheless in June of that year the City Council and Westhampnett R.D.C. agreed that the two road crossings should be culverted and filled in, on the understanding that the swing bridges could be reinstated at six months' notice.[7] Finally the Corporation formally closed and abandoned the canal in June 1928.

XIX

RESTORATION IN PART
1932-2005

Chichester Yacht Club takes out a lease (1932) – Salterns Lock restored
(1934) – wartime activity – The West Sussex County Council purchases the
canal (1957) – the formation of the Sussex Canal Trust (1973) – Chichester
Canal Society – its achievements – management action plans – The Chichester
Ship Canal Trust (2002)

Douglas Burrage recalls that in 1932 Denis Vernon, a yachtsman who had
cruised the south coast for many years and was aware of the limited winter
mooring facilities in the region, realised that the canal could meet this
need and without more ado obtained a 28-year lease of the canal from
Chichester Corporation.[1] Shortly afterwards he was joined by a former
merchant mariner, Mr J.H. Fuller, and established the Chichester Yacht
Company. The long stretch of water between the sea lock at Salterns and
Casher Lock near the Wittering road were put back in working order.
The tow-path was widened for motor vehicles and a pump brought in to
maintain the water level. By 1936 nearly one hundred craft were berthed
along the canal during the winter months.

There is (or was) a file marked *SECRET* in the archives of the Public
Record Office (now The National Archives) which refers to the part played
by the Chichester Canal in the preparations made in 1940 to resist possible
German invasion. The 4th Infantry Division, which had been given the
task of protecting the Sussex coast, immediately saw the potential value
of converting the waterway into an anti-tank obstacle.[2] Eighteen officers
and 800 other ranks of the Beds & Herts Light Infantry were engaged in
preparing defence works between Littlehampton and Chichester Harbour.
Their headquarters were at Climping with a battalion of the East Surreys
to the West. Upper Lock Cottage at Appledram was requisitioned by 30
Field Regiment RA and demolished. The military reported on 15 July 1940
that the erection of barbed wire fences, building of walls with sand bags
and the digging of communication trenches along the coastline had been
completed, that concrete pill boxes and road blocks had been set up and
were manned at night, four swivel bridges over the Chichester Ship Canal
had been dismantled and the water level raised three feet by building a

77   *The site of the former Hollinsworth swivel bridge at Barnham 2003. A total of 21 moveable iron bridges was built by Tickell of Southampton. Each bore the name of local landowners or committee members and the date 1820.*

dam above Cutfield Bridge. However, the boom across the harbour was still only partially complete and anti-tank block production was limited by a cement shortage. There was considerable air activity. Seven bombs had been dropped and one at least remained unexploded.

However, it was the driest of summers and the reach between the basin and Birdham Lock was little better than a wet ditch. The Royal Engineer officer, to whom the task had been given, consulted a former Inspector General of Irrigation in Egypt, who said, 'Fill it up by tipping water at the basin just as fast as you can and the clay puddle will probably swell and seal. This is a matter of the rate of supply of water. In this weather you won't ever win if you go at it slowly – it will all disappear down the cracks. However, the pipe from the river Lavant which led under the road was above the water level so that the first step was to build a concrete dam across the culvert which diverted the stream into Southgate Basin. To seal derelict Birdham Lock it was agreed a local firm should provide the sheet piling and pile driver in return for removing the disused iron swivel bridges and the lifting bridge of the Selsey Tramway.

It was not until August 1942 when plans begun to be made for D Day that the Admiralty requisitioned the waterway. The files of correspondence at the county record office mainly relate to the amount of compensation to be paid at the war's end to returning the canal to the state it was in three years before. A firm of consulting engineers estimated the cost at £12,475 of which the Admiralty's share was £2,272. A dispute then arose

78　*View of the aqueduct over the Aldingbourne Rife in 2003.*

as to whether this was payable to the corporation as landlords or to Vernon as tenant. The matter was not finally concluded until 1947.

In the early 1950s the tenants of the yards on the north side of the basin (including the Purchase family) relinquished their leases while the City Corporation considered the canal's future. At length the corporation decided that the cost of maintenance was an unfair burden on the ratepayers and in October 1958 the canal together with the surrounding land, the cottages and wharf at Hunston (plus the properties at Birdham which had been leased to the Chichester Yacht Club) was sold to the West Sussex County Council for £7,500.

It is surprising that, although the waterway lies so close to the city centre, no effort was made to plan its restoration until the formation of the Sussex Canal Trust in 1973. Under the chairmanship of Anthony Pagett it set out its intention to restore the Portsmouth & Arundel Canal to a navigable state. A distinguished group of supporters included the Duke of Norfolk as president, Christopher Chataway, MP for Chichester, Sir Alec Rose the yachtsman and Michael Marshall, MP for Arundel. However, after producing a dozen or more newsletters and holding several well attended meetings, the realisation that its aims were too ambitious caused the trust to fade away.

Meantime the Chichester Canal Angling Association had become leaseholders and were not encouraging other interests to use the waterway. Then, in 1979, John Cooper instigated a revival by forming the Chichester Canal Society with more limited objectives. Since 1981 management action plans have been formulated every five years to coordinate local interests.

79 *The two gasometers seen in 1962 shortly before they were demolished. The gas works in Stockbridge Road enabled Chichester to be lit by gaslight in September 1823. They were reconstructed in 1903, extended in 1921 and closed in 1958 when sea gas took the place of coal gas.*

By establishing good relations with the county council, the society obtained financial assistance in June 1987 for dredging to be restarted. Numerous other improvements by the society's volunteer working parties, assisted by funding from the county and district councils, have included new pathways around the basin and along the tow-path. A trip boat provides regular services during the summer months and enables both young and old to enjoy the waterway as well as contributing towards the cost of maintenance. It would be superfluous to describe in greater detail the activities and hard labour engendered by the volunteer workforce since this has been well recorded over the past twenty years by the editors of the society's newsletters. Progress in redeveloping the Chichester Canal has been slow for a variety of reasons, not least because of the substantial cost of building new bridges to carry the A286 to West Wittering and the B2201 to Selsey over the canal at Birdham and Donnington respectively. There was also the need to obtain the support of local authorities, the immediate neighbouring farmers, Chichester Harbour Conservancy and Premier Marinas Ltd, who lease the

80   *The warehouse depicted on the east bank of Southgate Basin in Malby's painting, seen here in 1963. The building was demolished in 2003 to make way for 18 town houses.*

81   *The* Richmond Arms *inn 1962. The flint and stone building was erected in the 1820s on the west side of the basin. It was too small to host the canal's celebratory opening dinners in 1822 and 1823 which took place at the* Dolphin *and the* Swan.

82 *The former engine house at Milton, depicted here in 1960, was built in 1821 to pump water from a huge well into the upper pound. The engine house provided accommodation for both the lock-keeper and the pump operator before being converted into a single dwelling house.*

Birdham end of the canal as well as owning Chichester Marina. In 1992 the canal was identified as a Site of Nature Conservation Importance (SNCI) and in 1995 Halcrow Consulting Engineers concluded that the estimated cost of restoration would be about £2.5 million.

In November 2002 it was agreed to rename the society the Chichester Ship Canal Trust. The chairman, a former mayor of Chichester, Mr Jim Payne, set out a new management plan which envisages the reopening of

83 *Sketch of the remains of the upper sea lock at Milton looking towards the lower lock in 1912. The bed was not filled in until after 1940.*

84 *The former bed of the Portsea Canal at Fratton was used to provide the railway's approach to Portsmouth station. The brick wall at right marks the line of the former embankment.*

the navigation by 2010. This document has been agreed by the county, city and district councils together with the Harbour Conservancy, the Sussex Wild Trust, the Environmental Agency and Premier Marinas Ltd. The biggest challenge now is fund-raising. A Heritage Lottery grant has been applied for, and a trading company established to run the trip boat and raise other money for the Trust. All environmentalists and pleasure boaters are urged to support the project. More recently has been the completion in 2005 of 20 three-storey two- and three-bedroom homes on the east bank of the canal basin. The property company has generally succeeded in preserving the original character of the site while ensuring a sensitive approach to its location.

Meanwhile the rebuilding of Drungewick Aqueduct on the Wey & Arun Junction Canal and its official reopening in May 2003 has presaged a major step forward in the attempt to restore this vital link which formed part of London's lost route to Portsmouth. Within ten years the canal will most probably be reopened from Loxwood to Newbridge, its former terminus where it joined the Arun Canal and, not long after, to the English Channel at Littlehampton. One expects too that by then an agreement will have been reached on how best to complete the restoration of the Wey & Arun at Bramley and the barge canal between Ford and Hunston.

EPILOGUE

The reasons for the failure of the Portsmouth & Arundel Canal Navigation are multifarious. Planned when war with France added to the dangers of navigating the Straits of Dover, it was built in a time of peace by a company whose management lacked business acumen. The route chosen was unsatisfactory. Indeed the scheme finally proposed by John Rennie was but a pale shadow of his own Grand Southern Canal project and he, in any case, took a poor view of the primitive Arun Navigation and its tiny tunnel. His choice of James Hollinsworth as engineer was unfortunate. Although he had worked for Rennie as a trusted assistant, his past record had not been without blemish. His relationship with the members of the management committee goes unrecorded since he is not mentioned by name in any available reports from the time he was appointed resident engineer. However, he was clearly unsuited to the task of controlling expenditure and supervising so large an operation. After his departure the contractors continued to have matters their own way and, lacking firm direction, continued to incur expenses which the company were unable to meet.

In any event the waterway was doomed from the outset. The cessation of hostilities with France, the fall in coastal shipping charges, the problem of promoting trade with five different navigational authorities, flood, ice, drought and the need to pass through 52 locks between London and Portsmouth precluded the chances of success. The detractors of the scheme before the initial Act was passed were soon proved right. The Portsea Canal proved an unmitigated disaster. The barge canal leaked profusely. Only the Chichester Canal was commercially viable. Eventually the winding-up of the company brought some slight compensation to the descendants of the numerous shareholders who could reflect on the unfortunate speculation of their forefathers.

APPENDIX A

Table of Locks and Distances from Queenhithe Wharf to Chichester and Portsmouth Harbour 1831.

From Queenhithe To	Shortest Distance (miles)	No. Locks	Navigation	Maximum size of vessel admitted by locks			
				ft.	in.	ft.	in.
Weybridge	30½	5	Thames	140	0	x 22	0
Guildford	45	15	Wey	73	6	x 13	10½
Godalming	49	19	Godalming	73	6	x 13	10½
Basingstoke	69½	36	Basingstoke Canal	72	6	x 13	6
Pulborough	73½	43	Wey & Arun Canal	68	6	x 12	2
Arundel	85	46	Arun Canal	68	3	x 11	9
Midhurst	84	51	Rother	73	0	x 12	0
Littlehampton	92	46	P & A	75	0	x 12	6
Chichester	100½	48	Chichester Canal	86	0	x 18	8
*Halfway-Houses	115½	52	Portsea Canal	101	0	x 24	1
Portsmouth Harbour	117	50	Portsbridge Cut				

Note: The P & A lock dimensions are from Bradshaw (1833).

* The Portsea Canal ceased to be used after 1825. The minimum draught throughout was 3ft. 1in.; the minimum headroom 7ft. The length of Hardham tunnel was 375 yards. The making of the cut in the Arun at Offham reduced the distance between London Bridge and places south of Arundel by ¾ mile after 1862.

APPENDIX B

ESTIMATE of the probable Expence of the proposed
PORTSMOUTH and ARUNDEL CANAL

FIRST DISTRICT.

The Canal to be 19 Feet 6 Inches wide at Bottom, 33 Feet at Top, and 4 Feet
6 Inches Deep.

From Ford, near Arundel, to Chichester Harbour.

	£
To cutting and forming the Canal from the River Arun, at Ford, to the Valley at Denges Burn, near Yapton	4149
To Embanking Valley at Denges Burn	1677
To making Canal from said Valley to a Valley West of Barnham....	598
To Embanking of said Valley	3683
To making Canal from the above Valley to a Valley near Lidsey, and Embanking said Valley.....................................	1200
To making Canal from ditto to Valley at the division of the Parishes of of Bersted and Oving	989
To Embanking said Valley	2638
To making Canal from ditto to Hunstone Common..................	2044
To Embanking at Hunstone Common	385
To making Canal from thence to the Tideway at Berdham...........	10,742
To two Sea Locks and two others................................	11,100
To six main and thirty occupation Road Bridges....................	9300
To four large and twelve small Culverts	1000
To Towing Path and Fencing	2898
To purchase of Land	7680
To a Steam Engine, Engine House, &c...........................	2760
Contingencies..	9427
	£72,270

ESTIMATE of the probable Expence of Deepening Wadeways at Thorney and Langstone.

	£.
To Deepening Thorney Wadeway	4970
To Ditto Langstone Wadeway	5800
Contingencies.......................	2144
	£12,914

ESTIMATE of the probable Expence of making a Canal from
Eastney Lake, in Langstone Harbour, to the Halfway-houses,
in Portsea Common, including a Basin at ditto.

		£.
To Cutting from Eastney Lake to the head of the second Lock		1163
To Ditto to the Basin at Portsea		2238
To two Locks		4600
To three roads six occupation Bridges		2680
To Forming and Fencing the Towing Path		583
To purchase of Land		1800
To Steam Engine		2452
To Basin and Contingencies		3102
		£18,618

*In the above Estimate nothing is allowed for the purchase of Ground
for Storehouses, or for the Storehouses themselves, as it is understood
these will amply pay for any expence that may be incurred; and their
extent will depend on the quantity of goods that may be stored.*

ESTIMATE of the probable Expence of making a Navigable
Canal from Portsmouth Harbour to Langstone Harbour, by
Wymmering.—Depth, 8 Feet.

	£.
To Cutting	5831
To two Locks	5000
To one Road and three occupation Bridges	1160
To Forming and Fencing the Towing Path	316
To Land	900
Contingencies	1981
	£15,188

RECAPITULATION,

	£.
Canal from the River Arun, at Ford, to Chichester Harbour, at Berdham	72,270
Deepening Wadeways at Thorney Island and Langston Harbour	12,914
Canal from Eastney Lake to the Halfway-houses, in Portsea Common	18,618
Canal from Portsmouth Harbour to Langstone Harbour	15,188
	£118,990

John Rennie
27 January 1816

Close inspection of the Giles's plan (see end-paper) reveals the proposed site of
the feeder to the engine-house above Sea Lock II at Milton, the planned road
diversion from Milton to the Sea Lock and the diversion of the Lavant stream at
Southgate Basin.

Appendix C

The Portsmouth and Arundel Navigation Company

Committee of Management

1817 Rear-Admiral Sir Peter Halkett (Chairman), Earl of Egremont, Admiral Viscount Keith, Sir Lucius Curtis, James Brown, William Cutfield, Thomas Edgcombe, Benjamin Goodeve, Moses Greetham, Trevor Letham, Robert Park, John Snook, William Turner, John Williams, William T. Williams.

Chairmen of Meetings*		Resident Engineer	
1817	Rear-Admiral Sir Peter Halkett	1818-1820	James Hollinsworth
	John Williams		Clerk
1818	Viscount Keith	1817-1819	George L. Greetham
	John Snook	1819-1822	J. Godwin Williams
1824	Lord Selsey	1823-1824	Jackson Muspratt Williams
	W. Charles Newland	1824-1832	James J. Fowler
1831	Edward Casher	1832-1851	Thomas T. Edgecombe
1832	George Palmer	1851-1888	Thomas Smith Edgcombe
1852	Reverend Arthur Perceval		

*A chairman was elected from those present at each meeting. The year is given of their first acceptance where known.

Appendix D

The Portsmouth and Arundel Navigation Company

Tonnage carried between the Thames and the Portsmouth & Arundel canal (1823-1840)

Year	To the Thames	From the Thames	Total
1823	425	1,475	1,900
1824	1,158	2,492	3,650
1825	1,001	1,581	2,582
1826	421	985	1,379
1827	193	78	271
1828	285	95	380
1829	125	77	202
1830	101	92	193
1831	115	296	411
1832	670	1,335	2,005
1833	1,102	1,458	2,560
1834	820	1,130	1,950
1835	409	721	1,130
1836	547	636	1,183
1837	303	602	905
1838	259	494	753
1839	285	502	787
1840	192	282	474
Total	8,511	14,204	22,715

PORTSMOUTH & ARUNDEL CANAL NAVIGATION[†]

Year	Tolls (£)	Tonnage
1822	142	3,000[*]
1823	669	10,000[*]
1824	827	11,500[*]
1825	944	12,500[*]
1826	1,010	13,351
1827	1,000[*]	13,000[*]
1828		
1829		
1830	1,028	

CHICHESTER SHIP CANAL

Year	Tolls (£)	Tonnage
1826	950[*]	12,000[*]
1847	104	3,000[*]
1858	191	5,111
1866	86	3,750[*]
1868	185	7,070
1874	46	2,000[*]
1882	57	2,500[*]
1883	58	2,600[*]
1884	57	2,500[*]
1885	85	3,800[*]
1886	66	2,900[*]
1887	58	2,600[*]
1888	133	6,001
1898	18	704

[*] Approximate.
[†] includes the Chichester Canal.

Appendix E

Bullion Traffic between Portsmouth and the Bank of England

Year	Number of Consignments	Total Tonnage
1824	6	110
1825	1	72
1826	2*	46
1827	3†	85
1828	2	45
1829	2	51
1830	4	97
1831	2	46
1832	2	32
1833	1	24
1834	1	5
1835	none	–
1836	1	4
1837	1	24
1838	1	4
Total	29	645 tons

Maximum consignment: 72 tons in February 1825
* 31 tons loaded at Chichester.
† 40 tons loaded at Littlehampton. 58 tons listed as 'money' not bullion.

BIBLIOGRAPHY

(I) ACTS OF PARLIAMENT

1817　An Act for making and maintaining a navigable canal from the River Arun to Chichester Harbour, and from thence to Langstone and Portsmouth Harbours, with a Cut or Branch from Hunston Common to or near the City of Chichester and for improving the Navigation of the Harbour of Langstone, and channels of Langstone and Thorney. (Portsmouth & Arundel Navigation Act)

1819　An Act for giving further Powers to the Company of Proprietors of the Wey and Arun Junction Canal, and to confirm an Agreement entered into between the said companies. (Portsmouth & Arundel Navigation Act)

1821　An Act for giving further Powers to the Company of Proprietors of the River Arun Navigation, and for confirming certain Agreements entered into between the said Company and the Company of Proprietors of the Portsmouth and Arundel Navigation. (Arun Navigation Act)

1828　An Act for granting further Powers to the Company of Proprietors of the Portsmouth and Arundel Navigation. (Portsmouth & Arundel Navigation Act)

1892　An Act to provide for the transfer of the Chichester Section of the Portsmouth and Arundel Canal Navigation to the Corporation of the City of Chichester and for other purposes. (Chichester Canal Transfer Act)

(II) BOOKS OF REFERENCE

1803　Robert Marshall, *An Examination into the Respective Merits of the proposed Canal and Iron Railway from London to Portsmouth*

1816　John Rennie, *A Report to the Subscribers to a Canal from Arundel to Portsmouth*

1817　Lake Allen, *The History of Portsmouth*

1826　I. Skelton, *A Topographical and Historical Account of Hayling Island*

1827　N.W. Cundy, *Reports on the Grand Ship Canal from London to Arundel Bay and Portsmouth*

1828   Henry Slight, *Chronicles of Portsmouth* (third edition 1838)

1831   Joseph Priestley, *Historical Account of the Navigable River, Canals and Railways throughout Great Britain*

1875   *Autobiography of Sir John Rennie*

1888   W.H. Saunders, *Annals of Portsmouth*

1900   W.G. Gates, *An Illustrated History of Portsmouth*

1916   W.T. Jackman, *The Development of Transportation in Modern England* (third edition 1966)

1932   *West of the Arun – a book of drawings by Students of the City of Chichester School of Art*

1936   Douglas Burrage, *An old Waterway Revived*

1951   F.G.G. Carr, *Sailing Barges*

1951   C.R. Fay, *Huskisson and his Age*

1958   F.D. Heneghan, *The Chichester Canal*

1961   Richard Esmond, *Portsmouth Not so Old*

1965   P.A.L. Vine, *London's Lost Route to the Sea* (fifth edition 1996)

1968   P.A.L. Vine, *London's Lost Route to Basingstoke* (2nd edition 1994)

1985   P.A.L. Vine, *West Sussex Waterways* (reprinted 1993 and 1998)

1987   Ted Cuthbert, *Portsmouth's Lost Canal* (republished 1991)

1987   Keith and Janet Smith, *Birdham & Itchenor: Then and Now*

1987   R.C. Riley, *The Industrial Archaeology of the Portsmouth Region*

1988   P. Moore, *Industrial Heritage of Hampshire and the Isle of Wight*

1989   Antony Triggs, *Portsmouth History in Hiding*

1989   John Webb, S. Quail, P. Haskell and R. Riley, *The Spirit of Portsmouth*

1990   P.A.L. Vine, *Hampshire Waterways*

1991   Hugh Compton and Antony Carr-Gomm, *The Military on English Waterways 1798-1844*

1994   P.A.L. Vine, *London to Portsmouth Waterway*

1995   P.A.L. Vine, *London's Lost Route to Midhurst*

1996   John Reger, *Chichester Harbour*

1999   Roy Philip, *The Coast Blockade*

1999   Ronald Tweed, *A History of Langstone Harbour*

2000   Saskia Heasman (ed.), *The Parish of Donnington*

2001   *Chichester Ship Canal – Management Action Plan*

2002   *Biographical Dictionary of Civil Engineers, Vol. I, 1500 - 1830*

2002   I. McGowen and G. Girling, *Mundham, Runcton & Hunston*

2005   A.H.J. Green, *The History of Chichester's Canal*

The Committee of Management Reports and the Annual Reports of the Portsmouth & Arundel Navigation Company (only those from 1816 to 1824 and for 1831 have been located), the reports in the weekly editions of the *Hampshire Chronicle & Courier* and the *Hampshire Telegraph & Sussex Chronicle* and files in the Public Record Office provided the main sources of information.

(III) PERIODICALS

'The Waterways of Sussex', Roger Sellman (*Sussex County Magazine*, January-
    May 1935)

'London's Lost Route to the Sea', P.A.L. Vine (*Country Life*, 27 March
    1953)

'Hunston Canal Bridge', A.H.J. Green (*Sussex Industrial History* no.31,
    2001)

Reference should also be made to the newsletters and publications of the
Sussex Canal Trust (July 1973-5), the Chichester Canal Society (1979-2002)
and the Chichester Ship Canal Trust (2002 to date).

NOTES

I Plans to Link London and Portsmouth (1785-1815), pp.1-6.

1. The full text of the bill can be found in *London's Lost Route to the Sea*, Appendix I (*see* Bibliography).
2. British Library, King's MS, 44 ff 3, 8-9, (1774).
3. *Derby Mercury*, 24 March 1785.
4. John Phillips, *General History of Inland Navigation* (1792).
5. C.E. Lee, *Early Railways in Surrey* (1944), p.12.
6. *Lewes Journal*, 5 March 1804. *See also* 'Considerations on the intended Junction of the Ports of London, Southampton and Portsmouth, by uniting the Basingstoke Canal (or the River Wey, at Godalming) with the river Itchin' 1807 and 'Observations on the Proposed Junction Canal between Winchester and the Basingstoke Canal' 1808.
7. *The Times*, 27 October 1809.
8. Robert Marshall, 'An Examination into the Respective Merits of the proposed Canal and Iron Railway from London to Portsmouth, 1803' (Patent Office Library). C. F. Dendy Marshall, *History of the Southern Railway* (1936), p.7. A similar pamphlet entitled 'Comparative View of the Respective Qualities and Advantages of an Iron Railway and a Canal with reference in particular to those projected between London and Portsmouth' examined the statements in favour of both and rejected most of the assumptions. The copy in Portsmouth City Library is undated, but since it refers to the Croydon railway being lately executed, it was probably published at about the same time as Robert Marshall's.
9. *Report and Estimate of the Grand Southern Canal*, John Rennie (1810). (Institution of Civil Engineers Library.)
10. Charles Hadfield, *The Canals of Southern England* (1955), p.113.
11. Portsmouth & Arundel Canal Committee of Management Report to the Subscribers, 5 August 1817.
12. *The Times*, 17 October 1811.

II The Portsmouth and Arundel Canal Project (1815-17), pp.7-16.

1. *The Hampshire Telegraph* and *Sussex Chronicle* or *Portsmouth and Chichester Advertiser*, 9 January 1815.
2. W.G. Gates, *Illustrated History of Portsmouth* (1900), p.574.
3. Lake Allen, *The History of Portsmouth* (1817), p.174. Lake Allen was a barrister, a fine classical scholar who 'possessed an extraordinary facility in the perusal of the various court texts used in ancient deeds and charters'. He died in 1823. (Slight, *Chronicles of Portsmouth*, 1828.)
4. *Hampshire Telegraph*, 14 October 1816. *The Sussex Weekly Advertiser* and *Lewes Record*, 11 August 1817.
5. MS, Rennie to John Wilson Croker, 17 April 1815 (ICE).
6. MS, William Turner to Lt-General Gother Mann, 10 July 1815 (PRO 44/532).
7. *Hampshire Telegraph*, 21 August 1815.
8. *Ibid.*, 25 September 1815.
9. Liverpool Papers BL 38191 f. 100 undated (probably autumn 1815). (Guildhall Library MS 13325.)
10. MS, George Thomas to Richard Corp, 16 November 1815.
11. John Rennie, 'A Report to the Subscribers to a Canal from Arundel to Portsmouth, 27 January 1816', p.11. Lord Keith had held a meeting the previous October to receive Giles's report.
12. *Ibid.*, pp 4-5.

13. Public Record Office, WO 44/532.
14. MS, John Staker to Richard Corp, 9 March 1816. (Guildhall Library MS 13325.)
15. *Ibid.*, 26 September 1816.
16. *Hampshire Telegraph*, 9 September 1816.
17. *Ibid.*, 23 September 1816.
18. *Ibid.*, 30 September 1816.
19. *Ibid.*, 14 October 1816.
20. *Ibid.*, 30 September 1816.
21. MS, Lord Egremont to Richard Corp, 21 September 1816 (Guildhall Library MS 13325).
22. *Ibid.*, 30 September 1816.
23. *Hampshire Telegraph*, 7 October 1816.
24. MS, Lord Egremont to Richard Corp 27 January 1817. (Guildhall Library MS 13325.)
25. *Ibid.*, 28 January 1817.
26. *Ibid.*, 28 January 1817. Egremonts's intervention met with success. The Governors were finally won over and agreed to sell the company ten acres or so of meadow land which would be used to excavate the first mile and a quarter of the canal bed leading from the river Arun.

III Parliamentary Progress (1817), pp.17-22.

1. *Hampshire Telegraph*, 3 March 1817.

IV Forming the Company (1817-18), pp.23-30.

1. *The Sussex Weekly Advertiser* and *Lewes Record*, 11 August 1817.
2. *Hampshire Telegraph*, 21 July 1817.
3. Portsmouth & Arundel Canal Navigation report, 5 August 1817.
4. MS, John Williams to Lord Egremont, 5 November 1817 (Petworth House Archives 8267).
5. *Hampshire Telegraph*, 2 February 1818.
6. *Ibid.*, 1 December 1817.
7. *Hampshire Chronicle & Courier*, 2 February 1818.
8. Alan Faulkner, *The Grand Junction Canal* (1972), p.35.
9. Charles Hadfield, *The Canals of South-Eastern England* (1969), p.183.
10. Jean Lindsay, *The Canals of Scotland* (1966), p.125; *Biographical Dictionary of Civil Engineers* (2002), pp.330-3.
11. *HC & C.* 11 and 25 May 1818. Hollinsworth resided at Rumboldswhyke.
12. Statement by Dyson & Thornton of Chichester to be put to the arbitrators (Arundel Castle archives MD 2525).

V Building the Waterway (1818-23), pp.31-45.

1. *Hampshire Telegraph*, 7 September 1818. See J. Dalloway (*County of Sussex*, vol.II, 1832, p.49) who reveals that 'the foundations of considerable buildings were discovered at Ford'.
2. Rennie, *Letter Book*, Vol.9, 25 August 1818 (I.C.E.).
3. 'Report of the Committee of Management' (RCM), 18 May 1819.
4. Rennie Reports, Vol.9, 6 February 1818 (I.C.E.).
5. *Ibid.*, 24 February 1818 (I.C.E.).
6. PRO WO 44/243. James Paine of Henley Park, Ash, was one of the land valuers employed to assess the damages caused by the waterway. In 1821 he assessed the compensation due to Christ's Hospital and their tenants at £444. This included payments for the inconvenience caused by navigators occupying the land on either side of the excavations, loss of crops, damage caused by carting bricks and for land used as a brickyard.
7. Rennie Reports, Vol.10, 22 February 1819.
8. *Ibid.*, 18 May 1819. The contractors were later to state that no price had been agreed and claimed £6,166 for excavating the basin and forming the new road.
9. *Ibid.*, 16 May 1820.
10. MS, John Rennie to J.W. Croker, 4 October 1827 (I.C.E.).
11. *Hampshire Telegraph*, 6 September 1819.
12. A Report to the Subscribers, 27 January 1816, p.14.
13. RCM, 16 May 1820.
14. *Hampshire Chronicle & Courier*, 16 August 1819.
15. *Ibid.*, 2 October 1820.
16. *Ibid.*, 11 December 1820.
17. *Hampshire Telegraph*, 1 June 1829.
18. Arundel Castle MS (MD 2525).

19. Report of the Committee of Management, 15 May 1821.
20. *Hampshire Telegraph*, 25 December 1820.
21. Shipping Register for Portsmouth, entry no 58, 16 November 1825.
22. RCM, 15 May 1821.
23. P & A circular to proprietors, 4 August 1818.
24. RCM, 15 May 1821.
25. An Act to authorize the Issue of Exchequer Bills and the Advance of Money out of the Consolidated Fund to a limited Amount for the carrying on of Public Works and Fisheries in the United Kingdom, and Employment of the Poor in Great Britain (16 June 1817).
26. *Ibid.*, 24 September 1821.
27. Pigot, *Directory of Hampshire*, 1823 *et seq.*

VI OPENING CEREMONIES (1822-3), pp.46-53.
1. *Hampshire Telegraph*, 1 April 1822.
2. *Ibid.*, 25 March 1822.
3. *Ibid.*, 15 April 1822.
4. MS, Arundel Castle MD 2525.
5. Report of the Committee of Management, 21 May 1822.
6. *Hampshire Telegraph*, 16 September 1822.
7. *Ibid.*, 23 September 1822.
8. *West Sussex Gazette*, 10 September 1936.
9. Reprinted in the *Brighton Gazette*, 5 June 1823.

VII THE PROSPECTS FOR SUCCESS (1823-5), pp.54-64.
1. MS, John Williams to C. Sandys (Wey Navigation), 31 March 1823.
2. Memorandum circulated to the Subscribers dated 29 May 1817 and reprinted in part in the *Hampshire Telegraph*, 2 June 1817.
3. MS, John Williams to C. Sandys, 31 March 1823.
4. *Hampshire Telegraph*, 9 June 1823.
5. *Ibid.*, 23 February 1824.
6. *Ibid.*, 30 June 1823.
7. *Ibid.*, 30 June 1823.
8. *Ibid.*, 13 February 1824.
9. *Ibid.*, 13 October 1823.
10. *Ibid.*, 23 February 1824.
11. 2 October 1824. I am indebted to Ron Davis for this information.
12. *Hampshire Telegraph*, 28 January 1824.
13. Proprietors of the Portsmouth & Arundel Canal v Messrs Thomas Dyson & Thomas Thornton. Statement of Claim by plaintiffs, 14 July 1823 (Arundel Castle MD 2525).
14. *Ibid.*
15. *Hampshire Telegraph*, 2 February 1824.
16. *Ibid.*, 12 April 1845.
17. *Ibid.*, 31 January 1825.
18. Simon Garfield, *The Last Journey of William Huskisson* (2002), *p.*96.
19. *The Speeches of the Rt. Hon. William Huskisson*, vol.II (1831).

VIII THE HAYLING ISLAND BRIDGE (1823-4), pp.65-68.
1. MS, Arundel Castle MD 2525.
2. I. Skelton, *Topographical and Historical Account of Hayling Island* (1826), pp.9-10.
3. *Hampshire Telegraph*, 13 September 1824.
4. *Ibid.*

IX THE STEAM PACKET, SIR FRANCIS DRAKE (1822-9), pp.69-76.
1. Jackson, W.T., *The Development of the Transportation in Modern England* (third edition, 1966), pp.457-9.
2. Pamphlet: 'Statement of the Probable cost of a Steam-Packet and the Advantages to be derived from the Employment of Vessels of that description between Portsmouth and the Western Ports on the completion of the Canal from London to Arundel and Portsmouth.' Plymouth, 3 April 1822 (National Library of Scotland MS 6480).
3. *Hampshire Telegraph*, 8 September 1823.
4. *Ibid.*, 13 October 1823.
5. *Ibid.*, 23 February 1824.

6. *Ibid.*, 17 January 1825.
7. Brunswick Annual Report, Plymouth, 5 December 1827.
8. MS, annotation dated 14 January 1828 to *Drake*'s Annual Report for 1827.
9. *Hampshire Telegraph*, 30 March 1829.

X   THE FAILURE OF THE PORTSEA SHIP CANAL (1822-5), pp.77-85.
1. Report of the Committee of Management, 20 May 1823.
2. MS, Dyson & Thornton to Thomas Edgecombe, 28 April 1824 (Arundel Castle MD 2525)
3. *Hampshire Telegraph*, 22 November 1824.
4. *Ibid.*, 6 December 1824.
5. *Ibid.*, 27 December 1824.
6. *Ibid.*, 3 January 1825.
7. *Ibid.*, 4 April 1825.
8. *Ibid.*, 14 August 1826.
9. *Ibid.*, 16 October 1826.
10. *Ibid.*, 18 September 1826.

XI   JOHN RENNIE'S REPORT (1827), pp.86-94.
1. MS, Sir John Rennie to J.W. Croker, 4 October 1827 with enclosures from Lord Egremont, Huskisson and Fowler. (I.C.E.)
2. MS Rennie to Lord Selsey, 20 November 1827 (I.C.E.)
3. The story of this project will be found in *London's Lost Route to the Sea*, chapter IX.
4. Wey & Arun Junction Canal Company circular letter, 25 May 1827.
5. *Autobiography of Sir John Rennie* (1875), pp.284-6.
6. *Hampshire Telegraph*, 30 March 1829. The idea lingered on. Frederick Homan, writing on behalf of the Hibernian Philanthropic Society for the Employment of the Peasantry in Ireland, advocated a ship canal from Galway to Dublin and quoted Lord Cloncurry's view that such a canal would be of great national benifit which 'in conjunction with the projected canals from Portsmouth to London and from Bristol to the English Channel would make the finest system of internal navigation in the world'. (*The Ballot*, 9 June 1831.)
7. *Ibid.*, 24 December 1827.
8. *Ibid.*, 31 December 1827.

XII   THE FOURTH ACT OF PARLIAMENT (1828), pp.95-9.
1. Henry and Julian Slight, *Chronicles of Portsmouth* (1828), p.12.
2. *The Spirit of Portsmouth* (1989), p.147. Rennie may not have been aware that the Thorney Island cut had not been attempted.
3. *The Bognor, Arundel and Littlehampton Guide* (1829), p.191.

XIII   THE COMPLETION OF THE NAVIGATION (1829-30), pp.100-11.
1. *Hampshire Telegraph*, 1 September 1828.
2. *Ibid.*, 13 April 1829.
3. PRO, C26/507.
4. *Hampshire Telegraph*, 20 April and 15 June 1829.
5. MS, Fowler to Burgoyne, 3 November 1829 (PRO, WO44/283).
6. LRCM, 7 June 1831. Rennie's estimate for the Portsbridge cut was £6159 (see page 90) to which £950 was now added.
7. *Hampshire Telegraph*, 19 October 1829.
8. *Sussex Weekly Advertiser*, 14 and 28 September 1829.
9. MS, Hodgson to Langton, 8 December 1829 (Lincolnshire Record Office).
10. *Hampshire Telegraph*, 5 and 19 April 1830.
11. *Ibid.*, 20 September 1830.
12. *Ibid.*, 25 May 1829.
13. *Ibid.*, 30 March 1829.
14. *Ibid.*, 1 June 1829.
15. *Ibid.*, 31 May 1830.
16. LRCM, 7 June 1831. Arundel Street was built upon the site of the canal basin.
17. *Hampshire Telegraph*, 27 June 1831.
18. *Ibid.*, 7 June 1830.
19. *Hampshire Telegraph*, 28 February and 7 March 1831.
20. Simon Garfield, *The Last Journey of William Huskisson* (2002), p.96.
21. *Hampshire Telegraph*, 7 March 1831. Mrs Huskisson sent Egremont a copy of the published volume

of her husband's Speeches and Memoir of his life. Egremont replied from Grosvenor Place on 15 July 1831: 'I am very much obliged to you. I have been shockingly ill since I saw you, and I am now hardly able to write. Ever truly yours, Egremont.'

XIV 'Our Last Gasp' (1831-3), pp.112-21.
1. MS, George Palmer to James Mangles MP, 11 April 1833 (SRO Acc 209).
2. *Hampshire Telegraph*, 24 November 1831.
3. MS, Palmer to the Thames Navigation Committee, 3 April 1832 (Surrey Record Office (SRO) Acc 209).
4. The company advertised that due to 'the great increase' in trade, 'additional barges would be employed between London and Portsmouth to provide a twice-weekly service in each direction' (*Hampshire Telegraph*, 16 April 1832).
5. SRO Acc 209.
6. Figures extracted from the Wey Navigation ledgers to traffic to and from Guildford.
7. MS, George Palmer to James Mangles MP, 11 April 1833 (SRO Acc 209).
8. MS, Admiral Halkett to James Mangles MP, 29 April 1833 (SRO Acc 209).
9. MS, George Palmer to James Mangles, 2.30p.m., 30 April 1833.
10. *Hampshire Telegraph*, 26 August 1833.
11. *Ibid.*, 30 December 1833.

XV The Thames Traffic Dies Away (1834-40), pp.122-28.
1. PRO, WO 44/283, 9 August 1847.
2. *Ibid.*, 14 December 1847.
3. Portsmouth & Arundel Navigation Company report, 21 December 1824, p.3.
4. *Bristol Journal*, 4 January 1834; *see also London's Lost Route to the Sea* (4th edition, 1986), p.109.
5. Parry, J.D., *An Historical and Descriptive Account of the Coast of Sussex* (1833), p.380.
6. *Hampshire Telegraph*, 27 June 1836.
7. Elwes (D.G.C.) and Robinson (C.J.), *History of the Castles, Mansion and Manors of Western Sussex* (1876), pp.275-7.
8. Horsfield, T.W., *History of Sussex* (1835), Vol.II, p.114.
9. Compton and Carr-Gomm, *The Military on English Waterway* (1991), pp.47-9.
10. F.D. Heneghan, *The Chichester Canal* (1958), p.24.
11. Portsmouth City Record Office, CCR 1, p.53.

XVI The Arrival of the Railway (1840-65), pp.129-40.
1. Quoted by R.A. Williams, *The London & South-Western Railway* (1968), Vol.I p.121.
2. House of Lords Minutes of Evidence, 13 June 1845.
3. *Hampshire Telegraph*, 12 April 1845.
4. House of Lords Minutes of Evidence, 13 June 1844.
5. *Ibid.*, 23 March 1846.
6. *Ibid.*, 25 June 1845.
7. *Ibid.*, 28 July 1845.
8. PRO, Admiralty Papers 1848-63 (M.T. 19/94).
9. Memorandum by Queen Victoria, 26 February 1852 (q.v. *The Letters of Queen Victoria*, ed. Benson & Esher, Vol.II (1907), pp.452-3)
10. *Punch*, Vol.XXII, p.62.
11. MS, Arthur Perceval to Augustus Stafford, 3 June 1852 (PRO M.T. 19/94).
12. J.B. Dashwood, *The Thames to the Solent by Canal and Sea* (1868), p.27. Further evidence of the date of disuse is provided by George Boniface, the tenant of one of the cottages by the engine house at Ford, quoted by the Christ's Hospital's solicitor as stating in September 1878 that the canal had been disused for 22 or 23 years, was now overgrown with grass, had no fence to mark its limits or prevent cattle encroaching.
13. PRO, C 26/507.
14. John Morley, *The Wadeway to Hayling* (1987), p.15.
15. F.G.G. Carr, *Sailing Barges* (1951), p.173.
16. *Chichester Observer and Recorder*, 7 March 1888.
17. *West Sussex Gazette*, 14 June 1866.

XVII In Chancery (1888-96), pp.141-52.
1. Public Record Office C26/507.
2. Chichester Canal Transfer Act 1892, Preamble p.2.
3. *Hampshire Telegraph*, 25 July 1891.

XVIII   THE CHICHESTER SHIP CANAL (1892-1928), pp.153-61.
1. *Chichester Observer and West Sussex Recorder*, 16 November 1892.
2. *Illustrated Sporting and Dramatic News*, 8 March 1890.
3. *Victoria County History, Sussex*, Vol.II (1907), p.466.
4. *Chichester Observer and West Sussex Recorder*, 14 March 1906.
5. F. D. Heneghan, *The Chichester Canal* (1958), p.19.
6. In 1904 Chichester Corporation began to charge pleasure boats 5/- a day. (WSRO CA/13.)
7. Minutes of Chichester City Council, 6 June 1928.

XIX   RESTORATION IN PART (1932-2005), pp.162-69.
1. Douglas Burrage, *An Old Waterway Revived* (1936).
2. *Chichester Canal Society Newsletter* (November 1994).

INDEX

Page numbers of illustrations are shown in **bold** type.

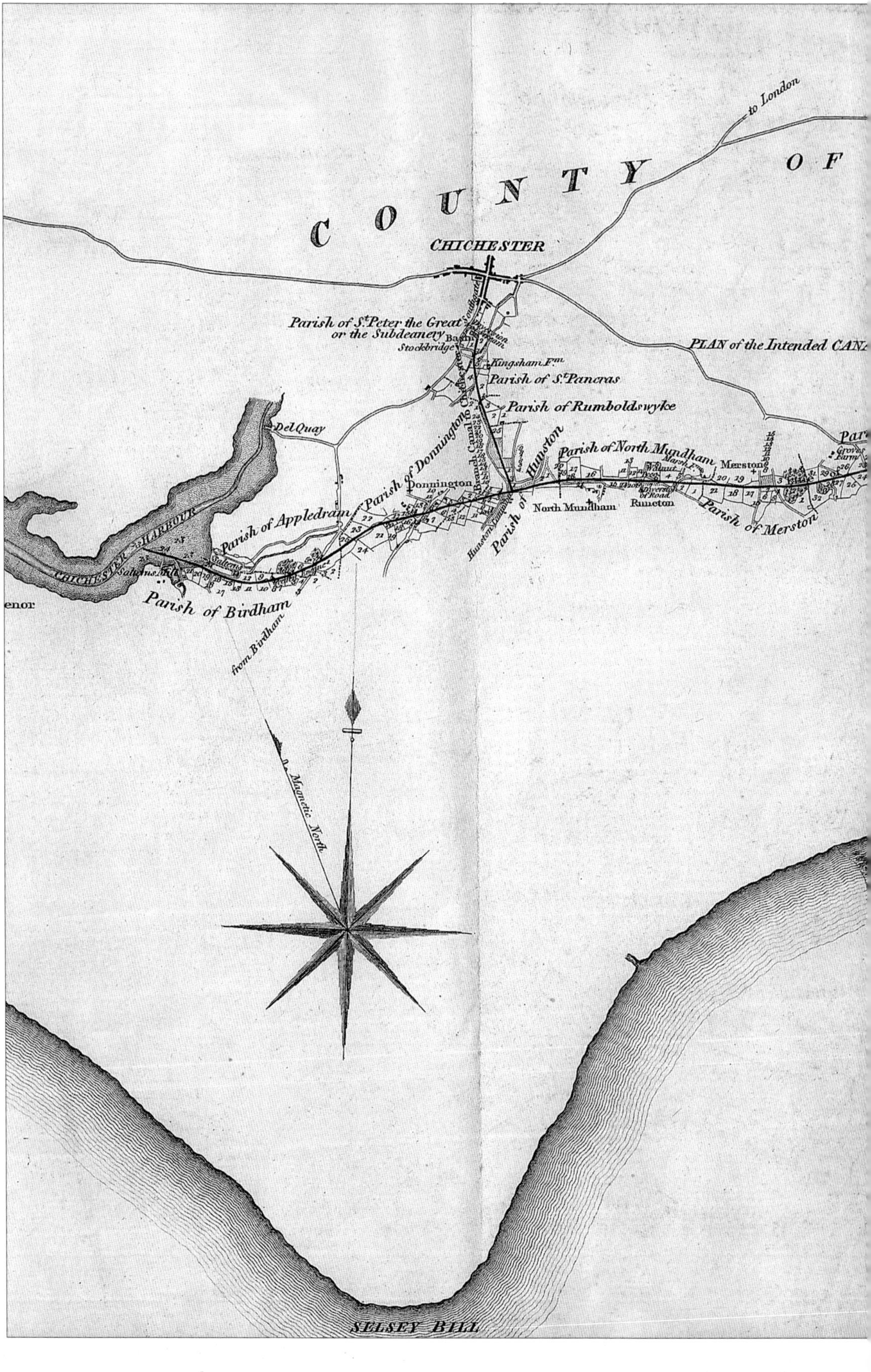

COUNTY OF

to London

CHICHESTER

PLAN of the Intended CANAL

Parish of St Peter the Great
or the Subdeanery
Stockbridge
Basin

Kingsham Fm

Parish of St Pancras

Parish of Rumboldswyke

Del Quay

Parish of North Mundham

Merston

Grove Farm

Par

Parish of Donnington

Donnington

Hunston

Parish of

North Mundham

Runcton

Parish of Merston

Parish of Appledram

CHICHESTER HARBOUR

Saltern Mill

Parish of Birdham

from Birdham

Magnetic North

enor

SELSEY BILL